DAILY
GUIDEPOSTS

2013

New York, New York

Daily Guideposts 2013

ISBN-10:0-8249-3175-0
ISBN-13: 978-0-8249-3175-9

Published by Guideposts
16 East 34th Street
New York, New York 10016
Guideposts.org

Distributed by Ideals Publications, a Guideposts company
2630 Elm Hill Pike, Suite 100
Nashville, TN 37214

Guideposts, Ideals and *Daily Guideposts* are registered trademarks of Guideposts.

Acknowledgments

Every attempt has been made to credit the sources of copyrighted material used in this book. If any such acknowledgment has been inadvertently omitted or miscredited, receipt of such information would be appreciated.

All Scripture quotations, unless otherwise noted, are taken from *The King James Version of the Bible*.

Scripture quotations marked (CEV) are taken from *Holy Bible: Contemporary English Version*. Copyright © 1995 American Bible Society.

Scripture quotations marked (ESV) are taken from the *Holy Bible, English Standard Version*, copyright © 2001 by Crossway Bibles, a division of Good News Publishers. Used by permission. All rights reserved.

Scripture quotations marked (MSG) are taken from *The Message*. Copyright © 1993, 1994, 1995, 1996, 2000, 2001, 2002 by Eugene H. Peterson.

Scripture quotations marked (NAS) are taken from the *New American Standard Bible*, copyright © 1960, 1962, 1963, 1968, 1971, 1972, 1973, 1975, 1977, 1995 by the Lockman Foundation. Used by permission.

Scripture quotations marked (NIV) are taken from *The Holy Bible, New International Version*. Copyright © 1973, 1978, 1984, 2011 by Biblica, Inc. Used by permission of Zondervan. All rights reserved worldwide. www.zondervan.com

Scripture quotations marked (NKJV) are taken from *The Holy Bible, New King James Version*. Copyright © 1982 by Thomas Nelson, Inc.

Scripture quotations marked (NLT) are from the *Holy Bible, New Living Translation*. Copyright © 1996, 2004, 2007 by Tyndale House Foundation. Used by permission of Tyndale House Publishers Inc., Carol Stream, Illinois 60188. All rights reserved.

Scripture quotations marked (NRSV) are taken from the *New Revised Standard Version Bible*. Copyright © 1989 by the Division of Christian Education of the National Council of the Churches of Christ in the United States of America. Used by permission. All rights reserved.

Scripture quotations marked (RSV) are taken from the *Revised Standard Version of the Bible*. Copyright © 1946, 1952, 1971 by Division of Christian Education of the National Council of Churches of Christ in the United States of America. Used by permission.

Scripture quotations marked (TLB) are taken from *The Living Bible*. Copyright © 1971 by Tyndale House Publishers, Wheaton, Illinois 60187. All rights reserved.

Scripture quotations marked (TNIV) are taken from *The Holy Bible, Today's New International Version*. Copyright © 2001, 2005 by Biblica, Inc. Used by permission of Zondervan. All rights reserved worldwide. www.zondervan.com

Andrew Attaway's photo by Doug Snyder. Brian Doyle's photo by Jerry Hart. Oscar Greene's photo copyright © 2001 by Olan Mills, Inc. Edward Grinnan's photo by Jane Wexler. Rick Hamlin's photo by Nina Subin. Roberta Messner's photo by Jan D. Witter/Camelot Photography. Elizabeth Sherrill's photo by Gerardo Somoza.

Cover design by Müllerhaus
Cover photo by Corbis
Interior design by Lorie Pagnozzi

Monthly page openers by Dara Burge
Indexed by Patricia Woodruff
Typeset by Aptara

Printed and bound in the United States of America
10 9 8 7 6 5 4 3 2 1

We often wonder what is God's will and specific purpose for our life. First Thessalonians 5:18, "Give thanks in all circumstances, for this is God's will for you in Christ Jesus," is one straightforward and glorious answer!

This thankfulness that God desires for us is the challenge that our contributors took on in *Daily Guideposts 2013* as they focused on our theme "In Everything, Give Thanks."

Sadly, this year, we said good-bye to Madge Harrah and Keith Miller who passed away. John Sherrill stepped down after many years of inspiring writing; we will miss him!

We're also very excited and honored to introduce you to some new folks: Ashley Wiersma from Colorado, Camy Tang and Jim Hinch from California, Sharon Hinck from Minnesota, Erin MacPherson from Texas, Patty Kirk from Oklahoma, and Erika Bentsen from Oregon.

We have some exciting special series that we hope you'll enjoy. Karen Barber will start us off each month with "Operation Thankfulness." Carol Knapp will go into depth about "The Gift of Trees." In "Listening to My Life," Scott Walker will share his inspiring midlife journey. "A Mother's Journey through Grief" is Debbie Macomber's personal account of trusting God through the pain of losing her son. Gail Thorell Schilling writes about her experiences of God's provision in "Divine Abundance." Jon Sweeney will take us through

Holy Week in "Come to Me," and Gina Bridgeman will be with us during Advent and Christmas in "Good News of Great Joy."

As you join us on a path of greater devotion to God, it is our prayer that your year will be characterized by joy and thanksgiving.

CONNECT WITH US ONLINE

We love hearing from our readers!

Whether you tweet, Facebook or still love sending handwritten letters, we want to connect with you.

Find us here: DailyGuideposts.org, Facebook.com/dailyguideposts or follow us on Twitter @DailyGuideposts.

Write to us here: DailyGPEditors@guideposts.org or *Daily Guideposts* Editor, Guideposts Books, 16 East 34th Street, New York, New York 10016.

DAILY GUIDEPOSTS IN YOUR IN-BOX

Now you can enjoy the faith-building inspiration of *Daily Guideposts* wherever you are! Receive each day's devotion on your computer, tablet or smartphone. This is a valuable benefit Guideposts offers only to members of the *Daily Guideposts* family. Visit DailyGuideposts.org/DGP2013 and enter this code: DGP2013.

January

*...Giving thanks always
and for everything to God the Father
in the name of our Lord Jesus Christ.*
—EPHESIANS 5:20 (ESV)

Tue 1

I am growing and becoming strong in spirit, filled with wisdom, and the grace of God is upon me. —LUKE 2:40

A few times a year, our sons Henry and Solomon stand barefoot in the kitchen with their backs against the doorway molding and we put a line with the date alongside their name.

Over the years, we've added the heights of our extended family, my siblings and their children; even my mom has a line charted on our wall. This morning as the sun rose, I went to the kitchen to start the coffee. *Another year*, I thought. I stood in front of the height markings and looked down at the smallest line. I remember my husband delicately holding Henry in a light-blue sleeper and penciling in his length when he was all of three months old. Seeing the fragile line so close to the ground, it's hard to believe Henry was ever that small, that five years have flown by.

I touched the line right below mine, the line from my sister Maria who died three years ago. It feels like forever since she stood in my kitchen, and yet sometimes she's so close in my heart and memory it's as if she is still here. And then I traced my husband's line. My line, like his, is bold and strong from the dozens of times it has been redrawn over the years.

Not long ago Henry looked at the wall and said, "Mom's and Dad's lines don't grow. They always stay the same."

"No," I said, picking him up and holding him on my hip. "See, they change. They're strong and thick. It's not just your body that grows. Your inside grows too. The way you think and feel, the way you love."

Dear Lord, as we begin the new year, broaden my perspective to recognize every precious gift, to see every blessing that strengthens my faith and grows my heart. —SABRA CIANCANELLI

Digging Deeper: Ps. 126:3; JAMES 1:16–18

OPERATION THANKFULNESS

Wed 2

"The king stood by his pillar and renewed the covenant in the presence of the Lord—to follow the Lord and keep his commands. . . ."
—2 CHRONICLES 34:31 (NIV)

John Wesley's Covenant Prayer basically says, "I'm all yours, God. Do what You want with me."

I wondered, *Is that sort of commitment still around these days?*

Then I got to thinking about the day our son Chris graduated from college and was commissioned as an officer in the US Army. Since an officer in any branch of the US military can administer the oath, our older son Jeff who was in the Air Force did the honors. My throat was tight with emotion as our two sons faced each other in front of the American flag and Chris raised his right hand and repeated in a clear, strong voice, "I, Christopher Barber, do solemnly swear that I will support and defend the Constitution of the United States against all enemies, foreign and domestic . . . so help me God."

At that moment, it felt like the world had suddenly started turning in the opposite direction. Ever since the day my sons were born, I had been committed to support and defend them. Now they were committed to defend and support me through their service to our country. As a parent, I knew that commitment comes at a great price. With Chris, it came when he was later deployed to war zones in Afghanistan and Iraq.

Thinking about my sons' commitments to serve in the armed forces answered my question about whether all-out commitment like what Wesley talked about still exists today. As his Covenant Prayer says: "I am no longer my own, but thine. Put me to what thou wilt."

Father, I am grateful for those who are committed to serve in our churches, communities and nation. Help me to look to them as role models when it comes my turn to serve in this new year. Amen.
—KAREN BARBER

Digging Deeper: JOSH. 24:15; JOHN 12:23–26

Thu 3

"Go from your country . . . to the land that I will show you."
—GENESIS 12:1 (RSV)

It was two years ago that John and I left our home of fifty years, and I still haven't made the move emotionally. When I confessed this to my sister last week, she reminded me of a long-ago summer. Our family spent most warm weekends at the Connecticut home of my father's brother. Uncle Raymond had a rambling cottage on a river, with a wonderful knotted rope that swung out over the water. How I longed to drop from it into the river as our older cousins did!

Uncle Raymond hosted a procession of friends as well—boring adults to us children. Until that wonderful August when I was eleven and Uncle Raymond's houseguest was Johnny Weissmuller. Tarzan was my favorite movie character, and here was Tarzan himself sitting across the table, strange in jacket and trousers. Next day, he shed them for swim trunks, looking even more heroic than on the screen. More generous too. This five-time Olympic Gold swimmer spent hours teaching my brother and sister and me the flat racing-dive.

He himself preferred to dive from the rope, flipping in the air and slicing into the water with scarcely a splash. "It's like when you swing from tree to tree in the movies," I said to him. "It looks so hard!"

"You know the really hard part?" Mr. Weissmuller said. "Letting go. But you can't reach that next tree unless you do."

That week I finally dared to let go of that rope. Maybe soon I can let a house go too.

Father, teach me to release my clutch on what was, and reach for the next place in the lifelong journey to You. —ELIZABETH SHERRILL

Digging Deeper: 2 SAM. 22:31; HEB. 11:8–12

Fri 4   *"The Lord will fight for you; you need only be still."* —EXODUS 14:14 (NIV)

Scanning the checkout lines at the grocery store, I quickly steered my cart to line number three. There were only two women there, and neither had kids or, worse, coupons! The store was my first stop that morning, and I had a half dozen others on my list before meeting my husband for lunch.

Two minutes turned into ten, and I watched as the other lines moved quickly. I rustled my items on the cart and dug for my wallet, "subtle" hints to the cashier that it was time to get a move-on.

Finally, after fifteen minutes, I took a breath and sighed. Then I heard the cashier tell the women in front of me: "And just like that, he told me what she looked like and left one hundred dollars on the register to pay for her groceries. He said not to worry about the change, just give it to charity."

The story she was sharing had taken place in the produce department. An older man had witnessed a worn-out mama in need. Shopping for staples with kids in tow, she was sticking to her list and adding the items on her calculator as she went. The gentlemen said he had a little extra on him that day, so he left one hundred dollars to cover her groceries and, just maybe, add a little wiggle room to her budget.

After hearing about the man who had quietly served a fellow traveler in life, I realized that my hurry, angst and general frustration were misplaced. What's five extra minutes in a line to hear a story of a man sharing God's love? Suddenly, I knew I could wait.

January

Remind me, Lord, that fifteen minutes in traffic, on hold or in line is simply a guilt-free excuse to spend time with You. —ASHLEY KAPPEL

Digging Deeper: ISA. 26

Sat 5   *"Be faithful until death, and I will give you the crown of life."*
—REVELATION 2:10 (NAS)

A former student of mine called to say that his life is "a train wreck." He's okay, but he set me to thinking about all the train terminology in our language:

"All aboard" means to commit to a project.

"Making the grade" is about measuring up to a task.

"A whistle stop" is a short break from work.

"A berth" is an easy, high-paying job.

"Sidetracked" means to be distracted from your real job.

"Caboose" means you are in last place.

Then a letter came from a woman in Baltimore whose husband had suddenly died, leaving her penniless. She has no skills, so she is going back to school. She closed with, "I know I'm on the right train and the train is on the right track, but where it's taking me is a great mystery."

What a lovely image of the life of faith, I thought. We are "all aboard" for heaven. Our Conductor is God. The road to heaven is steep, but we can "make the grade" if we don't get "sidetracked" or forget to take a "whistle stop" now and then. Each bend in the road is indeed a mystery but exciting, too, with new vistas and fresh challenges.

The most productive thing I can do on the railway of life is just to keep chugging along until I arrive at my eternal home. Whether I am in a "berth" or I'm just the "caboose," the important thing is to be faithful to the end.

Lord, life is longer than I thought, with many diversions. Help me stay on track and not give up until my run is over. —DANIEL SCHANTZ

Digging Deeper: Ps. 32

Sun 6

Ask me and I will tell you some remarkable secrets about what is going to happen here.
—JEREMIAH 33:3 (TLB)

It was a dreary afternoon when I sat in front of the fireplace with our dog on my lap, writing in my prayer journal. As I flipped through the pages, I saw that I'd been praying for some of the same things for years. A sense of discouragement came over me.

Our younger son's life was in constant chaos; would Dale ever find the pathway to sobriety? I have had issues with my weight since the time I was in grade school. Would my weight be a constant thorn in my flesh? I'd watched my dear friend Jane, who suffers from multiple sclerosis, deteriorate each year; would a miracle drug be discovered that would change her life? Again and again I'd poured out my heart to the Lord about a variety of subjects, and even though I'd been faithful in my Bible reading and prayer, nothing had changed. In some cases, the situations had even gotten worse.

I closed my prayer journal and questioned God. "Aren't You listening? Don't You care?"

On the wall directly across from where I sat was an elaborately framed and eloquently written Bible verse that I'd purchased years ago. All at once the words from Jeremiah 33 took on new meaning: *"Ask me and I will tell you . . . "*

Since that afternoon, when I write out my prayers, I take a moment to pause. Sometimes I feel God speaks to my heart. Other times He directs me to Scripture. Slowly, bit by bit, I'm learning what it means to simply listen.

Lord, keep my eyes open and my mouth shut that
I might hear You. —DEBBIE MACOMBER

Digging Deeper: Ps. 40:1–4

<u>Mon 7</u>

"See, I have given you this land. Go in and take possession of the land the Lord swore he would give to your fathers—to Abraham, Isaac and Jacob—and to their descendants after them."
—DEUTERONOMY 1:8 (TNIV)

Let's live in Scotland," I proposed in the weeks before my marriage. "Or Spain."

I had spent the previous decade abroad—Germany, China, Switzerland—and the concept of stasis was as foreign to me as venturing forth was to the Oklahoma farmer I was about to marry.

There was the farm to consider, Kris reminded me. His livelihood.

Also his mother, a widow in her seventies, who lived across the road.

Kris's mom was a key motivation to my wanting to live elsewhere. The two of them did everything together.

After we married, I demanded feats of cleaving, like refusing her meals and moving his tools out of her garage. Kris passed these tests, and our marriage proceeded amicably.

Nevertheless, I viewed marriage as a sacrifice. I'd relinquished distant friends, family, exotic food, speaking other languages, the freedom to leave whenever life grew difficult.

After seven years, I took a yearlong sabbatical from teaching to write. I set up my computer in the living room, between two windows. Between bouts of writing, I observed and considered the life I'd been given. The pink morning skies. Deer emerging from the woods at dusk. Birds everywhere. New friends and family surrounding me. Somehow I had been blind to these and many other delights. Considering them now, I was smitten with gratitude and eagerly entered the magnificent life I had been given.

Oh, my Father, Who loves to give me good things, help me to recognize the life I have been given as my promised land. Help me to enter it with enthusiasm.
—PATTY KIRK

Digging Deeper: DEUT. 27:3; 1 CHRON. 16:34

Tue 8   *We can rejoice, too, when we run into problems and trials for we know that they are good for us—they help us learn to be patient.* —ROMANS 5:3 (TLB)

I turned sixty-five in 2010 and was excited to qualify for Medicare. It saved me over three hundred and fifty dollars a month in medical insurance, money I put away for a thirty-six-day summer adventure to Alaska I was planning with my brother Joe and sister-in-law Linda.

As the trip got closer, I began to worry that I might not be able to keep up with my brother, nine years younger than I, and his wife, seven years younger than he. We'd be camping much of the time, something I'd done only once, years earlier.

A week before the trip, I developed a condition in my hip that required pain medication and a much slower, more deliberate walking pace. When I arrived in Alaska, determined not to even grimace in pain lest I spoil the adventure for Joe and Linda, I was relieved when she told me that my brother had experienced much the same thing the year before.

At night, I shimmied up over the seat and into the back of the van where I slept. During the day, I climbed steep hills, hiked craggy paths and biked numerous times over bumpy gravel roads. One day we even white-water rafted for four solid hours, wearing dry suits with suction cups attached to the wrists, ankles and neck in case we fell in the thirty-six-degree water. I loved it!

Thanks to a few pain pills, the compassion of my "I know what you're going through" brother and my own determination not to be a drag, I sailed through my Alaskan adventure with ease. This grandma of eight learned firsthand that age is a matter of mind: If you don't mind, it doesn't matter.

Lord, give me courage every day to do what looks difficult. Remind me that reaching for the gusto is what makes this amazing world You created truly sizzle. —PATRICIA LORENZ

Digging Deeper: DEUT. 31:6; PS. 30:10; 2 COR. 12:8–10

Wed 9 *In your anger do not sin. . . .* —EPHESIANS 4:26 (NIV)

I exploded at one of my kids this afternoon. The child had been difficult for two hours and had given me plenty of provocation, but I was beyond mad. Fortunately, one of my other children shouted, "Mom, you have to stop!" So I grabbed a jacket and left the apartment, trusting that if my heart could not move itself to a better place, my feet could do the job.

It was pouring, and I strode into the wind in fierce, long steps. The cold rain did not wash away my anger. Ten minutes into my adrenaline-driven power walk, an observation slipped into my thoughts: The strength of my reaction was out of proportion to the offense given. I pushed the idea away like the wet hair falling into my eyes, but it returned to drip uncomfortably in my mind.

A block later, I stopped under a store awning, smeared my glasses clean with a wet finger and considered the facts. My child had done wrong, and I had legitimate reason to be upset. But a few drops of righteous anger had been lost in a torrent of self-righteous indignation. *Show me the difference, Lord. I can see my child's sin. Show me mine.*

I sighed and shivered. The part of my heart that moments before had burned with anger now stung with cold, sticky regret. *I'm sorry, Lord. I am so sorry.* I turned toward home and caught a glimpse of myself in a storefront window. I did not look beautiful, and, yet, I did. For a contrite heart is a glorious thing, and what the rain can't wash clean, Jesus can.

> *Lord, cleanse my heart of the seeds of sin.*
> —JULIA ATTAWAY

> *Digging Deeper:* Ps. 51

DIVINE ABUNDANCE

Thu 10   *Use hospitality one to another without grudging.* —1 PETER 4:9

Brushing toast crumbs off the morning newspaper, I consider eating my oatmeal out of the cooking pot to save dishes. If Jacqui were still alive, how she would frown upon such casual dining! I smile at her memory, spoon my cereal into a proper bowl and remember my former Boston neighbor that first year I was married.

When my neighbor Jacqui first invited me for a potluck supper, I quickly discovered that this was not a clean-the-fridge affair. My Welsh-born friend set her table with a lace cloth and dozens of choices: entrées, sides, salads, desserts and breads.

Our friendship deepened over the next forty years and I learned that Jacqui genuinely enjoyed feeding family and friends, either by serving them at her table or by giving them food gifts. Over the summer, Jacqui made jellies from local grapes and berries, and pickles from the cucumbers and onions in her garden. She began holiday baking in November—mounds of cookies and tea breads.

My most recent visit with Jacqui coincided with a twice-canceled early morning hair appointment, so we talked late the night before, knowing we would miss each other the next day. When I rose, I found the breakfast table set with willowware on floral placemats. Honey, jam and butter awaited the scones. Coffee was brewed; orange juice poured. She had even partially browned the bacon, ready to be crisped by her husband when he cooked the eggs.

I savored my meal then and will remember it forever, for my beloved friend died suddenly a few weeks later. Like a benediction, the love in Jacqui's last breakfast will continue to nourish me for a long time.

Our Father, Who gives us our daily bread, thank You for the friends who feed our bodies and our souls.
—GAIL THORELL SCHILLING

Digging Deeper: JOHN 15:15; 1 PET. 4:9

Fri 11   *Say to those who are of a fearful heart, "Be strong, do not fear! Here is your God.... He will come...."*
—ISAIAH 35:4 (NAS)

My grandmother Gaia turned eighty this year. Gaia and I had only gotten closer as I'd grown up. Her honesty about her upbringing, in a family that didn't respect a woman's right to self-expression, helped me not only understand her better but also appreciate the barriers the women of her generation had to overcome.

So there was no way I was going to miss her birthday. I flew from Texas to New Jersey, and drove to Gaia's house with my parents. I greeted her, wished her a happy birthday and milled around the party, eating hors d'oeuvres and meeting her very best friends in the world.

Then, Gaia did an amazing thing. After everyone arrived, she had all of us gather in the living room. "I am so grateful that you are all here," Gaia said, "and I want to tell each one of you how much I love you." Several of her friends, more comfortable acknowledging others than being acknowledged, protested that it was *her* birthday, but Gaia was undeterred. She spent the next forty-five minutes publicly thanking every person at the party, highlighting their many good deeds. She acknowledged their work as therapists, social workers and volunteers; as helpers of the blind, the dying, the elderly and sometimes just regular people who needed comfort. She did this with a face full of life and God's love.

I was inspired. She was showing a strength she had hinted at before but had never displayed so clearly. I was witnessing a holy transformation, from a good-hearted but frightened person to a woman with the courage to be grateful and say it out loud.

And I understood that my fears didn't need to own my life. If my eighty-year-old grandmother could be courageous, then so could I.

Thank You, Lord, for Your messengers who lead us toward Your way of life. —SAM ADRIANCE

Digging Deeper: PROV. 4:8–10; 2 COR. 3:18

Sat 12

Moses answered the people, "Do not be afraid. Stand firm and you will see the deliverance the Lord will bring you today. The Egyptians you see today you will never see again."
—EXODUS 14:13 (NIV)

Millie is not a fearful or aggressive dog. True, she's wary of the car because we got into an accident when she was a puppy and she has never forgotten the Jeep flipping over. Otherwise she is kind, patient, curious and extremely friendly. Nothing really troubles her. Except horses.

For reasons I can't fathom and God refuses to explain, my dog Millie goes berserk at the sight of a horse. I mean she totally loses it. Roaring like a lion and snapping her jaws, she will practically pull me off my feet if she sees a horse-drawn carriage or mounted police officer.

The actual presence of a horse is not even required. The mere scent of one or the sound of equine hooves clacking on the pavement will drive her into a frenzy. Even after a horse is no longer on the scene she will have outbursts of barking, like some kind of canine maniac.

"Well," a friend said, "she clearly has an irrational fear of horses."

Can dogs have irrational fears? Are dogs even rational? I thought about that. Anyone who's had a dog knows they can figure out things, especially if it involves food. Therefore a dog can be rational and can have irrational or unreasonable fears. *Poor Millie!* I thought.

Then again I am not without my own irrational fears. I sometimes fear the future or pain or loneliness or failure. Yet I know no failure is final, my family and friends will never abandon me, pain can be endured, and God is as much in the future as He is in the present. Still there have been moments in my life when I have given in to fear, when I should have held more tightly to my faith.

One of these days I'm going to figure out Millie's equinophobia. In the meantime, I will keep her in my prayers and learn a lesson.

God, You protect me from many dangers. Most of all, protect me from my fear. —EDWARD GRINNAN

Digging Deeper: Pss. 27:1–3, 107:6; ISA. 41:10

Sun 13   *O come, let us worship and bow down: let us kneel before the Lord our maker. For he is our God; and we are the people of his pasture, and the sheep of his hand. . . .*
—PSALM 95:6–7

David Simpson is a bright, verbal four-year-old with a stream of consciousness that can run like the wind, especially during our Sunday school lessons. His enthusiasm for all that crosses his path is hard to contain. "Hold that thought, Davis," I'll say. And he tries.

One Sunday, our lesson was about Jesus, the Good Shepherd, Who takes good care of His sheep and knows everyone by name. Davis, sitting next to me in the semicircle of children, was his usual talkative self, chatting about a birthday party and his favorite planet. Each time, I brought him back to the fold. I showed the children the green grass, the clear, still water, and how God watches over them through danger.

"Who are the sheep?" I asked.

"We are," the children said.

At the end of the lesson we had prayer time, and I asked the children if there was something they'd like to say to God. After a long silence, Davis began, "Thank you . . ." Then he stopped. "Thank you," he began again.

He held out his arms as if searching for a word that was big enough to hold it all. Finally it spilled out of him, all his enthusiasm pulled together in one pithy sentence that summed it up for the whole class. "Thank You, God, for life!"

Lord Jesus, thank You for the simple joy of being and for children who exude it.
—SHARI SMYTH

Digging Deeper: DEUT. 6:7; Ps. 34:11; PROV. 22:6

Mon 14

"And forgive us our sins, just as we have forgiven those who have sinned against us."
—MATTHEW 6:12 (TLB)

As every TV police drama will tell you, a crime requires three elements: motivation, method and opportunity. Here's something I've learned about myself: At any random moment, I can be a total pain in the neck. I often have the motive, I always have the method, and I don't have to wait for the opportunity—I'll create my very own inappropriate occasion. Catch me on any workday morning on I-279 inbound, and I'll provide a vivid demonstration of my peevish ways.

Consider this: Think of a time you were unkind toward someone you loved. I'll bet you can remember every detail, much to your chagrin. You know what you did (acted like something less than a human being), and you know you're capable of doing it again. No one has to show us how; we seem to know instinctively.

Now think of a time when you made a genuine, positive difference in another's life. Think of a time when you were fully human: open, vulnerable, giving, full of agape rather than sour grapes. I'll bet you have far fewer details about that experience. It was more of a feeling, a stillness, a smile.

Why God chooses to love our species is beyond me. We are so skilled at hurting each other through myriad schemes; we seem to have an endless source of treachery. But compassion? Commitment? Not so much. Each act of humanity, each act of random kindness surprises us, as if we're treading virgin ground. Strangely, we had a very, very good Teacher to show us how, yet His lessons seem new every time.

So, a resolution this year: Mea culpa (mea maxima culpa) to those I love for my many transgressions.

> *Lord, please be patient as I learn (relearn, for the millionth time) how to act like a human being, how to act as I was taught, how to embrace the better angels of my fallen nature.* —MARK COLLINS

Digging Deeper: ROM. 8:1–11; COL. 3:13–15; 1 PET. 4:8

THE GIFT OF TREES

Tue 15

The king made... cedars as plentiful as sycamore trees that are in the lowland. —1 KINGS 10:27 (NAS)

Sycamore stories begin as far back in the Bible as the Egyptian plagues—when God "destroyed their vines with hailstones. And their sycamore trees with frost" (Psalm 78:47). They are a humble tree... mostly gone from Israel now. Related to the fig, their fruit is not as sweet. In the time of Jesus, only the poor ate sycamore figs.

It was a wealthy man who climbed the sycamore the day Jesus came to Jericho. Zaccheus had cheated to make himself rich as chief tax collector. But he couldn't make himself tall. The sycamore's burly, low-spreading branches were ideal for a glimpse of the One everyone was abuzz about.

Luke relates how Jesus saw him in the tree, told him to hurry down and announced Himself as

Zaccheus' next house guest! Before they'd even arrived home, Zaccheus said, "Lord, half of my possessions I will give to the poor, and if I have defrauded anyone of anything, I will give back four times as much" (Luke 19:8).

Jesus answered, "Today salvation has come to this house . . . For the Son of Man has come to seek and to save that which was lost" (Luke 19:9–10).

It's amazing how an encounter with Jesus invites a person to unload baggage. My daughter once confessed a major lie to me, asking forgiveness. Moments later when she questioned me about something I'd been keeping hidden, I told the truth. I could not lie before the Light of Christ shining in her. A long journey lay ahead, but I had taken that first honest step.

Truthful Savior, remember way back when I used to call the sycamore a "more sicker" tree? Call me out of there to find a lifetime of fresh, healthy beginnings in You. —CAROL KNAPP

Digging Deeper: LAM. 5:21; EPH. 4:22–24;
I JOHN 2:5

Wed 16

"My presence will go with you. . . ."
—EXODUS 33:14 (RSV)

When my brother and sister and I traveled to Jordan two years ago, each of us had one place we wanted most to visit. For Caroline, it was the ancient city of Petra with its tombs carved in the sandstone cliffs; for Donn, Lawrence of Arabia's desert vastness of Wadi Rum; for me, the pinnacle of Mt. Nebo from which Moses saw the promised land.

Petra was even more fabulous than its reputation. Wadi Rum overwhelmed us all. And I was sure Mt. Nebo would be more spectacular still. We drove toward it across a barren landscape that got us talking gloomily about the future of our planet. What kind of polluted world, I asked, would our nine-year-old great-grandson Adin inherit?

At last we reached a low, very unspectacular hill crowned with worship sites and centuries of ruins: Mt. Nebo. We stood as Moses did, looking out across a vast dry plateau, the same harsh, desert terrain we'd been traversing all day.

"*That* is the promised land?" Caroline said out loud what I was thinking.

I thought of Moses seeing from here the goal of forty years wandering and wondered how he'd felt. He knew he could not accompany his people into that demanding land, just as I cannot accompany Adin into the future. Did Moses despair, looking at that daunting landscape, as I so often do, contemplating our threatened environment? Or did he entrust those he loved to the God Who had promised him and them and us: "My presence will go with you."

Father, help me know, with Moses, that Your promises are forever. —ELIZABETH SHERRILL

Digging Deeper: GEN. 12:1–9; JER. 31:16–18; 2 PET. 1:3–5

Thu 17

In Your light we see light.
—PSALM 36:9 (NKJV)

A brass candleholder sits on a ledge in my living room, where it unobtrusively supports a short white candle. I strike a match and light the wick only on special occasions, just as company arrives for dinner. No one ever seems to notice the solitary flame, protected from drafts by a glass chimney. I see it differently.

The light's container connects me to my natal family; it was one of my parents' seven distinct brass candlesticks, each a different height and form, each representing one of their children. In the estate, the tallest went to the oldest; mine is one of the smaller—not that I feel shortchanged.

The burning wax ties me to my faith community. I don't buy new candles but pick up giveaway stubs that have blazed out their first half-life at the church, behind the altar.

Then there's the fire itself. Last night it caught my eye soon after seven girlfriends settled around a tray of appetizers. When Friend A noticed the stress of Friend B over hospitalized Friend C, she offered a suggestion: "Could we just stop and pray right now?" All agreed, and I took the lead.

Before I closed my eyes, the sight of the flame drew my spirit toward God's gracious light shining in our midst. After the "amen," it seemed the reflection of the candle in a mirror confirmed my guests' place in the good company of God's large family—and consequently mine.

Lord, may my family and home, like a brass candlestick, hold Your gracious light as it shines on, in and among my guests. —EVELYN BENCE

Digging Deeper: ISA. 60:1; JOHN 12:45–47

Fri 18   *Peace, peace to him that is far off, and to him that is near....*
             —ISAIAH 57:19

My wife Corinne and I were going to extend a business trip I had to make to Colorado and enjoy a few days of vacation. I couldn't wait. The last year of my life had been more than mind-boggling, and merging households and lifestyles had proven to be more difficult than we thought it would be.

We had both been single and career-oriented for many years. I had been raising Harrison, my eleven-year-old son; Corinne had her career plus the new responsibility of creating a home for someone other than herself. Our work schedules were different, and we both had our own sets of friends. Sometimes it seemed we were swimming upstream.

No wonder I had grabbed this time to take my fairly new bride away from it all. After my meetings, I found myself alone with Corinne. Acres of pure white powder covered a pristine mountain; a big blue sky spread above us. The sparkling snow created an aura of simplicity and peace. I was reminded of why we had fallen in love. We wanted to create a life together, something good, worthwhile...a place of peace.

I thought ahead to the chaos of everyday life back in Nashville, Tennessee. We couldn't stay on this mountaintop forever, but we could create spaces of peace wherever we happened to be. Together, we needed to be more choosy about the activities we took on, take turns with household chores and create more family space. After all, there were sunsets waiting, chances for early morning coffee, long talks and night walks. The choice to move toward a life of peace would always be ours.

> *Father, give us the wisdom to search for and*
> *find Your perfect peace.* —BROCK KIDD
>
> *Digging Deeper:* ISA. 26:3; 1 THESS. 5:23–24

Sat 19

> *"Their sins and their lawless deeds I*
> *will remember no more."*
> —HEBREWS 10:17 (NKJV)

For me, January is always the month of beginning again. I have packed away the bright trappings of Christmas, and our post-holiday house has a simple feel. We crave vegetable soup and cornbread, baked sweet potatoes, hot oatmeal.

The time is right to consider the year that lies ahead. I smile, suddenly recalling the words I used to say to our son Brock each night as I tucked him into bed: "Tomorrow's a clean blackboard with all the mistakes you made today erased away!"

I can almost hear God saying the same thing, as I remember a long-ago teacher choosing me to clean the blackboard. This coveted assignment involved standing on a chair and erasing every word on the blackboard and then gathering the erasers and going out to the back of the school building. There, I pounded the erasers against the wall until fanciful clouds of chalk dust floated toward the sky.

I laugh out loud, imagining God pounding the chalk from His big eraser after He has wiped our slate clean. A year's worth of my mistakes would seem to cloud the horizon, but God promises the opposite.

I am free to choose. I can leave my mistakes, my disappointments, my bad attitudes to yesterday. I can rewrite myself as a person of hope. I can get up each morning with an attitude of appreciation and turn every event into an occasion of thankfulness. If my life is too complicated, I have the power to make simpler choices.

God has tucked me in with His promise. I wake to a new day; my blackboard is clean; my mistakes have dissipated into the wind. How will I choose to write the new year?

Only You can make me brand-new, Father. Thank You. —PAM KIDD

Digging Deeper: Ps. 25

Sun 20 *How good and pleasant it is when God's people live together in unity!* —PSALM 133:1 (TNIV)

My husband turned to me with frustration on his face. "Yoshiko sent an e-mail. She doesn't understand why we want to sing the worship songs simultaneously in English and Japanese."

I was confused. "I thought we already explained that we want people to sing in their own language, so they won't have to stand there silent while we sing a stanza in an unfamiliar language. I don't speak Japanese, and I don't know if she understands my e-mails." Normally, my church has separate services so the English-speaking and Japanese-speaking congregations can worship in their own language, but once a year we have a joint service and a church picnic afterward. My husband and I are the worship leaders for the joint service this year, with two Japanese-speaking women joining the team. I was getting cranky because this language barrier seemed to be causing unexpected problems.

On the day of the service, even though I knew our decision about singing the songs in Japanese and English was a good one, I worried that the dual languages might make for a bit of musical chaos. At first, it did sound strange. But as the service went on, I saw people with eyes closed and hands raised, peace and joy on their faces as they praised God in their own language. I tried to imagine how God would feel to hear all these people praising Him at once, and I think God loves hearing different tongues raised in worship together, in unity as one body, bonded together by our love of Him.

Lord, open my eyes to ways I can help my church be a unified congregation, with our focus on You.
—CAMY TANG

Digging Deeper: JOHN 4:24; 1 COR. 12:2;
EPH. 4:1–3

Mon 21

And the people the men of Israel encouraged themselves, and set their battle again in array....
—JUDGES 20:22

A friend suggested that we go sightseeing in Washington, DC, to catch a glimpse of the Martin Luther King Jr. National Memorial.

In all honesty, I was weary when I began the day's journey. I am a dreamer and my plate always seems too full. There had been progress with some projects related to faith, homelessness, civil rights and justice, but there were always setbacks.

As Theresa drove us toward the National Mall, I smiled at her as we spoke, but inside I wondered if I should surrender. Maybe just find a quiet place where I could paint, bake and think about pleasant things. Other people have those kinds of lives. Why not me?

We rode past the Lincoln Memorial, the Jefferson Memorial... then I saw white granite peeking through the tree branches heavy with green leaves.

Dr. King worked tirelessly and sacrificed his life for a dream of justice and equality for all. As we walked through the memorial site, we were greeted by people of all races, ages and languages. The Inscription Wall read: "We shall overcome because the arc of the moral universe is long, but it bends toward justice."

I took a deep breath.

"I believe that unarmed truth and unconditional love will have the final word in reality. This is why right, temporarily defeated, is stronger than evil triumphant."

Tears clouded my vision. "Make a career of humanity. Commit yourself to the noble struggle for equal rights. You will make a greater person of yourself, a greater nation of your country, and a finer world to live in." I nodded, ready to begin again.

Lord, thank You for the soldiers and drum majors You have sent to encourage us and make life better. Strengthen us to fight on. —SHARON FOSTER

Digging Deeper: JOHN 16:25; 2 TIM. 4:6–8

Tue 22

And even the very hairs of your head are all numbered.
—MATTHEW 10:30 (NIV)

As my body glided into the MRI machine, I'd never felt so alone. The odd jackhammer sounds battered me as I focused on breathing and staying still. Doctors needed a peek inside my brain, which I already knew was a scary place.

Brains are so complex. Damage can wipe out memories, cause system-wide physical problems, even change personalities. Why couldn't they be looking for something a bit more straightforward, like a broken bone?

As the machine shifted to a new round of clacking noises, God whispered the words from Matthew into my heart. God knows each hair on my head. He also knows each cell in my body—even the beautiful, complicated brain cells that provide home for so much personality, communication and memory. After all, He created them. Even the wisest doctors have limited understanding of how our bodies work. Yet none of it overwhelms or confuses God.

My muscles relaxed as I remembered that I could trust God's love, whatever the future would hold.

Lord, thank You for knowing me intimately and holding me close through each uncertainty in life's journey. Amen.
—SHARON HINCK

Digging Deeper: 2 SAM. 22:3; PSS. 31:14, 139:1–3

Wed 23

Cast all your anxieties on him, for he cares about you.
—1 PETER 5:7 (RSV)

"My nanny called in sick today!" a fellow mom grumbled at an open play space. "This couldn't have come at a worse time! My husband is on a business trip and my housekeeper's on vacation!" Her mellow daughter was quietly playing with a doll as my two boys were running around in circles, rowdy and loud as always.

My husband wasn't on a business trip; he was in Texas after asking for a divorce. I'd never had a nanny to help with my children and could only dream of a housekeeper to clean the mess that was waiting for me at home.

The mom continued to complain and all I could do was nod, fighting the urge to scream. *What do you know about suffering?* I wanted to ask. *What do you know about being lonely and tired with no one to help you at all?*

Playtime was over. I wrestled my two toddlers into their coats and shoved the double stroller through the snow, praying they'd nap when we got home. They did.

As I sat down for a rare moment of rest, I turned on the television. A commercial showed a mother holding her hungry, dying child. She looked right at me, and I could hear her asking: "What do you know about suffering?"

My pain could never compare with hers, just like the grumbling mom's couldn't compare with mine.

God loves each of us and cares about our sadness and frustrations, be they great or little. Each of us has a right to our pain, in whatever measure it comes. I also know, begrudgingly, this applies to the privileged, grumbling mom at the gym. God is there for everyone.

Despite my pain, God, I am thankful for Your love.
—KAREN VALENTIN

Digging Deeper: Ps. 86:15–16; 1 PET. 4:13

Thu 24

"You shall clear out the old to make way for the new."
—LEVITICUS 26:10 (RSV)

"Don't put it down; put it away." A friend passed along this tip that she'd read in Dear Abby years ago. Those seven words lodged in my brain and proved very helpful in my ongoing battle against clutter. Previously, I'd find myself with a ketchup bottle in hand, for example, and think, *I'll just set it here.* An hour later I'd be looking for it and wonder why it was on my coffee table in the living room. One day, in a grateful mood, I phoned my friend to tell her how much that saying had helped me with my goal of taming clutter.

After she thanked me for letting her know, we moved on to other topics. I immediately brought up an annoying customer at work who'd come in the week before and yelled at me for not finding any books on Julia Morgan, the famous architect. "She acted like I was an idiot!" I exclaimed. My friend cut in, "Linda, remember: Don't put it down, put it away!"

"Huh?" was my inelegant response. "We're not talking about clutter here."

"Oh, but we are. That's brain clutter. Why are you still carrying around a grudge against someone, when the event happened more than a week ago?"

There was no good answer to that question, so I put it away. I found that I was happier talking about my friend's graduation from college and the customer who'd complimented me on finding just the right book for her husband's birthday.

Lord, am I holding a grudge? Today, let me not just put it down, let me put it away. —LINDA NEUKRUG

Digging Deeper: Ps. 141:3–5; MARK 11:25; 2 COR. 2:5–7

Fri 25

The Lord is nigh unto all them that call upon him. . . . —PSALM 145:18

I had just read a passage in a book about prayer, explaining how God was always waiting to hear from us, that He longed for us to call, that He was always ready to listen. Something slightly cynical in me bridled at the notion. As ready as I usually am to yammer on about things, I couldn't quite see how God would be so ready and willing to listen to me.

Then in the middle of my morning, when I had a meeting in a half hour, tons of e-mails to be answered and a huge impatience with any interruptions, the phone rang. "Hello," I answered quickly, making sure my tone said, "I'm busy. Make it brisk."

"Hey, Dad." It was William, 7:30 in the morning his time of day. He was on his Blue Tooth commuting to work. All at once my tone changed. "William, how are you?"

He told me about the job he was on right now and how he found it frustrating. He talked about a good friend who had gotten a job in the Bay Area and was moving to his neighborhood. He described a dinner party a group of young women had thrown that Wednesday. I was able to ask him about the job interview, the final round he was going for on Friday afternoon. "At this point, if they offer me something, I'm really tempted to take it," he said. "Gotta go."

"Me too," I said.

Ten minutes was all, but they were the heart of my day. I'd connected with my son; he'd connected with me. For those ten minutes, even though I was intensely busy, I had all the time in the world.

Later I went back to that passage about prayer. I got it, or at least got why God is often compared to a father: He hangs on every word, and He's always ready to listen.

*Our Father, Who art in heaven—
glad You're listening.* —RICK HAMLIN

Digging Deeper: Ps. 5:1–3; Mal. 3:16

Sat 26

Enter his gates with thanksgiving and his courts with praise; give thanks to him and praise his name.
—PSALM 100:4 (NIV)

I've never been good at keeping New Year's resolutions, but it's not for lack of trying. For nearly a decade, I was religious in my approach. The day after Christmas, I'd hole away for an hour and log ten or twelve goals for the coming year, using "I resolve to..." language and everything.

I'd go strong through Valentine's Day, and then my once-laudable effort would fizzle and fall flat.

Five years ago, I adopted a new approach. I opted instead for an annual theme. Humility, for instance, was one. Then, faithfulness, gentleness, peace. This January 1, I declared it the year of gratitude, a focus that has refocused my days and my gaze. Both the mundane and the meaningful around me now birth abundant reasons to stop and give thanks.

While scrambling eggs at daylight's first squint: *Thank You, Father, for food, for refrigeration, for utensils, for nourishment that leads to strength.*

While putting my daughter's diapers in the wash: *Thank You for water and soap and electricity. Thank You for Prisca's development and good health.*

While reviewing a new contract for a book deal: *Thank You for work that I enjoy, for clients I admire, for subjects that make me want to live a whole and holy life.*

While melting into my husband's embrace: *Thank You for showing Your children how to love each other and You, and for being delighted when they do those things well.*

So far, the year has taught me that "thank you" is a muscle that either atrophies or grows strong, and that flexing it on purpose always changes me for the good.

Father, let me encounter each moment of today with a ready "thank you" on my lips. —ASHLEY WIERSMA

Digging Deeper: 2 CHRON. 30:4–6; EZEK. 40:1–3; HEB. 13:15–16

Sun 27

"I have loved you with an everlasting love...."
—JEREMIAH 31:3 (NIV)

With a heavy heart, I plodded to my office and reread my lesson plan. I felt physically, emotionally and mentally drained. Having been diagnosed with two autoimmune illnesses, fatigue could be the explanation, but that was no excuse. Teachers teach. And I'd been teaching Sunday school for twenty years. I needed to buckle down and try harder.

God, what's wrong with me? Fix me. Change me.

Silence.

I began to dread preparing my lessons, but I saw no way out. I couldn't shake the belief that God's love for me was based on my hard work. I called a dear friend and poured out my heart.

"Julie," she said softly, "God loves you whether you teach Sunday school or not."

What if she's right?

Impossible. Yet I sensed a flicker of hope rise in me, and I wanted to believe.

"That's the beauty of grace," she said. "Rest in it." Her words were like pink rosebuds for my soul— soft and sweet and light. They wooed me to venture into a wider place in my faith. The following Sunday morning, I finally told my class how I'd been feeling. They responded with hugs and kindness. A new eager teacher volunteered, full of enthusiasm.

As the sun rose last Sunday, I tiptoed outside and sat on my front porch, watching birds at the feeder. In the lavender predawn light, I experienced something alive and fresh—a timeless love from my Father that didn't depend on what I did for Him.

Lord, even when I'm resting You still love me!
—JULIE GARMON

Digging Deeper: GEN. 2:1–3; 1 KINGS 8:56;
1 JOHN 3:1–3

Mon 28

"Where you go, I will go; Where you lodge, I will lodge. . . ."
—RUTH 1:16 (NRSV)

The photo was tacked to a bulletin board in the family room. I passed it every time I opened the door to the garage. This time I stopped to look. There were the four of us: Kate, me, our kids Frances and Benjamin. Wrapped in parkas against the winter cold, we stood on our old New

York street in front of our apartment. A friend took the picture moments before we left New York for California. We're smiling but we look apprehensive.

Six months later I still felt apprehensive. Past the door to the garage was our new car. *We didn't have a car in New York. We took subways. I like subways. I don't like the suburbs,* I thought.

I sighed. I missed our apartment too. *I wonder who lives there now?* I remembered gazing out our third-floor windows at the honking streets below. Rocking the kids to sleep in the glow of nighttime streetlights. Watching snow fall on the churchyard next door.

"It doesn't help to dwell on the past," Kate often reminded me. Easy for her to say. She liked her new job as rector of an Episcopal church. "Our true home is with God," she always added.

I stared longingly at the photo. *Wait a second*. Actually, that wasn't our apartment in the background. It was the apartment across the street. How come I'd never noticed before? I was so full of self-pity I'd simply assumed it was our apartment. I'd made up an entire story about that photo, but of course it wasn't about the apartment at all. It was about the four of us: Kate, me, Frances and Benjamin. We were together there just like we're together here.

Our true home is with God. I struggled with those words here in this new place. But surely being together with family gives us at least a glimpse of God's eternal love. In New York. In California. Anywhere.

Help me feel Your presence, God, wherever I am.
—JIM HINCH

Digging Deeper: PSS. 91:1, 139:7–10; ACTS 2:28

Tue 29

"For the Lord your God goes with you; he will never leave you nor forsake you."
—DEUTERONOMY 31:6 (NIV)

"How are you?" I asked my daughter-in-law Alexandra in a mid-morning telephone call. A few weeks earlier she delivered their fourth child.

"We all have doctors' appointments this afternoon," she answered, coughing. "I think we've caught something."

"How will you manage?" I wondered out loud.

"This is my life," she responded with teeth-gritting determination. "I can do this!"

"But you don't have to do it alone," I said. "I'll go with you."

So there we were, Alex carrying the newborn, me wheeling a stroller for two-year-old Gracie, who was wheezing, and six-year-old Genevieve and nine-year-old Gabi straggling along. Within the next hour, Alex was diagnosed with pneumonia,

Genevieve given a prescription for antibiotics, and Gracie hooked up to oxygen. "We're getting an ambulance to take Gracie to the hospital right now," the doctor told us.

Alex needed to ride in the ambulance with Gracie, so she handed me the baby who'd never been more than an arm's length from her nursing mommy. She started to cry.

"I have to go to the bathroom," Genevieve said. "Right now!"

At that moment, a woman behind the desk said, "Let me help you. I'll get that prescription for you."

Within minutes we were headed for the car. *I can do this!* I thought, looking at the girls in the rearview mirror, *but I don't have to do it alone.*

Father, I remind others about Your promise that we don't face our challenges alone. Sometimes I need to be reminded too. —CAROL KUYKENDALL

Digging Deeper: EXOD. 13:16; ISA. 40:29; PHIL. 4:12–13

Wed 30   "*If my people, which are called by my name, shall humble themselves, and pray. . . .*"—2 CHRONICLES 7:14

"G ene," I begged my husband, "Will you come with me to look for a coffee table?" His expression said it all; Gene hates to shop. "Never mind." I'd just go myself. I was still hopeful that I'd find the table of my dreams.

Sure enough, I found the ideal one: oval shaped with a glass top—from the 1950s. The owner of the shop and I struck up an impromptu friendship and had a lengthy conversation. She was helping me carry my find to the car when we heard screeching brakes, a horrifying thud and then high-pitched screams. We quickly put down the table, and she sprinted into the street with some other pedestrians. I froze in the doorway of her shop. Obviously, someone had been hit. *Should I run into the street?* However, I sensed silent instructions: *Stay put and pray.*

"Oh, Father, have mercy. Let them live and not die." The screams continued; so did my prayers. After two ambulances carried the victims to the hospital, I drove home, still shaken, still praying.

The next day, I read that a father and two children had been hit. The mother and another child had remained on the sidewalk. "Miraculously, everyone was okay," the article stated. Putting aside the newspaper, I settled down in my prayer chair with my journal and Bible on my new table—and a new sense of urgency about prayer, and obedience.

Father, failure to pray isn't an option for Your people, is it? —MARION BOND WEST

Digging Deeper: MATT. 11:29; ROM. 5:3–4; 1 COR. 3:13–15

Thu 31

He comforts us in all our troubles so that we can comfort others.
—2 CORINTHIANS 1:4 (NAS)

Because of a tumor in my back, I sometimes have difficulty walking. Today, at the veterans hospital where I work as a nurse, I had to hold on to the railing in the hallway in order to make my rounds. I struggled to take a step and then came to a complete halt.

My eyes met a patient's, in a wheelchair. I'd seen him around the hospital, but I didn't know his name. He had wavy brown hair and flew Old Glory from the IV pole on his chair. A makeshift bumper sticker proclaimed, "America is #1."

"I just got some great news, nurse," the gentleman told me. "They aren't going to have to take my leg off after all."

I smiled at his worn tennis shoes, completely unprepared for what he would say next. "I didn't have anyone to tell, and then I saw you having trouble getting around. I knew you'd understand."

If I hadn't been suffering today, that veteran would never have identified with me. And I wouldn't have had the opportunity to hug him and say, "Thanks for choosing me to share your good news. I'll be praying for you, sir. And, thank you for your service to America. I appreciate everything you did for our freedom."

*There's nothing like the comfort You provide, Father.
Help me to pass it along to others in my path.*
—ROBERTA MESSNER

Digging Deeper: ISA. 66:13; JER. 31:13;
2 COR. 1:3–4

GIVING THANKS

1 _____

2 _____

3 _____

4 _____

5 _____

6 _____

7 _____

8 _____

9 _____

10 _____

11 _____

12 _____

13 _____

January

14 _____

15 _____

16 _____

17 _____

18 _____

19 _____

20 _____

21 _____

22 _____

23 _____

24 _____

25 _____

26 _____

27 _____

28 _____

29 _____

30 _____

31 _____

February

*By him therefore let us offer the sacrifice
of praise to God continually, that is, the
fruit of our lips giving thanks to his name.*

—HEBREWS 13:15

OPERATION THANKFULNESS

Fri 1   *"Who dares despise the day of small things . . . ?"* —ZECHARIAH 4:10 (NIV)

As I was turning my husband Gordon's running socks right side out to throw into the washing machine, I thought, *My life seems like an annoying series of dull, ordinary things. Drive to the store because we're out of bananas and milk for the second time this week. Sort through the mountain of junk mail on the kitchen desk. Replant the winter pansies the deer ate.*

Then I remembered the first time I sat at my computer, trying to write an e-mail to our son Chris after he was deployed to Iraq. I kept hitting the Delete button because everything I started to write seemed trivial and unimportant. Gordon, who had been stationed overseas in Okinawa in the US Army before I knew him, gave me some good advice. "Chris doesn't really want to hear a lot of great fun and exciting things going on here because it will make him feel like he's missing out. Just write about the ordinary stuff that goes on every day. Trust me. He'll like it."

Suddenly, I recalled the long, blessedly uneventful letters my mother used to write to me. "It's really dry here, but we got some rain yesterday. The corn is just about ripe. We've been getting a lot of okra, and I froze ten quarts. The dogs went with us on a nice walk down to the church..." Each letter, though filled with mundane details, was like a heavenly minivisit home—comforting enough to be reread right before I got in bed, helping me drift off into a peaceful sleep.

Gordon's advice was golden. During Chris's deployment, I filled my e-mails with little details of ordinary life. "Dad had a guy come out and fix the riding lawnmower. Last time he did the lawn, it looked like a very bad haircut because the blade was so uneven...."

Dear Father, thank You for the ordinary rhythms of daily life that bring peace, balance and grace to my life. Amen. —KAREN BARBER

Digging Deeper: 2 TIM. 2:14–16

Sat 2   *Start children off on the way they should go, and even when they are old they will not turn from it.*
—PROVERBS 22:6 (TNIV)

Ever since my daughters became teenagers, with minds and desires of their own—minds that questioned every truth they'd ever been told and desires that rejected the church they've attended from babyhood—I've wakened each morning with the same prayer: "Father, let them turn to You. Let them know You."

As soon as I pray these words, though, I unpray them.

"How can God make them turn to Him?" another voice in me asks. "Surely, if any aspect of faith is up to us, it's that initial impulse to know one's maker."

This year I attended a faculty workshop in spiritual formation. We returned repeatedly to the questions at the root of my morning prayer-struggle. Does God *make* us believe, or are we on our own? Can our strategies as teachers or parents— can our prayers—inspire spiritual growth in another?

I like to think of believing as work. The only work of God, in fact. When asked what work God requires, Jesus answered, "The work of God is this: to believe in the one he has sent" (John 6:29, TNIV).

After the workshop, a colleague offered a devotion about Peter's unsettling dream in which God deemed permissible all the foods forbidden in the law.

"This story isn't about food or even the law," he told us. "It's about Peter's growth as a believer."

And he showed us how, in the story—before, after and even while Peter dreamed—a stranger named Cornelius was praying on Peter's behalf.

My colleague's teaching—his prayers—grew me, and I have prayed confidently for my daughters' spiritual development ever since.

Father, let the ones I love come to know You and love You. Thank You for hearing my prayers.
—PATTY KIRK

Digging Deeper: DEUT. 4:29–30; PS. 42:1–2

Sun 3

The fruit of the Spirit is love, joy, peace, patience, kindness, generosity, faithfulness, gentleness, and self-control....
—GALATIANS 5:22–23 (NRSV)

During Lent, several local congregations join together for simple suppers—bread, salad, soup—followed by theological lectures. When our turn came round, our church set out a good spread. I made a potful of my old standby, vegetable beef.

At the end of the evening, diners inquired about recipes. At the end of the week, I received a formal e-mail from Coordinator Lisa: First the compliment: "The soups we offered this year were a big hit." Then the request: "Would you be willing to submit your soup recipes for publication in the church newsletter?" Lisa obviously wanted precise measurements and replicable results.

Oh dear, what should I say? I'd watched my mother make soup, and then I'd tried to improve the flavor. I sent a reply. First the appreciation: "Lisa, thank you for organizing the evening." Then the response: "NSR—No Such Recipe. It's a splash of this, a bunch of that..."

I could list ingredients that always land in the pot and contribute to the dish. But the amounts and even the proportions vary from batch to batch, depending on how much supply I have on hand, how many people need nourishment. It often depends on how the spirit moves as I assess and stir the pot.

When I consider the biblical list of the fruit of the Spirit, I sometimes wish Scripture had given a specific, replicable formula: How much love? How much self-control? What's the proper proportion of peace to joy? But I'm learning that it's a case of NSR. How much of one or another depends on my spiritual readiness, the current need and how the Spirit moves.

Holy Spirit, creatively work through me to produce a medley of spiritual fruit. —EVELYN BENCE

Digging Deeper: ZECH. 4:6; JOHN 15:1–3; ROM. 7:4

Mon 4

Ye shall seek me, and find me, when ye shall search for me with all your heart. —JEREMIAH 29:13

On a clear day, my sister's husband Mike boarded a small plane for a business trip with five colleagues. The plane made it off the ground but then circled to land, obviously in trouble . . . and crashed at the airport. When the fire was put out, there was only one survivor: my brother-in-law Mike, barely alive.

I got a flurry of calls at work: "Ricky," my older sister called, "please pray. There's been a terrible accident." My mom called: "I'm heading down to the hospital, honey. We need you to pray. Please pray." I confess all I could do was yelp and groan, "*Noooo*, God, *noooo*."

All those guys with wives and children—it was too much to take in. And for our own family—lucky or unlucky, it was hard to know how to cope. But "*Noooo*, God, *noooo*"? Couldn't I do better than that?

The prayers continued on Web sites, Facebook, phone calls, in the silence of the night when sleep was hard to come by. Prayer provided a common language for people of many faiths and some with no faith at all, just this longing for God to be present in unfathomable suffering.

For twenty-four hours it was touch-and-go, with Mike kept alive by some combination of medical know-how, drugs and those prayers we'd been saying. He was taken to a burn unit where he was treated for two months and then went to a rehab hospital. At home, he continued therapy so he could walk, talk, go to his girls' soccer games, see a movie. He's a strong guy and a man of strong faith, but he's not the person he was before the accident. Neither are the rest of us.

I wouldn't have said "*Noooo*, God, *noooo*" was much of a prayer, but it's what held me together when there was nothing else to say. It kept me connected—by a thread. And that was enough.

God, You are always present. I need only turn to You.
—Rick Hamlin

Digging Deeper: Pss. 46, 145:18; Acts 17:27

Tue 5

And thou shalt not only while yet I live show me the kindness of the Lord. . . .
—1 Samuel 20:14

My best friend Bonnie and I used to go on vacation together, driving around New England or the Pacific Northwest, depending on where we were living at the time. No matter our destination, she enjoyed going there and I just wanted to *get* there. To me, the journey was a means to an end.

On a morning recently when my husband had an errand to run before we went to Tai Chi, I waited for him to pick me up on the street in the crisp winter chill. Time passed and still no Keith. I was cold, uncomfortable, starting to lose patience and growing very angry. And then I heard quacking.

Across the street, marching down the sidewalk, were seven large ducks, waddling purposefully along, looking curiously at the traffic and me. They got to a yard, slipped under the fence and walked in. They were clearly on an errand but not in any hurry, enjoying one another.

Minutes later, the ducks came back, marching in their line under the fence and up the sidewalk in the direction from which they'd come. There was an air about them of "This is what we do every morning. What's the big deal?" If I had not been there, I never would have seen that wonderful little parade. Whatever their mission, whatever their purpose, they were just like Bonnie—they had a marvelous time going there and back.

I began to relax. The morning was beautiful. And by the time Keith finally pulled up, I was happy I hadn't missed the simple journey of the ducks.

Lord, thank You for reminding me that there can be beauty and fun even at times when I have been forgetting to notice them. —RHODA BLECKER

Digging Deeper: EXOD. 33:14; 1 CHRON. 16:7–36; PROV. 12:25

Wed 6

And Sarah said, God hath made me to laugh, so that all that hear will laugh with me. —GENESIS 21:6

Lord, help me get through this day" was my fervent prayer. It was funny, I mused, before I'd gotten this job, I had prayed, "God, if You just let me get this job, I will never complain about anything again." Well, that had lasted about a month. Now I was five years into the job and constantly bemoaning my hurting legs, my swimming head, my small paycheck...

I forced a smile and said, "How may I help you?" to the next customer in line at the information desk. Secretly I prayed, "God, *I'm* the one who could use some information. How can I get through this endless night?"

The customer was a twentyish guy, and I have to admit I was surprised when he asked me, "Can you tell me where the section on Relationships is?"

"I'll show you," I told him. As I led him there, I commented, "You know, I've worked here for five years, and in all that time, you are only the second *man* to ask for the Relationship section."

He looked embarrassed. "Well . . . my brother is getting married this Sunday—"

"Aww," I said, touched.

"I want to get him a gag gift."

I laughed, then so did he. And I noticed that when I was laughing, my feet stopped hurting. So did my brain! I continued working the rest of the night with a smile on my face.

Thank You, God, for the gift of laughter. No matter
what mood I am in, You can help make things better
by showing me something to laugh about.
—LINDA NEUKRUG

Digging Deeper: PROV. 15:13–15

Thu 7
For my thoughts are not your
thoughts . . . says the Lord.
—ISAIAH 55:8 (RSV)

My husband and I had a house-sale prayer that had never gone unanswered. We'd prayed it often for friends: "Father, You know that Jim and Marge need to sell their home. You also know the particular family who needs this particular house. In Your perfect timing, Lord, we ask You to bring these needs together."

And soon the friends would call to say they'd found the perfect buyer. So when the time came to put our own home of fifty years on the market, we prayed those words ourselves and made the move to another state without waiting for the sale we were confident would speedily occur.

But a month passed, two months, six months . . . When the Realtor had no success to report after a full year, we panicked. God, it was clear, didn't know about the bad housing market. It was up to us. We lowered the price. We advertised in newspapers and on the Web. We even offered the house to a charity in exchange for an annuity.

Twelve more months passed with no buyer.

Then came a phone call from a young woman who'd just seen a photo of the house on the Realtor's Web site. "I knew right away that this was our home!" she told me. They had three children the ages of our three when we bought it. We had close friends who, it turned out, were also their close friends. The more we learned, the more we knew that the fit of this family with the house that's now theirs is something only God could have brought about.

Father, I forgot three little words of the house-sale prayer. Remind me that "Your perfect timing" doesn't mean "on my schedule." —ELIZABETH SHERRILL

Digging Deeper: DEUT. 7:9; 2 SAM. 7:27–29; ECCLES. 3:11

Fri 8   *Lord, you have been our dwelling place in all generations.*
—PSALM 90:1 (NRSV)

Just recently, I had to turn down a job opportunity I really, really wanted. I was pretty bummed—until one day, in the hallway, I saw a student's class graduation picture on the wall and remembered a conversation I'd had with him.

"Texas or Minnesota?"

At first, I thought it was a question about that night's baseball game, but it wasn't that at all. A student at the school where I teach just got two job offers, and he was polling me about which he should select.

"Which one do you want to take?" I asked.

"Well, the job description for the one in Texas is perfect," he replied.

"Well, that sounds like it might be the right one," I said, to which he quickly replied, "But Minnesota would be more of a challenge. And we're supposed to challenge ourselves, don't you think? You know, use God's gifts wisely."

"Of course, I'm a better spiritual match for Texas. But then again . . . " He went on for about five more minutes, tying himself up in knots, and then walked away before I could get in another word.

I saw him two weeks later. "Have you decided yet?" I asked, afraid he still might be so wildly uncertain.

"Minnesota," he said with a quiet confidence that belied our previous conversation. "I figured out that no matter where I chose, God was already there. After that, it was easy."

You are here, Lord. Open my eyes to the opportunities You have put before me in the very place that I am today. —JEFFREY JAPINGA

Digging Deeper: EXOD. 15:13; PS. 31:3

Sat 9

Trust in the Lord with all your heart and lean not on your own understanding; in all your ways submit to him, and he will make your paths straight. —PROVERBS 3:5 (NIV)

While doing ministry at Guideposts Outreach, I began a weekly Bible study. Within three months, we moved into a community center for Sunday services. The group got bigger, and we moved again to a local hotel. As the church expanded, so did my pastoral tasks and responsibilities.

Over time, the weight of being a bi-vocational pastor was taking a toll on me. People would ask me, "How are you doing?" I would say, "I'm tired but well." I didn't want to let down the people at the church, yet I could no longer do both ministries at the same time.

Many times I cried out, "Show me the way, Lord!"

Following eight months of praying, an answer came. After a Bible study meeting, Terry, one of the church leaders, said, "I understand if you decide to leave our church and continue your ministry at Guideposts. The Lord might need you where you are because you're touching people around the world. You are doing a lot of good work." His words caught me off guard. Except for my wife, no one at the church knew about my prayer request. I asked, "Did anyone talk to you about this?" "No, I just felt like sharing that with you."

On my drive home, I felt God's peace. I clearly understood that things were going to work out for the church and for me.

I trust in You, God. —PABLO DIAZ

Digging Deeper: PROV. 16:9; PHIL. 4:6–7, 10–12

Sun 10   *My soul waits....*
—Psalm 130:5 (RSV)

I sat, head down, studying my ring. Somehow I had lost a stone. On the side where the sapphire had been was an empty place.

A thought flitted through my mind: *My ring is like the church; all those years and now an empty place.* When David decided to leave his position as senior minister at Hillsboro Presbyterian Church, we understood that in the Presbyterian tradition we would not attend until the new minister invited us back. But the process was taking a mighty long time, and I missed my church family.

Now don't get me wrong; in most ways this time in our lives is more wonderful than it has ever been. David is actually married to *me* now, rather than the church. I delight in the new appreciation he seems to have for me, and it's great fun to see parts of him that he held back for so long. In the past months, he set off cross-country on his motorcycle, joined me in my community activities, and we've made new friends together. And I certainly don't miss Saturday nights when David huddled over his computer half the night, refining his sermons.

But when Sunday morning comes, I can't help missing my church family. From time to time, I visit a church where David is helping out or accept an invitation to hear special music somewhere. But it's useless. I don't want to replace my old church family with a new one.

I looked at my ring again. Even in the fullest life, there are bound to be empty places. Sometimes they become sacred ground, a place of memories. Other times they wait to be filled.

Father, give me the patience to wait. —PAM KIDD

Digging Deeper: Ps. 62; Isa. 8:16–18

DIVINE ABUNDANCE

Mon 11   *But unto every one of us is given grace.... —*EPHESIANS 4:7

I'm just stupid!" wailed my daughter Tess, then twelve, as she slammed her bedroom door. She had tried to make macaroni and cheese out of a box; unfortunately, she hadn't drained the water before adding the cheese powder. Now her siblings teased her about her "orange soup."

"Dear Lord, this child needs a success, quick! What can I do?"

Try again. Cook something easy with her. Don't give up or she will too.

When I invited Tess to make dessert, she zeroed in on a new recipe, Pink Angel Pie: pre-fab piecrust, a can of cherry filling and some meringue. How hard could that be?

First, she jerked the plastic wrap off the frozen shell, sending it skidding across the counter to shatter on the floor. Before she could cry, I picked up the pieces and swallowed my rebuke. "You know, Tess, pie dough is just like clay. You can just pinch it and press it back together."

Next, she opened the can of cherry filling and dropped the gooey lid on the kitchen rug. I stayed calm.

Now the tricky part: separating eggs. Once again, I withheld critique as she fished a few eggshell shards from the bowl, then beat the egg whites soft and high, splattering meringue on the cabinets. With a flourish, my increasingly confident daughter spread the fluffy topping on her creation and slid it into the oven for browning.

Well, Tess's dessert drew rave reviews from her siblings, and "orange soup" has become a family legend. Best of all, God gave both my daughter and me grace when we sorely needed it, thanks to Pink Angel Pie.

Gracious Lord, thank You for sending abundant grace wherever we are, even in a stained, meringue-spattered kitchen.
—GAIL THORELL SCHILLING

Digging Deeper: Ps. 21:6–7; LUKE 6:37–39

Tue 12

Pray without ceasing.
—1 Thessalonians 5:17

One of the nurses at the hospital where I work took me aside today. "A patient's wife asked me if I knew anyone who might pray with her," she said. "The chaplains are all busy. Would you care to say a few words, Roberta?"

I learned that Mrs. Devon's husband was having major surgery. While the couple was in their seventies, they were virtual newlyweds. Plain and simple, Mrs. Devon was terrified.

When I entered the hospital room, the patient was sleeping. A petite woman with short, white hair stroked his hand. I introduced myself, then explained that I would be honored to say a prayer with her. Truth was, I was afraid as well. Praying for someone I know is one thing, but this was a total stranger. What if I didn't say the right words?

I took a deep breath and asked God to help me. *The woman will tell you how to pray if you listen closely,* God seemed to say. *Just ask her about her concerns.*

"What would you like to talk to God about?" I asked.

"The strength to face whatever happens. Oh, and that I not be afraid." She dabbed her eyes with a tissue. "This is the first time we will be apart."

I placed my hand on her shoulder and repeated her petition. Then I closed it by saying, "And be with Mrs. Devon, Lord. Help her to feel Your love and peace at every turn."

The day after her husband's surgery, I stopped by for another chat. Things were better. While the surgeon did find a cancerous tumor, he was convinced that with treatment, it wouldn't spread.

"The staff here has been so kind to us," Mrs. Devon said, "but when you said that prayer with my name in it, that was the most personal thing that has happened."

Thank You for the privilege and power of personal prayer, loving Lord. Teach us to pray without ceasing.
—ROBERTA MESSNER

Digging Deeper: 1 KINGS 8:28; JOB 33:26; MATT. 18:19–21

Wed 13   *Rend your heart and not your garments.* —JOEL 2:13

The phone rang, and it was Maggie. "Mom, can we buy marshmallows and roast them over the candles you bought for when we had the hurricane? Daddy said we had to ask you."

It seemed a worthy use of wax and sugar, so I gave permission. The kids arrived home, only to realize they lacked skewers. Stephen solved that problem by retrieving some chopsticks from the kitchen. I found matches and lit the candles. The kids promptly set the marshmallows aflame.

"You should hold them further away," I advised, "So they don't burn."

"We like it this way. And it's faster," Maggie replied, waving a sugary torch.

"Hey, what's this gray stuff on my marshmallow?" demanded Stephen.

"That's ash," I replied. And with a start I realized that my city-bred youngest, who knows world-class museums but has never been camping, might never have seen ashes before. How odd.

After a moment Maggie asked, "Are ashes what's left after something's burned up?"

I nodded, adding, "Remember sackcloth and ashes in the Bible? Ashes are a symbol of repentance."

As my eyes tracked burning marshmallows, I thought of all the things that needed to go up in flames to reach repentance: pride, the desire for control, yearning for the admiration of the world, self-indulgence, selfishness . . . the list went on and on. *If we were to put on enough ashes to symbolize all that,* I thought, *we'd be covered from head to toe and unable to breathe.*

Which is why, I suppose, we use shorthand on Ash Wednesday, and our outward sign of inward repentance is applied in the shape of grace: the cross.

Lord, rend my heart and reshape it in Your image.
—Julia Attaway

Digging Deeper: Dan. 9:3; 1 Cor. 13:11–13;
Col. 3:9–10

Thu 14

We love because he first loved us.
—1 John 4:19 (NIV)

As I walk down the long card-display aisle at the grocery store, I recount the names on my Valentine's Day card list. Each year the number grows as our family grows, along with the addition of people I want to send love messages to because of some recent connection in our lives.

Seems like the card display has grown too. Thankfully, it includes special messages for different kinds of love relationships: husband and wife, parents and children, grandparents and grandchildren, siblings and friends. Valentine's Day is not just for sweethearts.

I have to admit, today this task of card-getting and giving feels a bit wearisome. I need to get the cards in the mail today, and it takes longer than I expect to find an appropriate message for my husband, a four-year-old grandson who's into cars and trucks, and a single friend who wishes she had a sweetheart. But it's a task I mostly like because I want to participate in this tradition of sending messages of love to others.

Finally, I complete my list and head home, where I spread the stack of cards out on my desk and begin addressing each one. When I reach into the desk drawer for stamps, all I have are leftover stamps with images of Jesus in the manger. Yet the idea of a Christmas stamp on a Valentine's Day card makes me smile; it's just the right reminder about the greatest truth regarding the source of love in our lives.

Lord, I love You with all my heart and all my soul and all my mind. When I do, all other expressions of love become more meaningful and less wearisome.
—Carol Kuykendall

Digging Deeper: John 15:9; 1 John 4:9–11

THE GIFT OF TREES

Fri 15 *Now Deborah, Rebekkah's nurse, died, and she was buried below Bethel under the oak....*
—Genesis 35:8 (nas)

I lost a close friend a few months ago. Delores was already seventy-six when we met, so our twelve-year friendship was a gift. One day I found myself doubled over the steering wheel in grief when I had to travel in the direction she'd lived, knowing that no matter how far I drove she wasn't at the end of the road.

Jacob, too, must have felt such loss when Deborah died. His mother Rebekkah's childhood nurse had journeyed with her by camel when she came as a bride to his father Isaac. Deborah undoubtedly filled the same respected nurse-confidante role for their sons Jacob and Esau.

She died soon after Jacob moved his family to Bethel, a town twelve miles from Jerusalem. I can picture him honoring his old nurse in his choice of a grave site. Burial beneath trees was an ancient custom. They were landmarks and places of meeting.

Jacob found an oak, likely a prickly evergreen called a Palestine oak. These oaks branch from their base and have stiff dark green leaves resembling holly. The Bible gives this burial tree a name: *Allon-bacuth* (oak of weeping).

Tears watered that oak the day Deborah was laid to rest. When my friend Delores was buried, I asked God how I could possibly say good-bye. I seemed to hear Him say, *Try to focus not on what you have lost but on what Delores has gained*.

I did try . . . and I can say that thoughts of heaven made dry the tears in a weeping heart.

Lord, when I encounter an "oak of weeping," gather with me there in comfort and hope. —CAROL KNAPP

Digging Deeper: 1 THESS. 3:6–8; 1 PET. 1:3–5; 1 JOHN 5:13

Sat 16 *The word of God is alive and active....* —HEBREWS 4:12 (NIV)

Although much of my correspondence is via e-mail or text, I still watch eagerly for the rural mail carrier. Why? Because tucked in among ads and bills, I often find joyful surprises. Sometimes it's a card from a far-off family member or a note from a *Daily Guideposts* reader. Occasionally it's an invitation to a wedding or anniversary celebration. More than twenty years ago I received a huge box containing a fake (but handsome) grandfather clock—twenty-sixth prize in a drawing! It still keeps perfect time.

Lately I've been cultivating that same sense of anticipation when I open my Bible. More often than not, I am surprised by a Scripture that speaks to a spiritual need or a situation I'm facing. Here are some examples:

"Don't be weary in prayer; keep at it" (Colossians 4:2, TLB, that morning there were seven prayer requests in my inbox).

"The Lord God has given me his words of wisdom so that I may know what I should say" (Isaiah 50:4, TLB, when a friend was overwhelmed with family and financial problems).

"Once more the autumn rains will come, as well as those of spring" (Joel 2:23, TLB, as crops were dying due to drought).

"For Christ himself is our way of peace" (Ephesians 2:14, TLB, when spiritual confusion troubled my heart).

Author and Finisher of the faith, thank You for the ever-fresh Word that guides my life journey.
—PENNEY SCHWAB

Digging Deeper: Ps. 119:105; 2 TIM. 2:15; HEB. 4:12

Sun 17

But He answered and said, "It is written, 'Man shall not live by bread alone, but by every word that proceeds from the mouth of God.'"
—MATTHEW 4:4 (NKJV)

Thankful? Me? Right now, this morning? Can we start slowly, in selfish fashion? Yes?

Oh, then, bless my soul, bacon and coffee. Slippers. Hot water. The dog *finally* closing the door behind himself with his moist epic nose when he slides in all muddy-pawed. The sweet, gentle, generous woman in the shower. The lanky boys snoring in their rooms. The wild clean plentiful water from the profligate sky. The heat vent with the missing screw so the vent plate shivers gently, which I should hate but which I love for its glorious unfixability, which is humbling and thus refreshing.

Being humbled but not crushed. Being alive, if creaky and sore. Being married, stunningly. Being a dad, miraculously. Being liked by the dog, although that is all about the bacon slice he gets for *finally* learning to close the door. Having a job that doesn't feel like work. Milk for the coffee. Hot water from the faucet. The slow dawn as the universe opens gently like a brilliant hand. The heron that commutes east at dawn and west at dusk.

The sudden tears that arise when I think how many millions of beings like me are cold and broken and dark and frightened this morning, huddled and starving. The snarl inside me as I think of small children. The thrash of ideas inside me as I dream of stories to tell to help them. The blessing of the woman's hand on my shoulder as she enters the kitchen. The gift of her silence as she sees my face; she knows. The prayer of her other hand on my other shoulder as we stand silent for a moment, girding for battle against the dark.

Dear Lord, You know and I know that no man on earth likes bacon and coffee more than me, but the food I need most is hope and light and laughter and courage. Feed me this morning? Please? —BRIAN DOYLE

Digging Deeper: LUKE 4:4, 11:10–12; JOHN 6:22–40

Mon 18

Come, let us bow down in worship, let us kneel before the Lord our Maker.
—PSALM 95:6 (NIV)

You know what I really love about gardening?" I asked my friend Lee, who'd stopped by my house and found me digging in my backyard.

"Planting new flowers?" she guessed.

I smiled and shook my head as I plopped a bright yellow pansy into its freshly dug spot. "It's the simple fact that gardening keeps me on my knees," I said, "and when I'm on my knees, it always leads me to prayer."

Then Lee shared a story with me. "There's a bronze statue of President Abraham Lincoln at the Washington National Cathedral in Washington, DC. He's kneeling in prayer, his head bowed and arms resting at his sides. Legend has it that the inspiration for the statue came from its sculptor Herbert Houck. His grandfather saw Lincoln kneeling in the woods in prayer just before he delivered the Gettysburg Address to the Union soldiers. It must have surprised Houck to see the president of the United States kneeling in prayer, but it probably wouldn't have surprised Lincoln's friends. It's been said that Lincoln once told a friend that he'd often been driven to his knees by the knowledge that he had no place else to go."

"You know," I said to Lee as I planted another pansy, "in some of the most difficult times in my life, I've picked up my gardening gloves, trowel and spade, and headed to my garden. It's down on my knees among the flowers, soil and mulch, that I think and I pray. And when I'm done, my head is clear, my direction is focused and my faith is restored.

"Perhaps that's what Lincoln experienced too," I said as I placed the last yellow pansy in its spot and spread the mulch over it carefully. "I sure hope so."

It's down here on my knees, Lord, when I can best look up to You. —MELODY BONNETTE SWANG

Digging Deeper: 1 KINGS 8:54; 2 CHRON. 7:2–4; Ps. 145:13–15

Tue 19

"Can you fathom the mysteries of God? Can you probe the limits of the Almighty? They are higher than the heavens above—what can you do? They are deeper than the depths below—what can you know?"
—JOB 11:7–8 (NIV)

I just don't get it!"

Those are the words of Richard Dawkins, one of the world's leading evolutionary biologists and, most notably, a preeminent atheist who has made a reputation bashing religion.

I like Dawkins, though I don't agree with him. He is honest, intellectually rigorous and very entertaining. He sees the world and sees no need for the existence of God. I see my life and find the need for God as absolute.

One of Dawkins' staunchest and most respected allies in his somewhat controversial theory of progressive evolution is Simon Conway Morris, the respected Cambridge paleobiologist and . . . Christian. Morris is as outspoken about his spirituality as Dawkins is about his lack of it. How did Dawkins account for his brilliant colleague's beliefs?

Dawkins fumbled for an explanation and then simply shook his head, exasperated. "I just don't get it!" he finally told the interviewer.

Eureka! as scientists might say. Because that's sometimes how I feel about my own faith. There are days when I am a doubter. Not in God but in my ability to serve God; to accept that what I can't understand about the world, God understands for me. I look at my faith journey with its twists and turns and seemingly uncertain direction and think, *I just don't get it!*

Belief reinforces belief, and the more I trust, the deeper that trust takes root in my life. It is not a trust that can be explained scientifically. Yet it does evolve. And on that point, perhaps, Professor Dawkins and I are in agreement.

My faith is a work in progress, Lord, evolving toward
an ever more complete understanding of your grace.
I may doubt in myself but never in You.
—EDWARD GRINNAN

Digging Deeper: JOHN 1:4–5; ROM. 1:20–22

Wed 20

By faith we understand that the worlds were prepared by the word of God, so that what is seen was made from things that are not visible. —HEBREWS 11:3 (NRSV)

The number of houses for sale on my walking route in New London, Connecticut, increased as the economy stalled. The largest, loveliest and most expensive homes stayed on the market longest, and the longer a property was on, the larger and fancier the For Sale sign became. Some even sported a photograph of the agent as if to say, "Trust this face with your future."

Proclaimed a Preferred Property by the prominent real estate sign, the most elegant house in the city is perched at the mouth of the Thames River, overlooking Long Island Sound. It had been for sale for more than a year when I walked by and realized something was different. The property landscaping is elaborate, so I wondered if they'd taken down a tree or added rose bushes or opened up a path to the river. Something had changed, but I couldn't figure out what. Later, passing by in the car, my husband observed, "Hey, the For Sale sign is down. Maybe they sold it?"

That was it! The sign was gone. As it turned out, they hadn't sold the house; a newer, bigger sign soon appeared. But the fact that I'd failed to miss something I'd walked by every day for a year reminded me of how much I take things for granted. There are times in my life when the goodness seems to go out of it, when I'm tired or depressed and something vital is missing, but I don't know what. It usually turns out to be God, and it is never Him missing me; it is that I am failing to see Him.

*Always-present Father, keep me awake and alive
to Your presence and guidance in my life.
Remind me to never take You for granted.*
—MARCI ALBORGHETTI

Digging Deeper: 2 PET. 1:5–11

Thu 21

*And God himself has said that one
must love not only God, but his
brother too.* —1 JOHN 4:21 (TLB)

When my brother Joe, his wife Linda and I
set out in Alaska in their not-so-new van
and a borrowed forty-nine-year-old, fourteen-foot
camper trailer, I didn't have a clue how much we
would come to depend on Joe. When the engine
overheated on a steep mountain road, he pulled off
to the side, stepped into his one-piece mechanic's
coveralls, shimmied under the van and changed the
spark plugs.

When it started to sprinkle just before supper, Joe
hauled out a huge blue tarp, strung it up, and moved
the picnic table over so we could dine in delicious
outdoor comfort.

One early morning at the campground, Joe pondered the fact that we'd be traversing steep mountain grades to get to our next destination. Once
again he slipped into his coveralls, pulled new brake

pads out of the van and replaced both front brakes in less than forty-five minutes.

Each morning he'd haul the folding bikes out of our trailer, get them ready for us to ride, then head back inside to fix breakfast on the camper stove. Pancakes, eggs, bacon, oatmeal . . . whatever Linda and I thought sounded good.

As the days went by, I noticed Joe would go out of his way to show us the most spectacular scenery one could imagine. I decided that having a brother is quite possibly the greatest thing one can be thankful for. Especially one who not only grilled the moose steaks, salmon, king crab legs and ground buffalo that a friend gave us, but also made the best darn home fries this side of the Yukon.

Lord, sometimes I take the people I love for granted. Help me not to do that ever again. And thank You for my brother Joe. —Patricia Lorenz

Digging Deeper: 2 Pet. 1:5–11

Fri 22

"For I am the Lord your God who takes hold of your right hand and says to you, Do not fear; I will help you." —Isaiah 41:13 (niv)

I sat in the hospital waiting room, not watching the muted television and trying not to listen to the doctor telling the woman three chairs over that he was pretty sure they got all of her husband's cancer, but they're not out of the woods yet.

I stuffed my hands in coat pockets and felt something in my hand. I pulled out the jewelry pin I had forgotten about. My sister Laura had asked me to hold it for her while she was in surgery. I studied the image of the cowardly lion on the face of the pin and the word engraved beneath it: Courage.

This pin makes its rounds in my family. My uncle had it a number of years ago when he suffered from a stroke and went through months of rehabilitation, learning to walk and talk again. The pin was with my cousin through a high-risk pregnancy, and now as my sister faces cancer she wears the pin on days she needs a boost of bravery.

The surgeon is probably starting the procedure, I said to myself. I said a prayer. I looked over the magazines on the table that I had no interest in reading and thought about the pin being sent where it was needed. Isn't that what courage is? Being there, facing what you must face.

I settled and watched the clock. Another hour passed. Finally, the surgeon walked toward me. I held my breath. He had good news.

Dear Lord, the strength of Your presence is always with me, right here in my heart, giving me the power to face anything. —SABRA CIANCANELLI

Sat 23

"But a Samaritan . . . saw him. . . . and took care of him."
—LUKE 10:33–34 (NIV)

D on't you think that's what Jesus is teaching us in this parable?" I might ask the weekly Bible study group that I lead.

"I don't think so," says Kip. "You're reading modern English translated from Greek translated from spoken Aramaic."

I met my friend Kip in 1973. Although our paths didn't cross often for many years, we see each other at least twice a week now: at church on Sunday and Bible study on Tuesday. Kip's continual but gentle disagreement might be frustrating if it wasn't for something that occurred in 1994. A wildfire threatened our home, so my wife and I gathered our possessions and stored them in a neighbor's garage, two miles north. Unfortunately, winds blew the fire north the next day. Kip met us at the garage and helped us move everything from the garage into our truck and his van. We could see flames curling over a ridge above us, and our hair was gray with pinion and juniper ash before we left for Kip's house. He let us store everything in his small home for as long as we needed.

I know for a fact that differing beliefs are meaningless during a wildfire. Kip was my Good Samaritan when our hair was gray with ash, and he is my Good Samaritan now that our hair is gray from age. If we are still attending Bible study when our hair is gone, I imagine Kip will disagree with me . . . and it will never be frustrating.

Dear God, thank You so much for those times when the Good Samaritan is far more than a parable.
—TIM WILLIAMS

Digging Deeper: Ps. 27:12–14; MATT. 12:35

Sun 24 *There is a reward for the righteous. . . .* —PSALM 58:11

Oscar night was over. I turned off the television and headed for bed, but I was thinking, *Some people work all their lives for an Academy Award, but that award is out of reach for most of us.*

Personally, I am more interested in having the applause of my own family, so you can imagine how proud I was to receive the following note from my ten-year-old, home-schooled granddaughter:

Dear Grandpa,

I am supposed to write a letter to someone I respect and love, so I chose you. You're not just a Christian college teacher, you're a friend and my grandpa. You show how happy a person can be when he has the Lord. You are a witness for God, just by riding your bike around town. People might say, "There goes the Christian teacher. He looks happy."

Love, Rossetti

Her letter is my Oscar. I was surprised that Rossetti sees me as a happy person because I see myself as inward and pensive. I learned something about myself that I didn't know, and I was pleased and relieved.

Rossetti herself is quiet, inward, but she has found her voice in her writing. She blesses the people she admires with her genial observations.

I don't have any Academy Awards to hand out to my friends, but perhaps, like Rossetti, I can be a kind of mirror to help them see how beautiful and valuable they are. Maybe I can see something in them that they don't see in themselves, something that will make them happier with who they are.

I thank You, Lord, for all the people who have helped me to discover who I am. —DANIEL SCHANTZ

Digging Deeper: MATT. 6:4; COL. 2:2;
1 THESS. 5:11–13

Mon 25

*Now faith is the substance of
things hoped for, the evidence of
things not seen.* —HEBREWS 11:1

Thank You, Lord, for purple martins! It's a prayer
that escapes my lips over and over as I watch
blue-black North American swallows catch wind
currents and glide effortlessly through the sky.
I hear their song and rush out to find them
flying around the birdhouse at the edge of my
pond.

"My birds are back!" I shout with joy to any neighbor within earshot.

The purple martins arrive every year in late
February, having flown thousands of miles from
as far away as Brazil. They get busy carrying pine
needles, mud and threads of oak tree moss into the
birdhouse to build their nests in preparation for a
new generation.

A few days into July, though, after they've hatched
a new brood of fledgling young, I awaken to silence.
Without so much as a warning, the purple martins
are gone, headed back to South America. Disappointed, I try to adjust to the eerily quiet morning. Doubt and fear creep in and grow. *What if the
martins don't return? What if the lab test results are
not good? What if my professor rejects the latest chapter
of my dissertation?*

The fear is still there at church the next day, distracting me from the sermon. I look up at the large wooden cross nailed on the wall behind the altar as the minister points to it and asks, "Do you know that what died upon the cross was fear?"

In that miraculous moment, I am redeemed. Jesus replaces my fear with a faith that assures me whatever happens, whatever news I receive, whatever work I still need to do, I will be okay. And, yes, the purple martins will return.

Lord, Your natural world is full of lessons in faith. Thank You for giving me one right in my own backyard. —MELODY BONNETTE SWANG

Digging Deeper: I CHRON. 29:10–12; JOB 19:25

Tue 26

Even so, I have noticed one thing, at least, that is good. It is good for people to eat, drink, and enjoy their work under the sun during the short life God has given them, and to accept their lot in life.
—ECCLESIASTES 5:18 (NLT)

I love dogs, but I had become convinced that my husband and I were too old to start over with one. Then we received a tearful phone call from one of my canine-rescuing friends. Thor was about to be put down all the way over in South Carolina. We live in Georgia, two hours away. Nevertheless, twenty minutes later, we were enroute to adopt a dog we hadn't even seen.

Sitting on the edge of a plastic, worn sofa in the get-acquainted room, we waited. Suddenly, a young yellow Lab with the strength of a mule headed for us, and after knocking me over, covered me with kisses. On the way home, Thor stretched out with his head in my lap, seeming to smile. When I finally stroked him, I had to smile too.

At our home, Thor gave me laser-beam eye contact as I explained things to him. His eyes matched his amber coat. Thor trotted right at my heels in the house or outside. He was eager to please, keeping his distance from our cats. He adjusted so perfectly that in just a couple of days, it was as though he'd always been ours.

When Gene and I watch television at night and I'm lying on the sofa, Thor rests his head on my chest until I look into his golden eyes. "Maybe we aren't so old," I told him, his face inches from mine. "Maybe you came to show us how much fun life still is."

Lord, help me live in Your plan daily.
—Marion Bond West

Digging Deeper: Deut. 5:32–33; Ps. 146:1–2

Wed 27

*For this God is our God for ever
and ever; he will be our guide even
to the end.* —PSALM 48:14 (NIV)

Sometimes God doesn't whisper lessons; He yells
them over the roar of a sixteen-foot moving
truck's engine.

I'd just pulled onto I-10, making my way from
Florida to my new home in Alabama, when I looked
up in panic. My rearview mirror had fallen off! Not
only had it fallen off, but it must have fallen out of
the truck, because it sure wasn't anywhere I could
see it.

I called my husband in a panic. "There's no
rearview mirror!" I squeaked.

"Sweetie," he said, "look behind you. What would
the rearview mirror show?"

I peeked quickly over my right shoulder to notice
the solid wall behind me that separated the cab
from the truck body. "There's no need for a rearview
mirror," he said.

Even after my discovery (sideview mirrors only),
I still found myself glancing up to check the cars
behind me. As I caught myself each time, I couldn't
help but wonder how much of my time in life I
spend looking backward.

The move that prompted me to drive a four-
ton vehicle six hundred miles was one fraught with
excitement and angst. I wasn't sad to leave Florida,

but I was nervous about what Alabama held for us. Even the knowns (a new job and first mortgage) seemed intimidating!

Thankfully, God took the opportunity at the first of my journey to remind me that looking back is fruitless. Instead, I should keep my eyes on Him—and the road—to see where I'm to go.

Lord, I can't always work my GPS or read my map correctly, but I know I'm safe when I'm traveling the highway of life with You.
—ASHLEY KAPPEL

Digging Deeper: ISA. 43:18–19; LUKE 9:61–62

Thu 28 "This is My commandment, that you love one another as I have loved you. Greater love has no one than this, than to lay down one's life for his friends."
—JOHN 15:12-13 (NKJV)

At a stoplight one morning, I burst into tears, thinking about my brother who will soon be dead from cancer, which no one says but everyone is thinking, and I get honked at by a huge angry guy in a car the size of a toaster, which makes me laugh while crying.

The rest of the day I think how thankful I am for fifty years of this brother, years of fist-fights and basketball and stealing shirts from each other and mud and laughter and surfing and post-cards and first terrible little goat beards and banging shoulders in the kitchen with our other brothers and picking on our mom as she piped imprecations, and silly gifts and awkward conversations and un-believably deep conversations, and digging cars out of the snow, and taking each other for granted un-til we didn't, and awkwardly holding hands while praying at funerals, and bobbing each other's kids on our knees, and a thousand thousand other things.

He stood up recently, tall and gaunt and fragile and illuminated, at our family reunion, and he said quietly that he loved us with a deep and inarticulate love, and that he was who he was because of us, and nothing in life ever made him so happy or so proud as to be milling around jostling with all of us, nothing, and if he had never been very good at saying that to us, he was sorry, but he felt that way most powerfully and deeply, and this was the time to say it, wasn't it? Which it certainly was. Which it certainly is.

And all day I have thought this: *Why do we not tell each other every hour that we love each other? Why is that? Because we should. Maybe right now, right after this sentence ends.*

Dear Lord, You have graced and blessed and inundated us with more gifts and glories than we can ever count, but the greatest of these is those we love. Thank You. —BRIAN DOYLE

Digging Deeper: 1 SAM. 18:1–3; 2 COR. 8:6–8; HEB. 4:15–16

GIVING THANKS

1 _____

2 _____

3 _____

4 _____

5 _____

6 _____

7 _____

8 _____

9 _____

10 _____

11 _____

12 _____

February

13 _____

14 _____

15 _____

16 _____

17 _____

18 _____

19 _____

20 _____

21 _____

22 _____

23 _____

24 _____

25 _____

26 _____

27 _____

28 _____

March

*Praise the Lord! Oh give thanks
to the Lord, for he is good,
for his steadfast love endures forever!*
—Psalm 106:1 (ESV)

OPERATION THANKFULNESS

Fri 1
    "If you have faith as small as a mustard seed, you can say to this mountain, 'Move from here to there'...."
    —MATTHEW 17:20 (NIV)

Before our mission trip to Romania, I ran out to the grocery store at the last minute for a small container of mustard seeds to use in Bible school. My bags were already packed, so I tossed them in my carry-on. We flew to Chicago for a flight out to Munich, Germany, but a central computer crash grounded the airline's entire fleet, stranding thousands of travelers without their luggage. I lacked the basics, such as pajamas. It seemed crazy that one thing I did have was a shaker of mustard seeds. Or was it?

At the terminal, as we waited in line for hours trying desperately to rebook our flights, we met a young man who was going to Amsterdam to see a young woman he was serious about. We gave him mustard seeds and said a short prayer. Later I struck up a conversation with a woman from Turkey. She listened with interest as she heard for the first time what Jesus said about the mustard plant, and she took a few mustard seeds, along with a little prayer that she'd soon be home.

We finally reached Romania two days later—without our luggage! The mustard seeds were the only item we had for our first day at Bible school. We tore out pictures of plants from a magazine, put a glob of clear fingernail polish onto each student's paper and dropped in a single mustard seed.

After being helped by mustard seeds for three days, I understood with renewed gratitude what Jesus meant about the power of mustard-seed faith. It doesn't always dissolve insurmountable obstacles; sometimes it simply gives us the determination and willpower to keep going until we reach the other side.

Jesus, thank You for Your promise that if I have a tiny bit of faith, I can trust You to strengthen me to get past this obstacle. Amen. —KAREN BARBER

Digging Deeper: 2 COR. 9:8; HEB. 11:1–3

Sat 2

I know that good itself does not dwell in me, that is, in my sinful nature. For I have the desire to do what is good, but I cannot carry it out.
—ROMANS 7:18 (TNIV)

My mother-in-law has Alzheimer's disease but still lives on her own in her house across the road from us. We are fortunate, compared to many others with ailing parents. My husband can schedule his hours around his mom's needs and my job. Between the two of us, we are able to look after her, and she has remained blessedly content.

I go by most afternoons to have coffee, fill her birdfeeders, and bake cornbread or biscuits, her favorite foods.

My part in caring for my mother-in-law is idyllic enough, as little is expected of me beyond friendliness and patience. I routinely fail, though, in both. Although it's not her fault that she can't remember anything, I answer sourly when she repeats a question.

I am in constant, hopeless prayer about my attitude in these small charities. *Let me be loving in spite of myself*, I beg. *Give me patience.* God never seems to grant these requests.

Recently, she found a box under her sofa. Together, we went through its contents.

At the bottom of the box was a thank-you card from me—or some unrecognizably sweet version of me from years before—that she had me read out loud. In it, I apologized for my crankiness and wrote, "I want you to know I really love and appreciate you. I don't know what I'd do without you."

"Save that!" my mother-in-law said, snatching it from my hand.

Weird—and so cheering—how this forgotten sentiment ministered to us both.

Holy and amazing God, Lord of what was, what is and what will be, thank You for listening to me always. And for sending Your Spirit to interpret my groans. And for Your astonishing replies.
—Patty Kirk

Digging Deeper: Isa. 51:6–8; Col. 3:12–13

Sun 3

"Come to me, all you who are weary and burdened, and I will give you rest."
—Matthew 11:28 (NIV)

Rest. It's a four-letter word that beckons me, but I've established a bad habit that often keeps me from finding it in my life. I assume that rest is something I do when everything else is done, so I don't deserve to sit down on the couch and read a book in a messy room.

Just last week something broke me of my bad habit. My two-year-old granddaughter Gracie was in the hospital for five days, and I offered to take a shift sitting with her early one morning. As I walked down the hospital hallway, I heard the sounds of her uncontrollable scream-crying. Her doctors had warned us that the medications would make her agitated. Add to that the confusing frustration of being tethered to her bed by an oxygen tube, with both arms in splints, so she couldn't remove the tube.

Derek, my son and Gracie's dad, who had been up with her much of the night, gratefully handed her to me, kissed her good-bye, and left to go home and sleep. So there I stood, holding Gracie and trying to comfort her. We sat down in the rocking chair next to her bed, and I began to tell her a story about a little girl named Gracie who didn't feel good but got better and went back home where she lived with her mommy and daddy and sisters and . . .

By the time I got through naming all of her dolls and stuffed animals, she started breathing more rhythmically. So there we sat, my chin gently tucking her head into my chest. I didn't even look up for at least forty-five minutes, but then I did.

The room was a total mess! Plastic spoons falling out of half-eaten containers of ice cream, a cup of cold coffee, wads of tissues, yesterday's newspaper. But all I cared about was rocking my grandbaby. I did that for three hours, which became a sacred, peaceful spot of rest, given and received.

Lord, You always know what I need most and what matters most. May I know what You know.
—CAROL KUYKENDALL

Digging Deeper: JER. 31:25; ROM. 8:26–27

Mon 4

*"For I know the plans I have for you,"
declares the Lord, "plans to prosper
you and not to harm you, plans to
give you hope and a future."*
—JEREMIAH 29:11 (NIV)

I got the job!" I screamed over the phone to my cousin Carmen. The financial burden I'd carried was finally lifted. I could get out of debt; the application for food stamps didn't have to be mailed.

For months I'd known that being a stay-at-home mom was no longer an option. Yet I'd felt helpless in finding an alternative solution. Outside of another freelance contract, I never thought I could find a job that paid enough to cover the bills and childcare. Now I had.

The thrill of my new employment disappeared when my little boys ran into my arms with overwhelming love in their tiny faces. I'd no longer be with them all day, every day, showering them with kisses, creating fun activities and taking them to interesting places. I now had to think of childcare options. Would their new caretaker be patient, teach them new things, play with them? Suddenly, I became bitter about my situation. The needs of my family were taking me away from them.

"So," Carmen said excitedly a few days later, "tell me about this job."

As I started to talk about it, the gratitude and excitement came back. This new path, I realized, was all God. The job came looking for me; I wasn't even job-hunting at the time. It was exactly what I needed, when I needed it. The position was something I had a passion for and knew I could do well. This was a hand-wrapped blessing from God, not a curse. It was a new beginning filled with promise of wonderful things to come.

My life and the lives of my children are in Your capable hands, Lord. —KAREN VALENTIN

Digging Deeper: ACTS 14:7; EPH. 3:20; PHIL. 4:19

Tue 5   *Likewise the Spirit helps us in our weaknesses; for we do not know how to pray as we ought, but that very Spirit intercedes with sighs too deep for words.* —ROMANS 8:26 (NRSV)

My oldest dream is to be a novelist, so this last year I applied to get my master's in creative writing. I resolved not to ask God for help in being accepted because I knew it would have been selfish and shortsighted.

My resolution was soon tested, however. In early spring, I was confronted by an endless stream of rejection letters. After opening my third ominously thin envelope in as many days, I started to feel desperate. In my darkest, most unreasonable mind, these schools were confirming what some part of me had always secretly believed: that I was worthless and unloved.

I finally asked God, "Please, just let me get in *somewhere.*"

More letters arrived, and they still said, "No." I couldn't understand what I'd done to deserve this, why God hadn't answered my prayer.

I was with Emily, my girlfriend of two years, when I got the seventh letter.

"What does it say?" she asked.

I tried to answer, but my voice faltered. Tears rushed out of me like they hadn't in years.

Emily held me. "I love you," she said. "I love you even if you don't get in anywhere."

I held her more closely. When I regained my voice, I told her what I'd only just realized: "You're more important than any school."

It was then that I understood. God hadn't given me what I'd asked for but what I needed—the chance to finally see the truth.

Thank You, God, for showing me You've given me everything I need for a perfect life. —SAM ADRIANCE

Digging Deeper: Ps. 63:3–5; PROV. 19:21; 1 COR. 15:28

Wed 6

"Every perfect gift is from above...."
—JAMES 1:17 (NAS)

Sitting in my first knitting class, I fumbled with my needles and stared at my fingers. *Behave! Act like you have some sense.* The other women zoomed ahead of me as though spinning straw into gold.

I'd wanted to learn to knit for decades. When I spotted someone knitting in a doctor's office or the airport, I would move closer. It looked incredibly difficult, but I was drawn to the peaceful motion and the idea of making homemade gifts. But who would want an uneven scarf or a crooked pair of socks? I suppose fear kept me from trying, but after turning fifty, I decided if not now, when?

"I'll probably never be fast," I whispered to the instructor.

"Knitting's not a race. It's about enjoying the journey. You'll catch on."

I took a deep breath and relaxed my shoulders. After a few rows of knitting, we moved to purling. Pretty soon, I made a mistake. "Uh-oh. Do I have to start all over?"

"Honey, did you notice the gorgeous handmade items hanging in the shop?" one woman in class replied.

"Sure, but I'll never be able to make anything perfect."

"If you look closely, every piece on display has a flaw. That's the beauty in art." She smiled. "And people—none of us is perfect."

Her words settled into my heart as though spoken from the Lord Himself. I continued purling and forgot about my mistake. After class, I took my tiny pink scarf home and completed it. During the winter, I made my daughters scarves and began knitting my first afghan. Each of my woolly creations is one-of-a-kind and beautifully flawed . . . just like me.

Wow, Lord, what a relief! It's okay to goof up in knitting . . . and in life. Only Your gifts are without fault. —JULIE GARMON

Digging Deeper: Ps. 139:13–14; Rom. 5:8

Thu 7 *They may forget, yet will I not forget thee.* —ISAIAH 49:15

Ever since I got that fiftieth birthday invitation to join AARP (and didn't join) I can't seem to remember names. "A senior moment," friends will say as we reach in the air for the name of that person . . . you know the one . . . she was in that movie with that other guy. Remember him? "Google moment" someone else calls it as we pull out our iPhones. Time and again, I turn to my poor wife and give her clues, like a game of charades, to help me come up with that name that should be so obvious.

And, yet, I keep reading these studies that show how you can improve your brain power and expand your memory at any age. You're supposed to do these mental exercises. *Fat chance!* I think. *How would I do that, and when would I have the time?*

The other morning it came to me: *Use your prayer time.*

Here's what I've been doing. I keep a note in my money clip with the list of people I've promised to pray for. Instead of just looking at it and reading it, what if I closed my eyes and tried to reconstruct it? It would be both good for my memory and good for my prayer life.

I won't be able to remember all these names, I thought. At first, I didn't. I'd have to go back and check the list, recovering a name. But I've found, with time, that my memory gets better, and each new name I add is a chance to both expand my spiritual horizons and jog my mind.

Yes, I still stumble over names and draw a blank sometimes. Call it a senior moment. Call it aging. I try to think of it as an opportunity for spiritual growth.

> *This one thing I will not forget, Lord: to trust You at all times.* —RICK HAMLIN

Digging Deeper: DEUT. 11:18–32; PS. 20:7; PROV. 7:3

Fri 8

And now, brothers and sisters, I want you to know what will happen to the Christians who have died so you will not be full of sorrow like people who have no hope. —1 THESSALONIANS 4:13 (NLT)

Today, my father-in-law's death feels imminent. He is eighty-six years old and frail, and in the past week he has undergone emergency quadruple-bypass surgery, developed severe pneumonia and lost 90 percent of his lung capacity. The outlook is grim. To make matters worse, my husband's parents live several states away. For the past six days, Perry and I have been relegated to riding the roller coaster of updates by text message: "He slept better last night . . . antibiotics seem to be helping." "Tough afternoon. Weakening by the minute." "Making jokes with the nurses . . . back to his old self." "Confused about where he is and what necessitated a hospital stay."

On the heels of one update in particular—Perry's brother sent word that all four siblings thought he should fly home as soon as possible, "just in case"— I came downstairs to find my husband standing on the porch, his fists pushed into his pockets, his eyes pressed shut, his face craned toward the hot sun and tears streaming down his cheeks. A brokenhearted smile curved his lips.

Tears clouded my own eyes as I took in the sight of my suffering husband, but something about his posture encouraged my soul. Seeking out light on the darkest of days—this is how we grieve as those who cling fast to hope.

God, during the highest of highs and the lowest of lows, remind me that You see me, You are with me, You care. —Ashley Wiersma

Digging Deeper: Pss. 29:11, 31:23–24; Rom. 5:5

Sat 9

So then, each of us will give an account of ourselves to God. Therefore let us stop passing judgment on one another. Instead, make up your mind not to put any stumbling block or obstacle in the way of a brother or sister.
—Romans 14:12–13 (niv)

I recently finished reading Kathryn Stockett's novel *The Help,* which looks at the lives of black maids in 1960s Mississippi and the white women who employ them. One of the recurring plotlines has to do with the unceasing efforts of doyenne Hilly Holbrook to set boundaries and establish the superiority of herself and those who are like her. She nags her friends and neighbors, for instance, to build separate bathrooms for their maids so that they won't have to use the same facilities. And she pointedly and repeatedly snubs Celia Foote, who has two devastating flaws: She comes from white trash and she married one of Hilly's former flames.

Wow! Thank goodness I am nothing like Hilly, I thought. I was deceiving myself though, because, in different ways and almost unconsciously, I do the very same thing. I inch away from the homeless person on the subway. I judge the outfits of people who ride in the elevator with me. I draw lines, creating clubs whose membership lists exist only in the secrecy of my mind. Occasionally, I puff up the importance of my self-created boundaries to think that they are so significant that I couldn't possibly associate with others, whether because of race or class, as with Hilly, or theology or ideology or politics.

It's human nature. But there was one person who never gave into the temptation to do this: Jesus. He's the One Who embraced the Samaritan, the tax collector, the woman at the well, all manner of have-nots. Ultimately, His example is all the help I need to erase the artificial boundaries I've drawn—and to focus on the ones He drew with His generosity and grace. Those are the lines that truly matter.

Jesus, help me to see people as You do. —J<small>EFF</small> C<small>HU</small>

Digging Deeper: M<small>ATT.</small> 25:31–46; L<small>UKE</small> 19

Sun 10

"Blessed are those who are invited to the marriage supper of the Lamb. . . ."
—R<small>EVELATION</small> 19:9 (<small>NAS</small>)

J<small>UST</small> before church began, our friends Charlotte and Mike joined us. Silently, she handed my husband an invitation—beautifully covered in pink roses. We were invited to their home for a soon-to-be dinner party. We both nodded and smiled. Then Gene hurriedly scrawled something with a pencil on the back of an offering envelope and handed it to Charlotte. She lit up and nodded back to him. Still smiling, Charlotte showed me Gene's scribbled message: "You 2 are our guests this Friday at 6PM at the Savannah Room to celebrate Mike's birthday."

I smiled . . . sort of. Wishing that our invitation could have been as charming in appearance as Charlotte's. To my utter surprise, she slipped Gene's invitation into her Bible, as if it was of great importance.

Thoughts of invitations lingered in my mind as I searched through the hymnal for our first song.

Instead, my eyes landed on an unfamiliar one, "An Invitation to Christ" by Dimitri of Rostov.

Come, my Light, and illumine my darkness.

Come, my Life, and revive me from death.

Come, my Physician, and heal my wounds.

Come, Flame of divine love, and burn up the thorns of my sin,

Kindling my heart with the flame of thy love.

Come, my King, sit upon the throne of my heart and reign there.

For thou alone are my King and my Lord. Amen.

Christ Jesus, yes. Yes! I accept.
—MARION BOND WEST

Digging Deeper: ROM. 10:9; 1 PET. 2:9

Mon 11

Seven times a day do I praise thee because of thy righteous judgments.
—PSALM 119:164

There's a little game my wife and I play whenever we have had a dark and futile day. As we are getting ready for bed, I will say, "Okay, name seven good things about this day for which you can thank God."

"What?" she balks. "Are you serious? There's not a single redeeming quality to this day."

"Well," I remind her, "you had a nice breakfast out on the deck, and I know how much you enjoy a good breakfast."

"But that's a small thing...."

"And our daughter Natalie called. You enjoyed that."

"Oh yes, I almost forgot that. And we didn't get any bills today. That's a plus."

Soon Sharon is up to seventeen things and then she turns on me. "Okay, Smarty, you name seven good things about your day."

"Oops, I was afraid you would get around to me. Sorry, there was utterly nothing about this day worth remembering. Zip. Zero."

"Well, you got that sticky garage door fixed. I'm amazed at how you can fix almost anything."

"That? I was just having fun. I love to fix things. My motto is 'If it ain't broke, break it, so I can fix it.'" I rub my knees and add, "The only good thing about this day is that my knees didn't hurt all day."

Soon I am up to twenty-five good things, and the next thing we know we are laughing, and the world seems a brighter place.

The Name Seven game has never failed us. Even on the darkest nights, the candle shine of gratitude is all the night-light we need to sleep blissfully.

Sometimes, Lord, the darkness is in me and not in life itself. Help me to notice the good things in life and not just the bad things. —DANIEL SCHANTZ

Digging Deeper: PS. 23:6; JER. 31:12

Tue 12   *"The Lord is my portion," says my soul, "Therefore I hope in Him!"*
—LAMENTATIONS 3:24 (NKJV)

I came into work feeling, well, just not right. Not achy, like a cold; or tired because I hadn't gotten enough sleep the night before; or low on energy because I hadn't been eating well. Just kind of . . .

"Blah," I told one co-worker that morning.

"No other symptoms?" she replied.

"None," I said.

When Deb cocked her head sideways and furrowed her brow, I knew something was up. "No other symptoms? Then you're the only one who hasn't noticed what a grump you've been the last two days."

"Well, Dr. Deb," I said—grumpily, I should note, "and what horrible disease might be causing this grumpiness?"

"Hurry sickness. You get it every time you try to do too much and think it's still not enough. When's the last time you simply spent a half hour with God?"

Every year I get a flu shot, so I don't get the flu. I take vitamins daily, so I can ward off colds. I try to eat right and exercise. But all of those things will not keep me healthy if I don't take my daily prescription for hurry sickness—at least twenty uninterrupted minutes of prayer and silence. God-time. Every day.

Feeling blah? Overwhelmed? Drained by a to-do list that keeps getting longer? I've learned to check myself for hurry sickness. I'm not always very good at preventing it, but at least I've learned the cure.

Fill me, God, with the health that comes only from You. —JEFFREY JAPINGA

Digging Deeper: PS. 61:1–3; MATT. 6:25–34; MARK 1:35

Wed 13

And even if is true that I have erred, my error remains with me. —JOB 19:4 (NRSV)

I watched the storyteller with barely disguised disdain. Dressed in an elaborate Mother Goose costume, she'd insisted that the children move from their desks to her special "snuggies" (blankets she'd arranged on the floor by her chair) and was now reading them a story in a voice that sing-songed back and forth. I found it hard to keep a straight face or to keep my eyes from rolling.

It was all part of a read-a-thon I'd agreed to attend. I'd already read from my own children's book, and the kids had seemed to enjoy it and their parents had been interested. Having answered a number of questions, I felt I could slip out while Mother Goose was onstage making a spectacle of herself. Last I looked, she was pretending to be a chicken.

Later I mentioned the event to my sister, who has taught six- and seven-year-olds for more than twenty-five years. When I started to describe Mother Goose, Lori said, "Oh, I know her. We have her at the elementary school. She's amazing. The kids really love her."

"Really? Honestly, it takes her longer to get the stage ready than to read the story. Don't you think she overdoes it?"

My sister gazed at me like I'd just dropped out of a tree. "Didn't you notice? The kids love that stuff. Whenever she reads a book, they all beg their parents to buy it."

I'd been too sure of my own opinion to think much about it, but the children had loved Mother Goose. Why hadn't I noticed? Just when I think I know it all, God shows me otherwise. His doses of humility are never wasted on me!

> *Lord, please help me to be less of an opinionated know-it-all and more of a quiet notice-it-all.*
> —MARCI ALBORGHETTI

Digging Deeper: MATT. 5:5; ROM. 12:15–16

Thu 14

And my God will meet all your needs according to the riches of his glory in Christ Jesus.
—PHILIPPIANS 4:19 (NIV)

My wife Rosie and I went to Liberia for a missions trip because some folks had heard about the work I do to break down racial barriers. They wanted me to preach this same message since their churches were similarly divided over tribal differences.

We met with many leaders, visited different churches and saw God's hand at work. We were excited about our involvement there and the way God was using us, but when we returned home, I felt exhausted. Late one night, Rosie rushed me to the emergency room, and the doctor diagnosed me as having malaria, acute respiratory disorder, and multiple blood clots in my lungs.

I don't have time to be sick, I thought. *God,* I pleaded, *I'm busy doing good work for You and Your people. Please get me back up on my feet. And soon!*

Slowing down is not in my DNA, but my doctor was adamant about eliminating extra stresses and getting plenty of rest. I took a hard look at my life and decided to cut out some activities and focus on the things that are most important: spending more time in the Word and with family and friends.

I felt a huge burden lift. During my fifteen-day stay in the hospital, I began to rejoice and even be thankful for this illness. I had plenty of time for prayer and Bible reading, and the Scripture once again became a place of celebration.

Lord, help me to relax in Your wisdom as You work out ways to supply all my needs. —DOLPHUS WEARY

Digging Deeper: Ps. 91:2; GAL. 6:8–10; HEB. 4:9–10

THE GIFT OF TREES

Fri 15

But he [Elijah] himself went a day's journey into the wilderness, and came and sat down under a juniper tree. . . .
—1 KINGS 19:4 (NAS)

For the umpteenth time, I gazed out the small north-facing bedroom window at the row of spruce trees on our property. They hadn't liked being replanted, especially the spindly one closest to me. Somehow, through winter's bitter snows and summer's oppressive thunderstorms, it had hung on.

I was back home after a year away. Some days my spirit felt cornered. Too much had happened between my husband and me. We struggled to survive it.

Elijah was struggling when he dropped beside the juniper tree; in Hebrew, *rotem-broom tree.* He'd run for his life and come to this dead end spot. Despairingly he "requested for himself that he might die, and said, 'It is enough'" (1 Kings 19:4).

Ironically, Elijah wanted to pack it in beneath a tree that persists—and even prospers—in extreme conditions. The juniper is a scruffy desert shrub, ten to twelve feet, with wandlike branches— good for stopping blowing sand. Its thick roots are used for a premium charcoal that burns for months.

Elijah did not die under the juniper. He carried on in the work of a prophet. My little spruce did not give up. It grew, inch by inch, through every distress. I'd see it and think, *If it can make it, so can I.* God was encouraging me from my own backyard.

Five years later, the spruce is standing firm—and so is our marriage.

God, in my wilderness, when the journey is hard, hold on to me so that I can hold on. —CAROL KNAPP

Digging Deeper: Ps. 107:28–30; 2 COR. 4:7–9; JAMES 1:12

Sat 16

Be joyful in hope, patient in affliction, faithful in prayer. —ROMANS 12:12 (NIV)

Spring, a time of rebirth, arrived early for me this year. On March 16, my wife drove me to the hospital because I just didn't feel right. "It's not cardiac," I assured each doctor and nurse who examined me, hooked me up to a monitor or drew blood. The heart specialist wanted me to undergo a stress test and echocardiogram. "It's not cardiac," I told him, but he tested me anyway. "It's cardiac," I said to my wife after I was placed on the gurney, given a nitro and wheeled into the cath lab.

I have been comforted by prayers before but never in emergency situations. Family, friends and church members prayed when I had a mole removed, when a test revealed that I had melanoma and when a biopsy indicated the cancer had not spread. Those prayers helped me to be "patient in affliction."

There is no time to be patient during a cardiac emergency. But when my wife informed me, just before a stent was being placed in a blocked coronary artery, that my family and friends were praying, I felt comfort such as I had never felt before.

Later that week, when the first day of spring actually arrived, I puzzled over the power of prayer. I will never know if the prayers on my behalf changed the outcome of the operation on my heart. I have learned that when people pray for us, the awareness of their prayers is positively heart-changing.

Dear God, thank You for the faithful people who surround us with prayers when we need them.
—TIM WILLIAMS

Digging Deeper: EPH. 6:18; 1 TIM. 2:1; JAMES 5:15

Sun 17

He shall receive blessing from the Lord, And righteousness from the God of his salvation.
—PSALM 24:5 (NKJV)

My birthday falls on March 14, just three days shy of St. Patrick's Day. So through the years, many of my birthday parties have conveniently adopted a St. Patrick's Day theme. Just imagine pots of fake gold for centerpieces, gold-foiled chocolate coins for favors, and lots of shamrocks and leprechauns perched on cakes. There's really no reason for me to imagine I have anything in common with Patrick, since my forebearers are as much Scottish and English as they are Irish. But since he always shows up at my parents' house on March 14, I decided to better acquaint myself with him.

The first thing I learned was that he was far from a saint in his early years. Okay, so we had that in common. Patrick was a self-professed pagan and only found the Christian faith during a stint in prison. He studied in a monastery where he found his life's passion. I'm not sure where the leprechauns, rainbows and pots of gold came in to the mix, but Patrick spent more than thirty years converting the Celtic Druids and building schools and churches across Ireland.

I also discovered that there is one truth hidden in all those birthday decorations my mom comes up with every year. It's hidden within the green shamrock. History says that Patrick used the shamrock in his sermons as a visual to represent the Trinity, showing how the Father, Son and Holy Spirit can all exist as separate parts of the same entity.

Not a bad takeaway for a sermon or, for that matter, a birthday party!

God, all I have to do is look and I can find You—
not just in celebrations, but in everything I see,
hear and do. —BROCK KIDD

Digging Deeper: JOHN 16:7–18

Mon 18

I consider that our present sufferings are not worth comparing with the glory that will be revealed in us. —ROMANS 8:18 (NIV)

My brother-in-law didn't leave a note, just an empty prescription bottle of pills he had filled that morning. It was impossible to rationalize that he had ingested them accidentally or for some other unknown reason.

The news and method of Mick's death were not necessarily a surprise to my wife and me. Yet still it was a shock. Death always is.

I don't think I ever knew anyone who struggled harder with life than Mick. He was big and talented: a graduate of the prestigious Iowa Writers' Workshop; an athlete and a poet. He moved to Houston and took a job working for the city, so he could have plenty of time to write the great book everyone knew he had in him.

But he fell on hard times and wrestled depression, then drugs and alcohol, then just booze and living on the streets. He was in and out of county jails, detoxes, rehabs, sober houses and hospitals. I can't remember how many times he would stay sober for a month, even many months, only to go tumbling back, falling a little deeper every time.

In the end, Mick only had Julee and me, loving him, praying for him, enabling him, cutting him off, taking him back, refusing to give him money, bailing him out. One Christmas we brought him to the Berkshires. Mick said it was the happiest day of his life. I had to turn away quickly because I didn't want anyone to see me crying. Mick could be manipulative, but that was real and it broke my heart.

Sometimes I fantasize that we will find that great book Mick finally finished hidden among his ratty things. In reality, though, he didn't even leave a note. I am glad he didn't. I think it would have been very painful. And there was to be no more pain.

God, no one but You can judge. No one but You can understand such pain. Cradle Mick's soul.
—EDWARD GRINNAN

Digging Deeper: Ps. 116:2–4; 2 COR. 1:8–11; REV. 21:4

Tue 19   *"If your gift . . . is serving, then serve. . . ."* —ROMANS 12:6–7 (NIV)

My daughter Keri and I were standing on a stage, being singled out for our work in Zimbabwe. A video showing the two of us surrounded by the children we serve played across the monitors amid thunderous applause. It was an incredible honor, but I felt removed.

Truthfully, we've always been "audience people" and had never envisioned this fifteen seconds of fame. Now, suddenly, we were on the other side, looking out on what seemed a never-ending wave of people, with hot lights glaring and huge monitors mirroring our images.

It was all pomp and circumstance, crystal trophies and citations. How could we reconcile the way it felt to dish out food to hungry children in a rural African schoolyard with this? The meaning was missing.

As we exited the stage, still half blinded by the lights, I saw a form spring from a seat and rush down the aisle in our direction. The man flung his arms around me, tears spilling from his eyes. "Thank you, thank you," he said. "I'm from Zimbabwe, and I want to thank you for what you are doing for my people there."

"Oh," I whispered to God as I found my seat in the audience, "so that's why You sent us here."

Father, beyond the bright lights are the faces of Your children. Keep me centered so that I never lose sight of the place where true happiness waits. —PAM KIDD

Digging Deeper: MATT. 5:16, 6:1–4

Wed 20 *Acquaint now thyself with him, and be at peace....* —JOB 22:21

It was 8:15 AM when Ruby and I reached the office of the glaucoma specialist. After weaving through heavy Boston traffic, we were on time. There was just enough time for Ruby's examination and for me to get to my speaking engagement.

Soon the clock read 9:15, and Ruby and I were still in the waiting room. I sighed loudly, crossed my legs and rattled the newspaper. At 9:30, the doctor entered, smiling and polite. I glared. Ruby disappeared into the examination room, and I squirmed.

Then an attendant eased in a wheelchair patient. The man was stooped and old beyond his years. Thick glasses hid his eyes, and he groped rather than saw. The attendant left the patient with, "God bless you. We're happy to have you back."

The patient sat motionless. Then, softly, he murmured to no one in particular, "I wish I had someone to love me, someone to call my own."

I blinked back tears. I had Ruby's love, good eyesight, excellent health and a bounty of gifts—gifts I had accepted without being thankful and had used without appreciation.

I was tardy for my speaking engagement, but as I left the office, I shook the doctor's hand, smiling, not glaring.

March

Understanding Lord, help me to slow down and enjoy the gifts You have showered on me.
—OSCAR GREENE

Digging Deeper: PROV. 18:22; ECCLES. 9:9

Thu 21

For since the creation of the world God's invisible qualities—his eternal power and divine nature—have been clearly seen, being understood from what has been made....
—ROMANS 1:20 (NIV)

My friend Kathi leaves Post-it notes around her house for her husband to find. On his bathroom mirror, she'll leave "Hey, Good Lookin'!" Or on the seat of his car, she'll say, "I'm so proud to have a husband who works so hard every day." Or on the kitchen table, she'll say, "I love spending time with you—you always make me laugh."

These Post-it notes are much more than simple words of encouragement; they're tangible reminders of how much he is loved and cared for.

On a much grander scale, God leaves us little Post-its.

The sticky-armed hug that my daughter Kate just gave me? Post-it: *I love you with a perfect love, My child.*

The shimmering full moon that blazed through my bedroom window last night? Post-it: *Find joy in the beauty of life; I made this world for you.*

The whisper of peace that just settled over my heart when my day seemed too daunting to handle? Post-it: *You can do all things, because I will give you strength.*

The verse that I just stumbled upon in my Bible which seemed written just for me at this moment? Post-it: *I know what you need, and I've given you everything you need to live fully and wholly.*

Post-it: *God made me. God understands me. God loves me.*

Lord, thank You for constantly reminding me of how big, how wide and how powerful Your love is.
—ERIN MACPHERSON

Digging Deeper: NEH. 9:6; ISA. 40:28

Fri 22　　*Each of you should use whatever gift you have received to serve others....*
—1 PETER 4:10 (NIV)

I walked into my daughter's house, laden with orange juice, crackers and chicken noodle soup. My three young grandsons were sick with the flu. One was curled up on the sofa, one on the love seat and one in the recliner. Each child was surrounded by pillows, stuffed animals and books. My daughter Misty stepped out of the kitchen.

"Honey," I said as I looked around the room, "you should have been a nurse! Look how you have the boys all settled in."

Misty, though, never thought about being a nurse. She began taking dance lessons when she was three years old and went on to graduate from college with a dance degree.

I thought back to when I was concerned that getting a degree in dance wasn't very practical. "Get a business degree," I'd advised. "That way you can get a good job."

"Mom," she had said, "I know that God has given me my talent to share with others." Then and now I knew she was right.

So, although at the moment, Misty was the perfect nurse, she'd followed her heart and become a professional dancer, employed in a school district where she teaches dance to at-risk teens. She shares with them her talent, her passion and her belief that when you answer God's call, He will see you through.

Lord, You have bestowed upon each of us special talents. Give us the faith to use them for Your glory.
—MELODY BONNETTE SWANG

Digging Deeper: ROM. 12:1–8

Sat 23

. . . Filling our hearts with food and gladness. —ACTS 14:17

We're having grapes," I told my husband Don when he asked about Easter dinner. "Grapes are the only food everyone likes."

We'd invited six guests to join us after church, only to find that each person had unique food needs or preferences. A child was allergic to wheat, corn, carrots, bananas, garlic, tomatoes and strawberries. A diabetic man needed a low carbohydrate diet. Four guests didn't eat white potatoes, and two wouldn't touch sweet potatoes. One didn't like salad, and another didn't eat much meat. I looked through some menu planners, but they didn't have ideas for pleasing people who didn't seem to like any of the same things.

"Grapes aren't very filling," Don observed. "Make a traditional meal. People will eat what they want, and it will be enough."

So I did. We had baked ham, sweet potatoes, green beans, a relish plate, rye *and* wheat rolls, salad without tomatoes, lemon freeze, and, of course, a big platter of grapes.

Everyone enjoyed at least three foods and the fellowship was great. Later, while I did dishes, I realized that our meal was similar to our faith community. We don't all like the same types of worship and music. Our theologies differ. But when we come together at the table of the Lord to share His bread and body in Holy Communion, the common meal satisfies everyone who partakes.

Lord, let me always remember that I'm not the only one feasting at Your table. —PENNEY SCHWAB

Digging Deeper: ACTS 2:42, 46; HEB. 10:25

COME TO ME

Sun 24

Morning by morning [the Lord God] wakens—wakens my ear to listen as those who are taught.
—ISAIAH 50:4 (NRSV)

PALM SUNDAY: WELCOMING THE MESSIAH

Rain is pounding on the metal roof that covers our porch. I live in rural Vermont with my wife and children, and this storm has already hit the big cities to our south. By midday, standing puddles have formed in the street out front. I refuse to even look at the crawlspace (which has a dirt floor).

Today is also Palm Sunday. It was on this day, long ago, that Jesus road into Jerusalem on the back of a borrowed donkey. It says in the Gospel, "Many people spread their cloaks on the road, and others spread leafy branches that they had cut in the fields. Then those who went ahead and those who followed were shouting, 'Hosanna! Blessed is the One Who comes in the name of the Lord!'" Today, I imagine laying down planks of wood over my sidewalk so that Jesus can get where He is going without being flushed away by the rain.

Jesus was traveling to the temple, in anticipation of Passover. My imagination turns there to the sacred places and moments of Holy Week, the special days when we recall, relive and commemorate Jesus' final days.

Meanwhile, the rain is pouring. But that crawlspace of ours is porous; water flows in and water flows out. In the same way, this is a week when it is especially important that I bring my cares and concerns to God. I need to bring them to Him and then leave them with Him. My soul is porous with concerns. They are always there, but like water flowing in and flowing out, they need not fill up and flood me all over.

> *I need You, Lord. I am reminded to turn my face*
> *toward You. I am listening. Speak to me—today and*
> *throughout this Holy Week.*
> —JON SWEENEY

Digging Deeper: NUM. 6:24–26; ISA. 59:18–20;
1 PET. 5:6–8

COME TO ME

Mon 25 — *You crown the year with Your*
goodness, And Your paths drip
with abundance.
—PSALM 65:11 (NKJV)

MONDAY OF HOLY WEEK: FEASTING OF JESUS

My wife and I bought a ton (yes, two thousand pounds!) of compost for our Vermont garden last year. A backhoe slowly made its way down our street. When it arrived at our driveway, our neighbor slammed the gearshift into park, keeping the backhoe's engine rumbling, and called out, "Where should I dump it?"

"That corner over there," I told him, pointing past the end of the driveway, "next to the garden!"

It took us days to spread all of that compost. In the late-day sunshine, when we were done, you could actually feel the heat of the soil radiating. Our garden was ready for planting, and in went the rows of beans, cucumbers, beets, carrots, broccoli and lettuces.

The words in today's reading are from Psalm 36:7–8 (NRSV): "All people may... feast on the abundance of your house, and you give them drink from the river of your delights." I love these words. What revelry that is from the psalmist to God and as a promise to us.

The soil in our garden is like my soul, waiting for God. The compost is like all of the spiritual activities I fill my life with: prayers, Bible reading, spiritual conversations with friends, helping my neighbors. Compost seasons the soil as prayer seasons the soul. And that backhoe? I imagine it is the church, particularly right now, when the services, traditions and people who make it up all come together to deliver what I need the most.

Abundant Gardener, show me today where I may cultivate deeper soil and well-watered roots to You.
—JON SWEENEY
Digging Deeper: NUM. 14:7–9; ISA. 61:10–11; JER. 17:7–9

COME TO ME

Tue 26

God chose what is foolish in the world to shame the wise; God chose what is weak in the world to shame the strong . . . so that no one might boast in the presence of God.
—1 CORINTHIANS 1:27, 29 (NRSV)

TUESDAY OF HOLY WEEK: THE HUMILITY OF THE CROSS

We knew that our garden was prepared for a great season. We had tilled the soil, spread in fresh compost and planted rows of vegetables. Then the woodchucks came.

The first time I saw one lumber into our garden, I walked outside to get a closer look at the adorable creature. Sadly, I scared this one off. The next time, I actually saw two as they nibbled our broccoli seedlings. That wasn't quite so cute! The following day, we fenced everything up tighter. No woodchucks were going to mess up my dream of fantastic salads. But two days later, three more unwanted visitors had burrowed underneath all of the fencing and continued their feast.

Today, we are reminded of the last week of Jesus and all that He experienced on His way to the Cross. The reading from I Corinthians illuminates what we know about the life and death of Jesus: He would die a gruesome death, the same sort used for the vilest of criminals. And yet the "foolishness" of that life and death would shame "the wise" who crucified Him and did not believe.

Rarely are there spiritual lessons to be had from woodchucks. But they were, for me, a good example of the "foolish" and "weak" showing me what's what. My "wisdom" assumed that I would change the course of a natural process. But the woodchucks had their way with me, and I suspect it was for my own good.

Lord, teach me humility. I thank You
for what I do not understand and
for reminding me that I don't.
—JON SWEENEY

Digging Deeper: EXOD. 35:31; MATT. 7:24–29;
PHIL. 2:5–11

COME TO ME

Wed 27

Therefore, since we are surrounded by so great a cloud of witnesses, let us also lay aside every weight and the sin that clings so closely, and let us run with perseverance the race that is set before us, looking to Jesus....
—HEBREWS 12:1–2 (NRSV)

WEDNESDAY OF HOLY WEEK: BLESSED BY A CLOUD OF WITNESSES

It was on the Wednesday before the arrest and Crucifixion of Jesus that Judas Iscariot made secret plans with the Sanhedrin to betray his rabbi for thirty silver coins.

Isn't it ironic, then, that on this day we are also supposed to remember the blessed people in our lives who have died? My mind turns, first of all, to my grandparents. The last of them died fifteen years ago, and a week doesn't go by when I don't think about at least one of them. They are part of the "cloud of witnesses" who watch me as I go through life.

Some people call this cloud "saints," and today is a day to remember them. Saints are ordinary-become-extraordinary people, such as the man or woman who mentored or cared for you. Such as the people who are popping into your mind right now as you read this. Saints are those people who show God at work in the world.

I love thinking about this cloud of witnesses because it is a teamwork approach to salvation. "How are you doing, Jon? Do you need to talk?" My grandfathers would ask me such questions.

Saints pray for one another, support one another, seek to improve one another. Sainthood doesn't have to be an exclusive club; we only need to look for and recognize it.

> *I thank You today, Lord, for all of those people who have blessed my life by showing me Your face and teaching me Your ways.*
> —JON SWEENEY

Digging Deeper: EXOD. 18:19–21; LEV. 10:10–12

COME TO ME

Thu 28   *"You call me Teacher and Lord—and you are right, for that is what I am."* —JOHN 13:13 (NRSV)

MAUNDY THURSDAY: FOLLOWING THE TEACHER

Every summer of my childhood, my family would pack up the station wagon and drive to the base of the Upper Peninsula of Michigan to a special island cottage. We would spend weeks there each summer, swimming, exploring and fishing.

Most of all, I remember enjoying following my grandpa around on that island. There were six of us boys, my brother and me and our four cousins, and we all revered Grandpa. He was funny and warm and smart. He was never scared when bats flew overhead at twilight, he knew where to catch fish in the local lakes and he even knew how to kill rattlesnakes! We would follow Grandpa around each day, listening as he told stories—many of them tall tales, for sure.

Jesus' disciples did this, too, with their master. They followed Him and listened to His every word. Jesus' stories were surely about more important things than my grandpa's were. But I think I can picture how the disciples listened to Christ because of how I used to listen to my grandfather: raptly, earnestly, honestly.

But this night, the one that we refer to as Maundy Thursday, is when things changed between Jesus and His disciples. This night is unlike all of the others for those followers of Jesus, for this is when one of them betrayed Jesus. Jesus, knowing the heart of His friend Judas as well as what he intended, still loved him. Jesus washed Judas' feet, just as Jesus washed the feet of all the disciples that night around the table of what we have come to know as the Last Supper.

Teach me today, Lord, to be a better follower of You. Teach me to listen to You with the careful attention of a child. —JON SWEENEY

Digging Deeper: DEUT. 4:40; LUKE 9:46–48; 1 PET. 5:5–6

COME TO ME

Fri 29

See, my servant shall prosper; he shall be exalted and lifted up, and shall be very high. —ISAIAH 52:13 (NRSV)

GOOD FRIDAY: THE TRANSFORMATIVE LOVE OF JESUS

What a holy day this is, Good Friday. But taken on its own, the events of this day feel anything but good.

Jesus, Who rode into Jerusalem on the back of a donkey only five days ago, is headed toward the Cross today. He gave up His life for His friends, most of whom stood aside and silently watched Him go to His death. The love that Jesus showed inspires me and spurs me to focus on the parts of my life where I live unaffected by God's love.

On this day, in many churches around the world, coverings are placed over the images of Jesus, including the Crucifix or crosses and any paintings of Him. This is a solemn act that's intended to direct us toward mourning. Similarly, there is a tradition in many churches to bury the alleluias we sing and say. *Alleluia* comes from Hebrew and means "Praise the Lord." Today, think of not saying it as a sort of verbal fast. When we hear, say and sing it again, two days from now, we will appreciate and mean it all the more.

I have never experienced Christ's love like a thunderbolt, but I've seen and been through a slow process of transfiguration at various times in my life—times when I have been affected by God's love. There was the year that I lost a lot of weight, the summer when I fell in love with my wife, the beautiful moments spent with my children or caring for someone. Transformations can come when we live a life with God. With Him, we "shall be exalted and lifted up, and shall be very high."

Giver of all life, today is the day that You died on a tree. For this I am full of love and gratitude and sadness. —JON SWEENEY

Digging Deeper: JOHN 17; ROM. 6:11; EPH. 2:4–7

COME TO ME

Sat 30   *O God, You are my God; early will I seek You; my soul thirsts for You; my flesh longs for You in a dry and thirsty land where there is no water.*
—PSALM 63:1 (NKJV)

HOLY SATURDAY: LISTENING FOR GOD'S VOICE

This is one of those few days on the calendar when we don't quite know what to do with ourselves. Some call it "Black Saturday." Jesus' body lies in the tomb on this day, and our churches are usually quiet and dark until tomorrow morning, when we begin to celebrate.

But before Easter Sunday comes, there is time to be quiet, to listen for God's voice. I listen for that divine voice in many places: walks in the woods, conversation with my wife, the loving touch of my children and, of course, in quiet prayer.

I seek refuge in God and I am always striving to know more and more how to do it, not because prayer is complicated, but because *things* (and I) often seem to get in the way. This reminds me of a story from the life of Francis of Assisi.

One evening Francis was sitting before a fire, when a novice drew near to speak with him about acquiring a prayer book. The novice, knowing how passionately the founder of the Franciscans felt about not owning things, was nevertheless asking for permission to own one.

"Then," Francis said to him, "you will want a fancy Bible too. And then you will seat yourself in a pulpit like a great priest and beckon to your companions, saying in a proud voice, 'Bring me my Bible!'"

Taking up some cool ashes from the nearby fire, Francis gently smeared a line of ash on the forehead of the novice, saying, "*There* is your prayer book."

Remind me, Lord of all, to come to You with just me,
and to listen for Your voice without fuss.
—JON SWEENEY

Digging Deeper: PS. 131:2; 2 COR. 3:5; JAMES 4:8

COME TO ME

Sun 31 "I have revealed and saved and proclaimed—I, and not some foreign god among you. You are my witnesses," declares the Lord, "that I am God." —ISAIAH 43:12 (NIV)

EASTER: LIVING IN THE LIGHT OF THE RESURRECTION

This is a day of resurrection. We no longer bury our alleluias, and the covers no longer drape the images of Jesus in church. Mary Magdalene and the women who were with her on that Easter morning were the first to know why. "Why do you look for the living among the dead? He is not here, but has risen," the angel told her (Luke 24:5, NRSV). The women hurried to the eleven remaining disciples to share what they'd seen and heard.

I find it interesting that many churches, today, will read the memorable passage from Luke quoted above because there are many cheering us on to live in the light of the Resurrection.

Like Mary Magdalene, my grandmother taught me to believe. Grandpa was a pastor, and Grandma was a mother, friend, counselor and teacher. While he would preach three-point sermons of theology from pulpits, she would quietly teach lessons just as important.

Some of my fondest memories are of watching Grandma teach the Bible in nursing homes. She did so with great patience, using a flannel board and flannel figures of Moses, Noah, Abraham, Jesus and the disciples. I have no doubt that thousands of elders, in their final stages of life, relearned the Bible with the help of my grandmother. "God loves you so much!" she would say, cheering them on.

A cloud of witnesses surrounds each of us as we run this race, as we live the resurrected life.

I thank You today, Lord, for the gift of new life and for the blessing of faithful family who have gone before me. —JON SWEENEY

Digging Deeper: ISA. 52:7; 1 COR. 9:24; COL. 1:28

GIVING THANKS

1 _____

2 _____

3 _____

4 _____

5 _____

6 _____

7 _____

8 _____
9 _____
10 _____
11 _____
12 _____
13 _____
14 _____
15 _____
16 _____
17 _____
18 _____
19 _____
20 _____
21 _____
22 _____
23 _____
24 _____
25 _____
26 _____
27 _____
28 _____
29 _____
30 _____
31 _____

April

Be anxious for nothing, but in everything
by prayer and supplication with thanksgiving
let your requests be made known to God.

—Philippians 4:6 (NAS)

OPERATION THANKFULNESS

Mon 1   *They urgently pleaded with us for the privilege of sharing in this service to the Lord's people.*
—2 Corinthians 8:4 (NIV)

As an inexperienced leader of a new nonprofit organization, one thing I absolutely dreaded doing was asking people for things. Money. Volunteer time. Anything. Problem was, I was wearing myself out trying to do everything. Then I remembered an e-mail our son Chris sent soon after his platoon arrived at his base in Iraq. "There's not a lot of stuff here at the BX. Could you send me my favorite shampoo? And I need coat hangers. I'm actually the only one here who has a couple of them; when we went out to meet the locals, an Iraqi private gave me some of his. It is offensive to refuse."

I tried to imagine Captain Chris Barber in full combat gear, helmet, goggles and gloves with a rifle slung over his shoulder on an official visit, carrying clothes hangers back to the Humvee.

After reading Chris's e-mail, the first thing I did was rush to my closet and start corralling handfuls of empty hangers to pack up to send. It felt wonderful to have something useful to give, even if it was inexpensive hangers.

Remembering this incident, I suddenly saw the error of my ways in being averse to asking others to help with the nonprofit. Our desire to give is a gift of joy that God puts into every heart, even if all we have to offer is a few wire coat hangers. Instead of wringing my hands about having to ask people for help, I decided to thank God for the opportunity to ask others to help so they might experience the joy of grateful giving.

Father, thank You for the desire to give, which You have placed in our hearts. Help me learn how to gratefully and gracefully receive when others give to me. Amen. —KAREN BARBER

Digging Deeper: 1 CHRON. 29:16–18; 1 COR. 10:31; EPH. 2:10

A MOTHER'S JOURNEY THROUGH GRIEF

Tue 2   *"My Father's house has many rooms; if that were not so, would I have told you that I am going there to prepare a place for you?"* —JOHN 14:2 (NIV)

DAY 1: WALKING JOYOUSLY TOWARD THE LIGHT

I woke early Easter Sunday. The house remained quiet as I sat at the kitchen table and reached for my Bible. Wayne and I would be joining our children and grandchildren later for church, followed by a big family breakfast.

Earlier I'd purchased each one of my four children a book I'd recently read about heaven. The story involved a four-year-old's near-death experience and his incredible telling of what life was like in the great beyond. The book had encouraged me, and I felt it was the perfect Easter gift.

I smiled at the rising sun and thought about the terrible price Jesus had paid for my passage into heaven. I closed my eyes, and as I did I had a vision.

The image was that of a tunnel, dark and bleak with a bright light shining at the end. It was like the one I'd read about so often from those who have stood on the precipice of death. It was Jesus Who had carved that tunnel. He died, descended and was there for three days. I often wondered what had happened during that time, and in that moment I understood. Jesus had freed the multitude of souls who had been awaiting His arrival.

Little did I know that just four months later, Wayne and I would stand brokenhearted over our son's grave. My solace was the knowledge that this was the very tunnel Jesus had carved out by His death and Resurrection. Jesus was there to greet

Dale walking joyously toward the light, following his Redeemer.

> *Father, thank You for Jesus, Who paved*
> *our way to eternal life with You.*
> —Debbie Macomber

Digging Deeper: Deut. 4:39; Luke 23:42–43; John 11:25

A MOTHER'S JOURNEY THROUGH GRIEF

Wed 3

For I am sure that neither death nor life, nor angels nor rulers, nor things present nor things to come, nor powers, nor height nor depth, nor anything else in all creation, will be able to separate us from the love of God. . . .
—Romans 8:38–39 (esv)

DAY 2: SAFE IN GOD'S HANDS

Dale suffered from depression, and recently he'd been going through a difficult patch. This was as much a spiritual battle as a physical one. He was on medication, but his problems were multiplied by a recent DUI ticket and what that would mean to his teaching career. Every morning, I faithfully brought our son before the Lord.

Three years earlier Dale had gone to the Holy Land with a pastor-friend of ours and was baptized in the Sea of Galilee. Dale joked with me and said, "Gee, Mom, all you had to do was send the other kids to Bible camp. Me, you had to send all the way to Israel." For a long time afterward, he was on the right path and then all of a sudden everything seemed to go awry.

One week before Dale turned up missing, I was praying for him as I did every morning, when a dark, oppressive spirit came over me. Words fail as I try to describe this heavy darkness that descended on me. For a moment, I could barely breathe and then I broke into sobs. When my husband asked me what had happened, I said, "Something's wrong with Dale. I can feel it. We're losing our son." I continued to pray for Dale every day, knowing he was in God's hands no matter what.

I called and talked to Dale later that day, and he assured me all was well. It wasn't. I believe now that was the day our son decided to take his own life.

Father, thank You for the assurance that the battle has already been won and Jesus is the victor for each one of us. —DEBBIE MACOMBER

Digging Deeper: Ps. 34:17–18; 1 COR. 15:54; 1 JOHN 5:4

A MOTHER'S JOURNEY THROUGH GRIEF

Thu 4

Even when walking through the dark valley of death I will not be afraid, for you are close beside me. . . .
—PSALM 23:4 (TLB)

DAY 3: THE GRACIOUS CUSHION OF GOD'S LOVE

Dale was missing. Our son had sent vague text messages telling us each of his love. I was convinced Dale had either entered rehab or run away, something he'd done before.

I didn't take the fact that he'd been missing seriously until his wife contacted Search and Rescue. Dale's car was found, and the family gathered together and prayed as bloodhounds searched the area. They found nothing.

Our older son Ted spent the night with Wayne and me. The next morning I rose and reached for my Bible; the verse for that day was John 6:39. In that moment I knew, as only a mother can, that Dale was dead. When Ted left, I called our two daughters, asking them to come to the house right away.

Instead of heading directly home, Ted stopped off at the area where the bloodhounds had searched only a short while before. While in the woods, he found evidence that his brother was close by. He contacted the sheriff's department and together they located Dale's body.

The leader from Search and Rescue told us that in thirty-one years, he's never had his dogs that close to a body and not find it. In retrospect, I understand that God didn't want a dog to find our son. Nor did God wish for a stranger to relay the news to us that Dale had committed suicide; our daughters were there with their father and me when Ted contacted us with the devastating news. God had placed His loving arms around us and given us the gracious cushion of His love.

Thank You, Lord, that You were so very present in the worst day of my life.
—DEBBIE MACOMBER

Digging Deeper: Ps. 71:20–22; 2 COR. 4:1; 1 THESS. 4:12–14

A MOTHER'S JOURNEY THROUGH GRIEF

Fri 5

Cast your cares on the Lord and he will sustain you: he will never let the righteous be shaken.
—PSALM 55:22 (NIV)

DAY 4: MY DARKEST HOUR

Dale's funeral was packed with family, friends and his former students. His brother gave the eulogy and his two sisters worked on the photo display and a video set to his favorite karaoke song "You're So Vain." Ted set up a Facebook page titled "Remembering Dale Macomber," and literally hundreds of entries were posted within a few days.

I'd been emotionally strong through the funeral and the reception, but when we reached the graveyard and I viewed my son's casket being lowered into the ground, I broke into sobs. How could this have happened? Why would our son who was always so loving and tender bring such horrific pain into our lives? None of this made sense; none of it felt real.

As we readied to leave, my husband placed his arms around Dale's wife and me and steered us toward Jody, our oldest child. "I want you to take Laurie and your mother home," he said.

I looked up at him in disbelief. Why wouldn't Wayne want to return home with us? If ever there was a time I needed my husband, it was now. "What are you going to do?" I asked.

My husband looked at me with tears in his eyes and said, "I'm not going to let a stranger with a backhoe bury our son. I'm going to do it myself."

Wayne and I have been married more than forty years, and in all that time, I never loved my husband more than at that moment.

Lord, in my darkest hour You were there. For me, for my family and all who grieve, I eagerly await the day You will wipe away each tear.
—DEBBIE MACOMBER

Digging Deeper: Ps. 17:7–9; Isa. 61: 1–3; Matt. 5:4

A MOTHER'S JOURNEY THROUGH GRIEF

Sat 6   *Do not be conformed to this world, but be transformed by the renewal of your mind, that you may prove what is the will of God, what is good and acceptable and perfect.* —ROMANS 12:2 (RSV)

DAY 5: TREASURING YOUR WORD

Each year I read the Bible from Genesis to Revelation. I was reading the book of

Lamentations when Dale died. Tears marked the pages when I made the notation in the margins of the date when we lost our son.

Dale's youngest son Jaxon was just seventeen months old, and I knew he was far too young to have memories of his father. As the days progressed, I made other notes in my Bible and decided that I would give Jaxon this Bible. He wouldn't remember his father, but he would have his grandma's Bible from the year his father died.

As the grieving process took hold, I realized I had a lot more to say to my youngest grandson than the date of his father's death, so I started making other notes in the margins, tidbits of wisdom I wished to pass along to this precious child. In Genesis, where Abraham gives Lot the choice of land when their servants come to odds, I added, "Jaxon, Abraham was a peacemaker. Be one too." When I started reading the Gospels, I made a notation when Jesus heals the man with the withered hand: "Jaxon, stretch out your hand for all the wonderful gifts God has for you."

I have come to enjoy this so much that I've decided to make a Grandma's Bible for each of my nine grandchildren. It is my prayer that the Word will bless them the same way Scripture has blessed me.

*Father, may my grandchildren treasure Your Word
and feel not only Your love but also mine.*
—DEBBIE MACOMBER

Digging Deeper: 2 TIM. 2

A MOTHER'S JOURNEY THROUGH GRIEF

Sun 7

"Fear not, for I have redeemed you; I have called you by name, you are mine. When you pass through the waters, I will be with you; and through the rivers, they shall not overwhelm you; when you walk through fire you shall not be burned, and the flame shall not consume you."—ISAIAH 43:1–2 (RSV)

DAY 6: STANDING WITH THE LORD

As the weeks progressed after we had buried our son, I struggled with guilt and doubts. Grief overwhelmed me, and I dragged myself from one day into the next. I trusted the Lord. Yet Dale was gone from us.

One morning, when my spirits were low and my doubts rampant, I reached for my Bible. I flipped it open to the reading for that day, which happened to be the story of Daniel. I must have read these verses a hundred times, but that morning the story took on new meaning to me. Like Daniel, I had prayed and still was thrust into the cage with a lion. I believed that God would set Dale on the right course and deliver him from his addiction to alcohol. And yet, despite my prayers, I was face to face with those hungry lions.

What struck me most was that despite his circumstances, Daniel continued to trust in the Lord. He didn't go kicking and fighting into that den. Instead, he walked in with his head held high and faced those beasts because he knew God would stand with him. In that moment, I knew God would stand with me too.

I continue to struggle with my grief, but I no longer feel alone. And when I feel the lion's breath coming over me, I stand strong because I stand with the Lord.

Father, thank You that a familiar Bible story can take on new meaning and offer reassurance when I need it most. —Debbie Macomber

Digging Deeper: Dan. 6; 1 John 4:4

Mon 8   *When pride comes, then comes disgrace, but with humility comes wisdom.* —Proverbs 11:2 (NIV)

As I opened the door, I held my breath and zipped passed the unwashed homeless men and women who sat at tables, waiting to be fed. It was my first week as the children's director at Graffiti Church and the first time I was introduced to Wednesday night meals.

Extra work kept me there later than usual, and I had to make the dreaded walk past them toward the resource room several times that evening. The second time, I prepared myself with a deep breath and my feet ready to go double-time. I took my first quick steps, but something made me slow down. The pastor, with his tall stature and friendly face, greeted these men and women like old friends. *Poor Pastor*, I thought. *He has to bear the smell a little longer as he says hello and good-bye.*

After I fumbled around in the resource room and collected what I needed, I went back out to zip past them again. The pastor was now sitting at one of the tables, talking and laughing with them, eating the same food.

I overheard one of the men sharing a war story, and he had the pastor's full attention. By the third time, I didn't even hold my breath; I was getting used to the smell. The food was gone, the tables moved, and they sat in chairs forming a big circle. The pastor was leading a Bible study.

I've always thought of myself as a humble person with a servant's heart. But, suddenly, all I could see was my own filth of self-righteousness.

April

The pastor began to lead them in a familiar song and noticed me. "Oh, Karen has a great voice," he said with a smile. "Maybe she can help us." Their faces lit up as I sang, and when I finished, they let out the most exuberant round of applause I'd ever received.

Lord, help me always to love and have compassion for everyone I meet as the precious children You created and adore. —KAREN VALENTIN

Digging Deeper: MATT. 9:35–38; MARK 2:15–17; 1 THESS. 3:12

Tue 9

And God said, "This is the sign of the covenant I am making between me and you and every living creature with you, a covenant for all generations to come: I have set my rainbow in the clouds. . . ." —GENESIS 9:12–13 (NIV)

I had just finished reading the Bible story of Noah's ark to my five-year-old grandson Frank, and we were looking at a picture of the rainbow that was a sign of God's promise to never again flood the whole earth. Under it, a white-bearded Noah raised his hands in thanksgiving.

Frank traced his finger across the rainbow. "I wish I could see a real one," he said.

"I do too, honey, but we don't get them here very often." In fact, only once in the fifteen years we'd lived in Tennessee had I seen one.

"Do they look like this?" Frank asked.

"They're much more beautiful," I said. He sighed.

Two days later Frank and I were coming out of a store after waiting out a heavy rainstorm. The sun had appeared, along with something else. Just as we were getting into the car, I looked up and saw a brilliant rainbow spanning the sky in a perfect arc. "Look, Frank," I whispered.

His eyes grew wide. "God sent us a rainbow!" We stood there, as if on holy ground, eyes and hearts lifted to this stunning gift from Noah's God and ours.

Almighty God, Whose faithfulness spans the generations, thank You for hearing a small boy's wishful sigh. —SHARI SMYTH

Digging Deeper: GEN. 9:1–17; PS. 139:4; 2 COR. 1:20

DIVINE ABUNDANCE

Wed 10

But others fell onto good ground and brought forth fruit, some an hundredfold. —MATTHEW 13:8

In spring when the first warm Chinook blew down the Wind River Mountains, raising temperatures thirty degrees in as many minutes, we folks in Wyoming's Lander Valley turned our thoughts to gardening. My own plot of rich, river-bottom soil consistently produced well for my family. As a single mom, I depended upon these vegetables. Then one particularly challenging year, when I worried incessantly about squeezing the buffalo off the nickel, God used pumpkins to remind me that He always provides.

While shopping, I discovered seeds for ten cents a package, perfect for my strained budget. I scooped up a supply for tomatoes, green beans, zucchini, lettuce, radishes, onions, beets, peas and pumpkins. Since I hadn't planted potatoes that year, I had space for six generous hills of pumpkins, which would sprawl and consume the vacant space.

That year frost held off, so by the end of September I had a bumper crop, a golden mound of pumpkins weighing five to ten pounds apiece. Even after the kids had chosen their jack-o-lanterns and I set aside some for pies, I still had pumpkins. As I shopped for potatoes the next day, I jokingly asked the produce manager if he needed pumpkins. "Sure do! I'll give fifteen cents a pound."

About a week later, I received a check for fifteen dollars, a modest windfall but a tremendous return on a ten-cent investment. Once again, I knew that if I would plant and tend my garden, if I would be a good steward of what little I had, God would take care of the rest.

Generous God, Your bounty amazes me always.
—GAIL THORELL SCHILLING

Digging Deeper: MATT. 25:14–30

Thu 11

Those who say, "I love God," and hate their brothers or sisters, are liars; for those who do not love a brother or sister whom they have seen, cannot love God whom they have not seen.
—1 JOHN 4:20 (NRSV)

I never liked one of my brothers very much. Growing up, we routinely got into philosophical shouting fits, each of us determined to be right. Usually he won, although I never acknowledged defeat. How could he not win? He's the image of our father in every way: big, loud, easily annoyed and more certain of his views than I have ever been. In our arguments as adults, I relived the deflating childhood experience of being outshouted in family debates. Following my modus operandi with anything upsetting, I took pains to avoid him.

That wasn't hard to do. I moved even farther away after I left our family's Southern California home. I went to grad school in New Orleans; lived in Boston for a time and then Berlin, Beijing and Hong Kong. I didn't actively hate my siblings. I merely distanced myself, leaving them in the past.

Eventually I returned to the United States, by then effectively chopped from the family tree.

Years later, I noted how often Scripture commands us to love our brothers. Inspired by my literalist husband, I set out to love my actual siblings. The result of this project surprised me. My brother had mellowed over the years, I discovered, and is now a prized conversation partner. We chat regularly about politics, relationships, God, the Bible. Invariably, I use up my phone's battery. Our voices breaking up, we fantasize about continuing the discussion in person someday. If we had more time to talk, we joke, together we could set this messed-up world right.

Father, You made me and all my siblings, and Your great desire is that we love one another. Help me to love my brothers and sisters deeply and inwardly.
—PATTY KIRK

Digging Deeper: GEN. 1:27; PROV. 10:12

Fri 12

I keep my eyes always on the Lord. With him at my right hand, I will not be shaken. —PSALM 16:8 (NIV)

If you've ever seen a Disney movie or known a little girl, you know that princesses are *the* thing to be. Princesses talk to animals, wear shiny dresses, and spend their days singing and dancing. What more is there to life?

At the theme parks, the magic comes to life when ladies appear wearing the costumes, makeup, jewelry, and wigs and bend to speak to pint-sized princesses-in-the-making.

"You should've seen it," Mom said as we put our feet up for a moment before starting our dinner. She was on her way home after a visit to Disney World with a handful of lucky grandkids. "The princesses knelt down and looked each girl in the eyes and spoke with them, asking their names, complimenting their dresses, and answering all their questions. They gave their undivided attention, and the girls felt like they were the only people in the world."

Mom was silent for a minute, then softly said, "I think I need to be more like the princesses."

I thought about what she said. How many times had I "uh-huhed" my way through conversations with my husband while trying to finish dinner or get the next load of laundry in? How often did

April

I let my mind wander to my to-do list at work while catching up with my ninety-three-year-old grandma? Was I in charge of my life or was I simply bowing to my constantly growing to-do list?

I can't always be like the princesses. At times, I really do just need to pick up my dry cleaning and be on my way. But when I can, I stop and really listen to my husband when he gets home (*Dinner will wait!*), or take the call from Grandma (*Where am I in a hurry to go?*). And every time, I am thankful that I did.

Lord, remind me today who is important in my life and allow me to focus wholly on them, if only for a moment. —ASHLEY KAPPEL

Digging Deeper: ESTHER 8; Ps. 30:5

Sat 13   *We are labourers together with God.... —*1 CORINTHIANS 3:9

William got up before dawn to catch his flight. I heard our son hoist his bags, the front door opened and closed, and then I heard him drop the keys through the mail slot, following instructions his mother had left on a note. I hated to hear him go. *He's twenty-three years old*, I told myself. We'd had a great visit with him. Why feel so sad?

But the ache was still there at breakfast before I did the chores. *I wish I could figure out how to pray my way through this one*, I thought. When would we see him again? In another three or six months? It seemed a lifetime. He lived two thousand miles away.

I went into his room and took the old stuffed animals off his bed, stripped his sheets and picked up his towel. In some ways, he still was a child. Independent, with a great job, a nice set of friends and a damp towel on the floor. I gathered everything up and put it in the washer. I noticed the books on his shelves, the ones we read to him and the ones he read. The progression from *Goodnight Moon* to *Infinite Jest*, from Dr. Seuss to Malcolm Gladwell went so fast, but wasn't that what we would have wanted?

It's a good thing, I thought. Soon I would e-mail him some article I'd seen, and he'd forward something he'd read. We were lucky to be able to stay connected through e-mails and texts and phone calls. I spread the clean sheets over the bunk bed, throwing the stuffed animals back to their berth. *Thank God*, I thought, *he hasn't completely outgrown them.*

There it was. The prayer I'd been looking for. It had been with me in cleaning the room, doing the laundry, making the bed. The ache had lifted into a sort of gratitude. "To work is to pray" is an ancient monastic saying. I slipped the clean pillowcase on his pillow, thankful for the years, looking forward to the ones ahead.

> *Give me work, Lord, that lets me pray.*
> —RICK HAMLIN

Digging Deeper: 1 SAM. 1:26–28; JOHN 14:12; 1 JOHN 3:1

Sun 14

Carry each other's burdens, and in this way you will fulfill the law of Christ. —GALATIANS 6:2 (NIV)

I volunteered to lead the men's group of our new church on an eight-week study guide titled *Life-Healing Choices.* I wasn't sure if the men would connect or open up, given our short time together as a church.

We were feeling our way until we got to the third session about disappointments and hurts. Billy, the youngest, shared, "I am deeply disappointed with myself. I expected to be farther down the road with my faith. I should have been doing more for the Lord."

Ken followed, and with tears streaming down his cheeks said, "I still grieve the loss of my older brother. He taught me everything. If only my two boys would have met him."

Anthony told how he regretted not playing sports with his father and said, "When I get to heaven, the first thing I want to do is play catch with my dad."

I, too, wanted to share my struggle, but a part of me didn't want to be honest. *What would they think of their pastor?* Yet I knew the moment was right. I mustered the courage and said, "I am spiritually tired. The pastoral ministry is taking a toll on me."

Ken softly responded, "Pastor, I have been concerned about your well-being."

Peter quickly added, "We're here to help you." At the end of the meeting the guys gathered around and prayed for me.

I have been in many groups, but this one was really special for me. I had found a band of brothers who helped me with my burden in a nonjudgmental and caring spirit. The last thing I expected was that these men, who I was supposedly leading, would deepen my faith through their unconditional love and care for me.

Dear Lord, thank You for these brothers in Christ who help carry my burdens. —PABLO DIAZ

Digging Deeper: EZRA 7:27–28; PROV. 18:23–24; 2 COR. 4:16

THE GIFT OF TREES

Mon 15   *On either side of the river was the tree of life. . . .*
—REVELATION 22:2 (NAS)

When my granddaughter Sarah was seven, she wrote a story about a food tree. On her tree grew: popcorn, apples, pears, bananas, blueberries, tomatoes, broccoli, celery and carrots.

The amazing tree of life pictured in Revelation grows along the river flowing from God's throne. It bears "twelve kinds of fruit, yielding its fruit every month" (Revelation 22:2). What delicious mystery! Our apple tree works months to produce a single crop. Imagine a heavenly tree continually bearing!

I see a tree of glorious grandeur laden with succulent fruit, filling heaven's environs with color and fragrance. A painting by Henriette Sauvant has a wonderful gnarled old tree bending its branches to offer a perfect pear to a young girl standing on tiptoe. I think of the tree of life offering its fruits like this.

Another fascination of this tree is its leaves for "healing of the nations" (Revelation 22:2). Many trees contain healing properties in their leaves, but what manner of vibrant dancing leaves might these be?

I imagine them the dark green of cedars deep in the forest. And fan-shaped like ginkgo leaves spinning on the breeze. They gather breath from God, water from the river of life, light from Jesus—and with these drape a holy peace upon all people who draw near. Oh, to rest beneath such a tree.

Great God of far reaching vision, all praise to You for Your most supreme tree of life! —CAROL KNAPP

Digging Deeper: GEN. 1:12; PS. 1:3; PROV. 3:17–19

Tue 16

You need to persevere so that when you have done the will of God, you will receive what he has promised.
—HEBREWS 10:36 (NIV)

D addy, can we practice riding my bike?"
I tensed. Frances, our four-year-old, hadn't asked this question in a while. Several months earlier, after her last failed attempt, she angrily announced, "I don't want to ride my bike. I'll ride it when I'm five." And that had been that. She hadn't touched the bike since. *Here we go again*, I thought. I wasn't a very good parent in these situations. I tended to get impatient with her impatience.

"Are you sure?" I asked this time. "You said you didn't want to learn to ride until you were five."

"I'm sure," she said. I sighed, knowing how this would end.

I pumped up the tires and wheeled the bike to the sidewalk. Frances hoisted herself onto the seat. "Don't let go, Daddy," she reminded me.

Frances' legs whirled. She seemed steady, so I withdrew my hand slightly from the seat. She stayed up. I jogged along beside her. I wasn't holding on, and she was riding! Suddenly, she veered into the grass and tipped over. I held my breath. She bounced back up and righted the bike. "Were you holding on?" she asked.

I shook my head. "You were riding by yourself." She grinned. "Let's do it again!"

We went up and down the block. I let go of the seat a little longer and then even longer. Finally, steeling myself, I stopped and watched her pedal down the street on her own. She was riding!

I have no idea what prompted Frances suddenly to get back on the bike. Whatever it was, her body somehow knew when it was ready. God knew when we were both ready.

"Get your bike, Daddy, and we'll ride together," said Frances. And we did.

Help me live according to Your time, God.
—Jim Hinch

Digging Deeper: Prov. 14:29; Eccles. 3:1

Wed 17

From these the maritime peoples spread out into their territories by their clans within their nations, each with its own language.
—GENESIS 10:5 (NIV)

D escribe something you miss about your country," I ask Suneetha, the young student from Sri Lanka.

"Oh," she says with a big sigh, "the food."

How do I get her to say more than that? "What kind of food do you miss?" She tells me, and I half understand her.

Every sentence that I draw out of these non-English-speaking residents of the United States is hard work on both sides. I have to make myself understood, and they have to understand. One of my favorite ways of doing this is to give them easy crossword puzzles that they can work on as a team. As they find words to fit empty squares, the volume in the room rises and everyone is trying out ideas.

Language is a gift that we so often take entirely for granted, but listening to an ordinary conversation, one can realize how incredibly difficult learning English is for these adults, who often have advanced educations from their native lands. Gregorio, for example, has lived in the United States for thirty years and can just manage a few stumbling sentences. He was living in a Hispanic community where English wasn't a priority until he wanted to help his grandkids with their homework. Now he never misses class.

At the end of a day, I visit with my son and hear Otto, his two-year-old, trying very hard to get his message across. "Vant dat," he says firmly several times, pointing to an orange on the table. He gets what he wants and sees from the very beginning the power of language. Language is the invisible thread that binds us all together.

Thank You, Lord, for both Your Word and the words You have given to us to reach others.
—Brigitte Weeks

Digging Deeper: Ps. 19:2–4; Prov. 18:10

Thu 18

Your Father knows what you need before you ask him.
—Matthew 6:8 (niv)

Being pulled over by the state police on the interstate is a frightening, heart-pounding and often expensive experience. And as such, I figured this day was as good as ruined. I'll be honest: I didn't even pray about it, didn't even ask God to help. What would be the point?

The officer had clocked me at four miles an hour above the speed limit, which he described as "pretty fast." Although I disagreed with his assessment, I don't like to argue with police officers, so I just nodded and maintained eye contact with him through the open passenger-side window where he was standing.

"What do you do for a living?" he asked.

"I give motivational speeches. Like at conventions, corporations and schools," I replied. "I'm actually driving to a speech right now."

He nodded and considered this. "What is it that you speak about?" he asked.

"Overcoming adversity."

"Well," he said, "I'm going to let you off with a warning so that in your speech you can talk about how you overcame this speeding ticket."

And just like that, my day was transformed. Not only did I not have a ticket to pay, I also drove away in an even better mood than I had been in before the incident. I brought that positive energy, along with a new funny story, onstage to my speech.

I had thought it was pointless to ask God for help, but even without my asking, He came through in a way I would've never expected.

Lord, thank You for looking out for me even when my first response is not to look up to You for assistance.
—JOSHUA SUNDQUIST

Digging Deeper: Ps. 100:5; ISA. 25:1; JOHN 16:33

April

Fri 19

Through the Lord's mercies we are not consumed, Because His compassions fail not. They are new every morning; Great is Your faithfulness.
—LAMENTATIONS 3:22–23 (NKJV)

I recently applied for long-term-care insurance and was promptly rejected. I shouldn't have been all that surprised, what with the serious neurofibromatosis I've battled since my teenage years. But when my agent called to notify me I'd been turned down, I found I was plagued by all manner of self-doubts. Chief among them was a comment the agent had made during the application process. "If you have good long-term-care insurance," he said, "you'll have greater access to the best nursing homes."

What does that mean? I wondered now. *Will I be left to suffer in some forgotten place during my later years?*

Then the words of the wonderful old hymn "Great Is Thy Faithfulness" came to me:

Great is Thy faithfulness!
Great is Thy faithfulness!
Morning by morning new mercies I see.
All I have needed Thy hand hath provided;
Great is Thy faithfulness, Lord, unto me!

It says in Lamentations that God's mercies are new every morning, so great is His faithfulness. That goes for nursing-home years, too, or whatever life holds for me. Each new day, when the pink edge of dawn peeks though my window shade, I will have opportunities anew to serve. I can encourage a nursing assistant going through a rough divorce, save back the lemon meringue pie on my lunch tray for a friend, go to wheelchair bingo and win a stuffed giraffe for my great-niece.

Thanks to God's promises, His mercies will follow me wherever I go, offering strength for today and bright hope for tomorrow. And with them will come everything I need . . . and still more to give away.

I'm standing on Your promises, Lord Jesus.
—ROBERTA MESSNER

Digging Deeper: DEUT. 7:8–10; 2 CHRON. 6:14; NEH. 9:31

Sat 20

I have shewed thee new things from this time, even hidden things, and thou didst not know them.
—ISAIAH 48:6

I have to admit I'm not a fan of change. I'm perfectly content if most things in my world go on today as they did yesterday and do the same tomorrow. I buy the same brand of pants year after year, in the same colors; all that changes is the waistline (expanding, contracting and then, alas, expanding again). I have my favorite spot for reading (the blue chair in the bedroom), my favorite route for walking (in and along the parks from our Upper Manhattan apartment building to a coffee shop just over the river in the Bronx), and my favorite drink (iced coffee, black, no sugar).

For someone as change-averse as I am, this past year has been challenging. I've seen changes in my career, in the configuration of our family (Elizabeth back to school and John back home), in my daily routine. I've told myself to take each change as an opportunity to grow, but that hasn't proved as easy as I'd hoped. I'm not a believer in karma, but all those years of doing the same things in the same way have taken their toll now that it's time to try something new.

I've done a lot of thinking and praying about my allegiance to the tried-and-true and I've decided it isn't just a matter of preference; it has deeper roots. One of them is pride: *My way is the best way, and I'm not going to change it!* And another is fear: *It's safer to stay in my comfort zone. Who knows what might happen if I don't?*

Now it's time for me to dig up those roots and begin afresh—without pride and unafraid. And I'm taking those words of Isaiah to heart: How can I know what God is showing me if I'm too afraid to look?

*Lord, renew my heart and give me eyes
to see the wonders of Your love.*
—ANDREW ATTAWAY

Digging Deeper: PS. 51:10–11; MATT. 9:17;
2 COR. 5:17

Sun 21

*As soon as I pray, you answer me;
you encourage me by giving me
strength.* —PSALM 138:3 (NLT)

I sat on the beach, watching my sons draw their names in the sand. The ocean was icy, too cold for me. The waves crashed at the shore. A few brave souls swam just beyond the rough surf where it was calm and peaceful.

I looked down at my book and then back at the water. Behind us, an older gentleman was helped down the sand dune over the beach grass by his wife and daughter. He wore dark blue swim trunks and held a cane in his hand, but the women supported him, guiding him slowly toward the lacey edge of the waves. The man approached the water with difficulty, dragging his feet in the unstable sand.

"You're doing it," his wife said. "We're almost there. Let me take your cane."

As they reached the water, they stiffened at the chill. "Cold," the wife said.

"Beautiful," the man said.

They continued on, deeper, arm in arm, shivering in their bathing suits as the rise of the rough waves reached their shoulders. Beyond the crashing surf, they stood in the calm water and stopped.

"Ready?" his wife asked. The man nodded. They let go. The man spread out his arms as if he were flying.

"You got it, Dad!" the daughter shouted.

The man lay on his back, floating, and lifted his feet so the tips of his toes rose to the surface. He smiled.

> *Dear God, thank You for these beautiful moments*
> *when I witness another's spirit soar and*
> *feel Your love in my heart.*
> —SABRA CIANCANELLI

Digging Deeper: ISA. 46:3–5; JOHN 6:63, 10:10

Mon 22

The Lord God made all kinds of trees grow out of the ground—trees that were pleasing to the eye and good for food. . . .
—GENESIS 2:9 (NIV)

One of my favorite dates with my husband is a visit to the local arboretum. Each time we stroll the grounds, we're surprised by new discoveries and overwhelmed by the evidence of God's creativity. Graceful willows shade the banks of creeks, while gnarled oaks stand like sentries on hilltops. Even the sound each tree makes is unique, from the gentle creaking of maple limbs to the rustle of aspen leaves when a breeze tickles them.

I'd read the creation story hundreds of times, but one day a new phrase jumped out at me: "trees that were pleasing to the eye." If the purpose of trees was to provide food, God could have created little black boxes that contained fruit for people's use. Instead, He chose to design them as pleasing to the eye. And not only did He form one beautiful, intricate, attractive shape, but He also made variety.

Trees come in all sizes and shapes, with leaves of various colors and bark of different textures. Ancient redwoods give me a small glimpse into the magnificence of God's power. An overflowing cherry tree reminds me of His generous provision. A weeping crab apple shows me a hint of His whimsy. Everywhere I look, nature teaches me that God is not merely concerned with the utilitarian, but also with beauty and limitless imagination. I love knowing that about God.

Psalm 19:1 (NIV) tells us, "The heavens declare the glory of God." So do all the elements of the world He's created. Each mountain, star, blade of grass, ocean or flowering tree shows us more of the limitless facets to God's love.

Lord, thank You for the beautiful world You made and what You have revealed about Yourself. Today, help me notice each tree, shrub or flower as a gift of Your love. —SHARON HINCK

Digging Deeper: Ps. 102:25; ROM. 1:20

Tue 23

One father . . . in you. . . .
—EPHESIANS 4:6

At the financial company I work for, we were fortunate to have many stories of success, and on this particular day, we had gathered as a group to work on ways to spread our company's good news with the community.

As the meeting started, an associate asked to go first. His suggestion was followed by accolades from our other partners. I, however, was unable to praise his great idea. After all, the idea just presented was mine. The week before, this so-called friend had invited me to lunch and had pressed me to share my thoughts on the coming presentation.

I wanted to stand up, bang the table and yell, "My strategy has been stolen!"

Suddenly, my thoughts took me back to an outing with my son. We were driving home after seeing "The Lion King." In the story, a young lion has lost his father and falls into a wayward life. "Dad," Harrison had asked, "how do you think Simba [the young lion] became such a great leader after messing up so much?"

"Well," I remembered answering, "I guess it's because he finally realized that his hero-father still lived within him."

Now that image filled my head: our Father God living within us . . . living within me. I looked across the table. I remembered my friend was going through a tough time in his marriage, and his most recent performance appraisal had been weak.

"So, Brock," the president directed the conversation to me, "what do you think?"

"I like Bob's idea," I said. "I think it's just right for our company's image!"

I caught Bob's eye and offered him a smile. I hope he saw a glimmer of love there.

Father, when I remember Who You are, I see who I can become. —BROCK KIDD

Digging Deeper: MARK 8:34–36; PHIL. 2:3; 1 JOHN 5:1–5

Wed 24

"Different trumpet blasts will be necessary to distinguish between the summons to assemble and the signal to break camp and move onward."
—NUMBERS 10:5 (TLB)

After camping for three weeks in Alaska, my brother, sister-in-law and I opted for a little luxury on a cruise ship for seven days. Shortly after boarding, we were required to attend a safety drill that I thought was an inconvenient waste of time.

That night after our set-sail party, luxurious dinner and live entertainment, we weary passengers fell into bed, dreaming of exquisite scenery about to enchant us at Glacier Bay. At 4:00 AM, we were stunned into consciousness by the loudest horn I'd ever heard. The captain shouted from the loud speaker, "Ladies and gentleman, get dressed immediately and report to your lifeboat muster station! We fear someone has been pushed or fallen overboard, and we are required by law to retreat back to that spot."

In a daze, we pulled jeans over our pajamas, grabbed our jackets and stumbled to our muster station where we stood outside in the freezing cold while the crew called the names of all two-thousand passengers. Thankfully, everyone was present. False alarm. The captain told us he'd never had to summon passengers from their beds in his twenty-three years on the seas.

As we stood there shivering, I remembered how I'd complained in the past about having to wear a seat belt or life jacket. I'd even complained about the commandment to keep holy the Lord's day. That night I decided safety devices are gifts as amazing as having God in my life. Someone smarter than me knows better than me.

Lord, help me to be thankful, not resentful, when asked to buckle up, wear the life jacket, helmet, harness; hold on to the hand rail; or attend church services every Sunday. —PATRICIA LORENZ

Digging Deeper: 1 COR. 6:12; GAL. 6:7–16

Thu 25   *As iron sharpens iron, so one person sharpens another.*
—PROVERBS 27:17 (NIV)

I've been struggling with physical stuff with my girlfriend, and I'd appreciate some prayer." The college student sat in his chair with his head down. "I'm having a really tough time following God."

It was our college group Bible study, and my heart went out to him because my husband and

I struggled with that ourselves when we were dating.

Then another boy who is usually very quiet spoke up. "You know, I admire you for being honest and sharing that. I've had struggles, too, but I try to read my Bible a lot when I'm alone. Then I somehow feel stronger."

The student who'd asked for prayer seemed encouraged by what the other student said.

The exchange made me realize that when I'm going through really tough times, transparency between me and my fellow Christians gives me comfort and support. When I am honest about my struggles and when those listening are honest about their own experiences, I'm greatly encouraged.

That kind of vulnerability can be scary because I worry about people rejecting me or condemning me, but true believers deal with each other in love, and love casts out fear. I hope the love we shared with that college student gave him strength to face his struggles.

Lord, guide me to the right person to share my struggles with so I can be transparent and feel encouraged by an equally transparent fellow Christian.
—CAMY TANG

Digging Deeper: Ps. 119:9; 1 COR. 10:13; 1 JOHN 4:18

Fri 26

More profitable than . . . gold.
—PROVERBS 3:14 (NIV)

K nowing how I relish packing my camera and setting off on lone adventures, my husband David gifted me with a trip to Paris. And now I'm in a quandary because I made a promise to my granddaughter Abby: "I will never, ever go back to Paris without you."

One ticket was a stretch; three tickets (Abby and I wanted her mom, Keri, to come too) would be impossible.

I did have two gold coins given to me at Keri's birth. I unearthed a few gold objects from forgotten boyfriends, a chain I'd never wear, an outdated bracelet. At the antique jewelry shop, I waited while they weighed, tested and calculated, and then left with a check just large enough for two fares to Paris!

Soon three generations of giggling girls were checking out our Paris hotel, walking down the Champs d'Elysees, belting out "I Love Paris in the Springtime" with Abby shushing in mortal fear that we might run into another eight-year-old from Nashville, Tennessee.

From there, we did Paris Abby-style. We ate dinner in the Eiffel Tower, gazed at the Mona Lisa from every angle, had tea in an ancient tearoom and studied the gargoyles at Notre Dame. We walked up and down the River Seine, sampled pastries, inhaled chocolate eclairs and ate our fill of croissants.

On the last day, Abby and Keri presented me with a little hand-cranked music box. Back home, when the house is quiet and the time is right, Abby hands me the music box and I turn the little crank. "I Love Paris in the springtime... I love Paris in the fall..." as Abby leaps and twirls and dances Paris all around the room.

God, You have yielded returns on my investment beyond imagining. I cannot thank You enough.
—PAM KIDD

Digging Deeper: PROV. 3:9–10; MATT. 6:33

Sat 27
The Lord pondereth the hearts.
—PROVERBS 21:2

Ten hours into my day, I was on the tractor, raking grass hay in one of the fields on our family cattle ranch. To stay awake until it was finished, I threw back my head and sang, *"Piove sull'oceano, piove sull'oceano, piove sulla mia identità..."*

To the casual observer, I am a cowgirl through and through, from my Wrangler jeans to my Resistol hat. It could be assumed that I work with cattle, ride horses and spend a great deal of time outdoors. But on the inside, I'm way more complex than that. I occasionally read Westerns, but more often I can be found deep in the pages of Jane Austen, Robert Louis Stevenson or even the Baroness Orczy. I like country music, but I also listen to rock, oldies and Celtic—depending on my mood. My favorite song is "Oceano," an Italian ballad sung by Josh Groban.

The thing is, I like to observe people when I'm in town. I make a game of guessing who they are, strictly by their appearance. Business suit: banker or lawyer, probably listens to classical music and NPR. Truck driver: definitely classic country, sports fan, never listens to the news.

But just as I can't be taken at face value, I'm sure I'm pegging them wrong too. Perhaps this is why God instructed us not to judge our neighbors. Jumping to conclusions is easy when we can plainly see people's façades, but only God can truly know their innermost hearts.

"*É per l'amore che ti do, É per l'amore che non sai . . .*," I belt out merrily at the top of my lungs over the rumble of the tractor. No one would guess I don't understand a word of Italian!

Dear Lord, You know our hearts. You alone can truly judge us. Please don't let me judge others.
—ERIKA BENTSEN

Digging Deeper: I SAM. 16:7; MATT. 22:36–40; LUKE 6:31–36

Sun 28

Great is the Lord . . . his greatness is unsearchable. —Psalm 145:3

Just outside our apartment, there's a little patch of lawn that catches the early morning light. The slanting rays backlight hundreds of tiny whirling insects just above the grass. Circling, dancing, darting, moving too fast for my eyes to follow any individual, they're a dazzling explosion of energy, and I always try to get outside before the sun climbs higher and the spectacle disappears.

I'd been enjoying it for days before it occurred to me that, of course, the phenomenon was not unique to that bit of lawn. It was simply the angle of the light that enabled me to see it there. The spinning mites must be all over—on other lawns, in grassy places everywhere, in unimaginable numbers.

The little light show, I thought, was an image of the cosmos itself: billions of galaxies, each with billions of stars—a reality too vast for the brain to take in. And equally inconceivable is the other end of the scale: billions of atoms in the bench where I sit, in the book on my lap, in my own body— each atom a little universe of revolving particles. My mind goes blank at such figures.

But for a few minutes every morning, a little patch of God's universe is illuminated for me. In the whirling specks I seem to see both the wheeling galaxies and the spinning atoms. And their dizzying dance says to me: At the base of all creation is energy, and the name of that energy is *joy*.

*Let me join today, Creator God, in
the universal celebration.*
—ELIZABETH SHERRILL

Digging Deeper: GEN. 1:1–2; PS. 147:4–5;
JOHN 1:1–3

Mon 29

*I have set before thee an open door,
and no man can shut it. . . .*
—REVELATION 3:8

My wife and I were lounging in the screened-in porch, admiring the antics of the humming-birds that buzz around our red glass feeder. I was thinking about one of my students who is unmotivated, wondering how I could jump-start him.

Then one of the little hummers wandered into our garage and couldn't find its way out. Over and over it bumped into the ceiling, thinking it was the sky.

"Look," I wanted to say, "you are not trapped in here. The overhead door is wide open. Just go that way and you will be free." It's frustrating, trying to help these feathered friends, when they know only one approach.

It's even more frustrating when I find myself locked into the same kind of one-way thinking. I have tried to be nice to my unmotivated student, but it just seemed to make things worse. I needed to look at other options.

What if I show him where he stands in the grade book? Maybe I need to work with him, one on one? Turns out, the grade book did the trick.

The hummingbirds that wander into our garage are not stupid. God made them brilliant aviators, but when they feel trapped, they panic and are blinded to the obvious answer to their dilemma.

The next time I feel frustrated, I must remember to take a deep breath, settle down and look around for an exit from my situation. It's always there, if I can just recognize it.

There are no mysteries to You, Lord. Show me the open door that's right in front of my eyes.
—DANIEL SCHANTZ

Digging Deeper: PS. 32:7; MATT. 8:23–27; REV. 3:20

Tue 30   *"Zacchaeus, make haste and come down, for today I must stay at your house."* —LUKE 19:5 (NKJV)

About five years ago, my niece Karin had to find a new home for her tabby cat. I hadn't particularly wanted a pet, but I opened my door. One sunny afternoon, five-year-old Kitty arrived.

On distinctive blue stationery, Karin had hand-written some care tips and detailed some of Kitty's personality quirks. I thanked Karin for her comments, noted the attached veterinarian's report and set aside the papers.

My friend Jane remembers asking me how I felt about my new companion. She says I smiled big and replied, "Head over heels." The years have slipped by, and now I can hardly imagine life without Kitty.

I occasionally looked for Karin's papers, but they never surfaced—until yesterday. Sorting through an untidy stack that I've cleaned around for way too long, I spotted the unmistakable stationery.

I scanned Karin's characterization of Kitty. No surprises there. But a relatively insignificant fact distressed me. Kitty is a year older than I thought. My mind raced ahead, imagining a closer-than-anticipated heartbreak: the day she's called to take her place on the graph that measures feline life expectancy.

All day long, when I saw Kitty, I felt sad. When she bumped me, I felt blue. Then last evening, she sat at the top of the staircase. I walked by and, as if to tease me, she ran down the stairs. Her burst of energy jolted me out of my anticipatory grief. Impulsively, I laughed and challenged her to a race. In the kitchen, I picked her up and thanked God for the joy of the *present* presence.

April

Lord, help me to appreciate the delights of today rather than anticipate the griefs of tomorrow.
—EVELYN BENCE

Digging Deeper: GEN. 3:8; PSS. 23:4, 139:7

GIVING THANKS

1 _____

2 _____

3 _____

4 _____

5 _____

6 _____

7 _____

8 _____

9 _____

10 _____

11 _____

12 _____

13 _____

14 _____

15 _____

16 _____

17 _____

18 _____

19 _____

20 _____

21 _____

22 _____

23 _____

24 _____

25 _____

26 _____

27 _____

28 _____

29 _____

30 _____

May

And let the peace of Christ rule in your hearts,
to which indeed you were called in one body.
And be thankful.

—COLOSSIANS 3:15 (ESV)

OPERATION THANKFULNESS

Wed 1

Many, Lord my God, are the wonders you have done.... Were I to speak and tell of your deeds, they would be too many to declare. —Psalm 40:5 (niv)

One morning I was driving alone on a rural section of I-85 near Anderson, South Carolina. *Whack! Whack! Whack!* The front end of the car began vibrating violently. I gripped the wheel and managed to safely get over to the shoulder of the road. Flat tire! I called the highway patrol and the dispatcher said they would send a roadside assistance vehicle.

I moved over to the passenger's seat and waited. Ten minutes. Fifteen. The longer I waited, the more I hated being stuck there. Then my eyes fell on a wild yellow Carolina jasmine vine blooming on a fence post. *Well at least I'm stuck in a shady spot with something pretty to see. Hmm*, I actually felt a bit better.

I fished a notebook and pen out of my bag and began to write a prayer of thanksgiving about my situation. "I'm right in front of mile marker 24, so I could tell the dispatcher my location. My cell phone is working. I was in the right lane with light traffic when the tire blew. It's not dark. I'm not in an unsafe area." Soon, I had seventeen specific things I was thankful for on the list!

The roadside assistance truck arrived forty-five minutes later, and in no time my spare tire was on and I was on my way. As I continued my interrupted journey, instead of being upset over the lost time, I thought, *Who would have thought I could find seventeen reasons to thank God stranded at mile marker 24? I guess that when you take time to count your blessings, your quality of life improves dramatically.*

Dear Father, show me the small, beautiful blessings of where I am so I can thank You for this very minute. Amen. —KAREN BARBER

Digging Deeper: EPH. 5:20; JAMES 1:2; 1 PET. 1:5

Thu 2   *When I became a man, I put the ways of childhood behind me.*
          —1 CORINTHIANS 13:11 (NIV)

On a rainy Friday night, I stand in the walkway at Lincoln Center, waiting to pick up my Student-Rush-ticket-obsessed twelve-year-old from the ballet. I watch a family tickle a baby in a stroller as they take shelter from the downpour. Suddenly, I miss Elizabeth. I check the time, and then text her: *Howz life?*

I smile when my phone beeps that I have a message. She writes back: *Decent! Had a kinda rough week, 005 p-set was crazy hard, but it's done now.*

That's MIT-talk for saying her computer science homework was more than unusually difficult. I text back: *Do you like the class?* I know it's on algorithms, though I have only the vaguest idea what that means. She says it's hard but pretty cool overall. My how-stressed-is-she meter registers in the normal zone, and I'm grateful that texting allows for the appearance of nonchalance.

John doing okay? she writes, then asks after the others. I provide short updates, tapping out letters one by one on my cell phone. Texting makes for a highly edited version of life, but there are enough ties to bind us—years, prayers, love—that I don't worry if a few details are lost. Besides, long-distance parenting requires different skills and methods. My daughter is growing up; how we stayed close in the past matters less than finding ways to grow close in the future. Which tells me one thing about devotion: It's more about being open to love than about sticking to the same old methods.

May

> *Lord, open my eyes today to new ways to grow
> closer to You.* —JULIA ATTAWAY

> *Digging Deeper:* Ps. 119:18; JOHN 15:5–8;
> 2 PET. 3:18

Fri 3

And a little child shall lead them.
—ISAIAH 11:6

It was just at dusk when the ranch owner's eight-year-old daughter and I found the lone pair. The cow and calf were half a mile from the rest of the herd. As we came closer, we saw what was wrong: The cow was completely blind.

Susan and I looked at each other. I'd only been working at the ranch a short while and was new to handling cattle. I understood we couldn't leave the pair here—a mountain lion would make short work of the poor cow—but our corral was miles away.

"What about over there?" Susan pointed at our neighbor's corral a quarter mile away. I wasn't so sure. To move a cow with only one eye, the person on its blind side talks so the cow knows someone is there. But a totally blind cow?

Show me what to do, Lord, I prayed inwardly while trying to exude confidence. I was supposed to be in charge, but was little Susan right? "Okay," I said at last, "let's try it."

When we dropped the fence, the strangest thing happened. Instead of racing away when we drew near, the calf circled around and came up alongside the cow, her side touching the cow's flank. The calf brushed against her mother as she walked forward until the cow's chin was resting on the calf's back. In a practiced move, the calf paused for a moment and then slowly stepped forward. To our utter amazement, the cow started forward as well, keeping her chin on the calf's back. Slowly, but surely, the baby led its mama across the field and into the neighbor's corral.

> *Lord, when I am blind to Your path, let me trust*
> *the guide You send . . . even if it's a child.*
> —ERIKA BENTSEN

Digging Deeper: EXOD. 13:21; ISA. 42:16

Sat 4

To the weak I became as weak, that I might win the weak. I have become all things to all men, that I might by all means save some.
—1 CORINTHIANS 9:22 (NKJV)

One of my favorite dishes has always been a classic of Cantonese cookery: steamed whole fish bathed in soy sauce and hot oil and garnished with copious amounts of fresh julienned ginger and scallions. Friends of mine who did not grow up with chopsticks in hand have never quite taken to the presence of the whole fish (head, tail and all), while others find navigating bones an unwieldy exercise. "My people have moved on to the fork," one friend always says wryly. And it was a pain to figure out how to steam the fish, given that I don't have my mom's trusty, elongated steamer.

So I set about trying to reconfigure the recipe, to make it a more accessible eating and cooking experience. Instead of a whole fish, I opted for user-friendly filets. Instead of a steamer, I decided to oil-poach in the oven. The dish itself did not change—not the essential ingredients nor the fundamental flavors. And it worked spectacularly, so much so that over time, my friends have "graduated" to the whole-fish dish.

This, in essence, has been a form of evangelism. With the Gospel as with fish, we don't just shove the whole thing in someone's face and tell them to eat it. We translate the good news into their language, without losing the central ingredients. We adapt it to their cultural context, not in such a way as to steal its essence but rather to make that central truth comprehensible. We meet others where they are, accounting for their needs and hoping that they will come to love what we love.

*Jesus, help me be an effective—and
passionate—ambassador for You, everywhere I go.*
—JEFF CHU

Digging Deeper: MATT. 4:19; ACTS 1:8;
ROM. 10:17

Sun 5

*But one thing is needful: and Mary
hath chosen that good part, which shall
not be taken away from her.*
—LUKE 10:42

W hy don't you stay an extra day?" our daughter Kendall asked when I called her and described the spectacular mountain view from our balcony in Telluride, where her dad and I were spending the last night of our five-day road trip through the Colorado Rockies.

"We can't," I answered way too quickly. "We have things to do at home."

"You never do spontaneous stuff like that," she countered.

After I hung up, I looked at a list of our obligations for the next day. We had to get home. Or did we?

Could Lynn and I make a few calls to cancel some things and stay here another day? The decision seemed harder than it should have been. But we felt pulled by our ingrained habit of sticking to the plan and fulfilling our obligations.

"Let's stay," Lynn finally said.

So I got up early the next morning and sat outside, breathing in the texture and color and sounds of the beauty around me. I knew that I was on the edge of a "gift day" and didn't want to let the moments slip through my fingers. Instead, I wanted to hold and savor each one gratefully.

I let God enter my soul, filling a deep reservoir with His presence that I would surely draw upon in all those days ahead when I tackled the obligations on my calendar. For this day, though, I was right where I was supposed to be.

Lord, the beauty of Your creation fills me up. You have given me a sacred gift of a day, and I receive it with gratitude. —CAROL KUYKENDALL

Digging Deeper: 1 SAM. 16:23; ISA. 40:31; MATT. 6:34

Mon 6   "*My grace is sufficient for you, for my power is made perfect in weakness.*"
—2 CORINTHIANS 12:9 (RSV)

Another trip to the playground. I sighed. Plenty of work waiting on my desk back home but for now, still looking for child care in our new town, I spent most of my time walking to the playground, pushing one-year-old Benjamin on the swings, watching four-year-old Frances master the monkey bars. I felt guilty thinking such thoughts. What kind of parent was I?

Suddenly, Benji looked up from his stroller and cried, "Mell! Mell!" It took me a moment to understand. He meant *smell*, as in, *Daddy, please stop the stroller, so I can smell these flowers.* Beside us a garden bloomed with red and white roses. I wondered how on earth Benjamin knew about smelling flowers. Then I remembered. His sister, Frances, who is four, stops to smell, examine or proclaim about nearly every natural object we pass: flowers, snails, dead bugs, unusual sticks. Benjamin wanted to be like Frances. He wanted to smell the roses.

I stopped the stroller and Benji buried his face in a red bloom. He didn't smell. In fact, he blew out. Nonetheless, he emitted a satisfied "Mmm," just like his sister does when she smells a flower.

Benji hadn't smelled a thing and yet he was delighted. It was as if he was practicing for the day he really would be able to. He seemed to take it on faith that if you act as if you can . . . one day you will.

We arrived at the playground, and Benji tottered off toward the swings. I thought of myself as a parent. My clumsy attempts to balance work, faith and fatherhood. Act as if you can . . . one day you will. I chased after Benji, looking forward to the flowers we would smell on the way home.

God, turn my weakness to strength. —JIM HINCH

Digging Deeper: EXOD. 15:2; PS. 19:14; 2 COR. 13:4

Tue 7

The Lord has established His throne in heaven And His kingdom rules over all.
—PSALM 103:19 (NKJV)

By the end of high school, I'd developed a very close-knit group of friends, the best of whom were Ted, Ross and Dan. When we all went off to college, we rarely talked, though we did see each other over winter breaks and summers.

I always assumed I would see less of them as I got older. We would all have our separate lives and wouldn't be returning to our parents' houses. But the summer before our senior year, when we started thinking about what we'd do after college, that outlook started to change.

Dan would have an extra semester to finish at Brown University in Providence, Rhode Island. Ted and I wanted to go to graduate school, and Ross wanted to get into the restaurant industry there. Part of me thought God was working to bring us together, but another part thought there were too many moving parts—it would never happen.

Then, a few things started to fall into place. Ted got into Brown's MFA program, and Ross got exactly the kind of job he was looking for. I was the only one left. *Would I get into Brown?*

I didn't; I was rejected. Not only had my dream of going to school there ended, but so had the chance to be with my best friends.

But I was wrong again. As graduation approached, I realized I wasn't confined to any particular place. For one year, at least, living with my closest friends might outweigh my best job prospects.

The first night we spent in our apartment, playing board games like we were in middle school again, I knew the situation was perfect. God hadn't made it easy for me; He hadn't made all the pieces magically fall into place. Rather, He made it so I could fit them together on my own.

Thank You, Lord, for always showing me how to create what I want. —SAM ADRIANCE

Digging Deeper: Ps. 37:23; ISA. 48:17

Wed 8 *I press on toward the goal to win the prize for which God has called me heavenward in Christ Jesus.* —PHILIPPIANS 3:14 (NIV)

I balked when the doctor told me I'd not be able to jog anymore. I was dealing with a chronic back injury, and his advice was to start walking instead. I wasn't too happy. I'd been a runner my entire adult life. I'd started in my late twenties with one-mile races and eventually moved up to running a little more than five miles a day. I'd even run a marathon.

But now it looked like those days were over. "I want you to stick to walking one mile a day," my doctor advised. "I'll see you back here in a couple of months."

By the time I left his office, I decided to quit exercising. *Why bother if all I can do is walk one mile a day?* I thought.

A few weeks later, a group of students at a local elementary school showed me otherwise. I was at their school to produce a video highlighting their physical fitness program. "We run marathons!" the young children told me.

"Really?" I asked, doubting their claim.

"Yes!" they all said in unison.

A little girl stepped forward. "We run one mile a day, and in a month we'll have run enough miles to have completed a marathon. Isn't that awesome?" she asked as she jogged off.

"Absolutely!" I replied.

That evening, I knew what I needed to do. I put on my running shoes and walked the big loop around the neighborhood pond. It equaled just about one mile.

A month later I was back in the doctor's office. "Well," he asked, "how'd you do?"

"Great!" I exclaimed. "I just finished a marathon!"

Step by step, Lord, I just need to walk with You.
—MELODY BONNETTE SWANG

Digging Deeper: JOSH. 1:9; 2 TIM. 4:7

Thu 9   *"I was ... in prison and you did not visit me."* —MATTHEW 25:43 (RSV)

Many innocent people of the Bible spent time in prison: Joseph, Daniel, Paul, Peter and Jesus, who was beaten and imprisoned shortly after explaining to His disciples that "whatever you did for the least of these brothers of mine, you did for me."

If one of my friends was wrongfully accused and convicted, I would certainly visit that "brother of Christ" in prison! It would be easy to do so. Maybe that's why Jesus said, "My yoke is easy and my burden is light" (Matthew 11:30). Light and easy— that's the kind of command I can obey.

Well, recently a friend of mine was accused and convicted, and he is in prison. But he isn't innocent. I visited him in our county jail before his sentencing, and it wasn't easy at all. I hated going,

May

I hated being searched, and I even hated my friend for being in jail.

My friend "Sam" is now serving time in a state prison. The only way I can visit him is by exchanging letters. The first year I wrote to him, it was never easy. He answered my letters immediately. I could answer his only after weeks of prayer and procrastination.

I can't say that Christ's command will ever be easy, but it is slightly lighter this year. Before writing to Sam, I sit down at my desk and mentally write the heading "Dear Jesus." I then write a letter that I hope would cheer Daniel, that would bring a smile to Paul and that would lift the spirit of Jesus.

Dear God, help us to be grateful for friends who love us and for friends who need us. —TIM WILLIAMS

Digging Deeper: ECCLES. 4:9–12; JOHN 15:13–15

DIVINE ABUNDANCE

Fri 10   "*Though He slay me, yet will I trust Him. Even so, I will defend my own ways before Him.*" —JOB 13:15 (NKJV)

Some call it Depression Cake, others Eggless Cake, but I still call this rich chocolate confection Wowie Cake, the name I learned when I was eleven. My best friend Lynda and I wanted to make our own Wowie Cake. Mrs. Dennison agreed, shared her recipe and let us loose in the kitchen. Since Lynda and I didn't buy groceries yet, we scarcely understood the real "wow" of the budget recipe: no butter, eggs or milk. We thought Wowie referred to the required vinegar! Surely, this was a mistake. Even we fifth graders knew that vinegar belonged in salad dressing, not in a cake.

Mrs. Dennison, however, assured us that the ingredients were correct. Deeply skeptical, we followed the directions exactly, didn't dare to lick the bowl and shoved the pungent batter into the oven, hoping for the best. Within half an hour, our cake rose dark and glossy, smelling of chocolate sweetness.

I hadn't made a Wowie Cake for decades until recently when I had promised a cake for a morning meeting and discovered late at night that I had run out of eggs.

While my cake baked, I pondered: Just as vinegar is necessary to make this cake rise, so can the acid events of my life trigger unanticipated changes. The career detour that leads to the perfect job; the harsh words that soften into reconciliation and deeper love; the loss that provides an opportunity for others to show they care. Like two little girls who trusted their batter, I'm learning to trust the vinegar times, the sharp, eye-watering moments that set in motion changes to sweeten my life.

> *Even in the midst of tumultuous change, Lord,*
> *You are with me. Please strengthen my trust.*
> —GAIL THORELL SCHILLING

> *Digging Deeper:* GEN. 50:19–21; JER. 32:42;
> LAM. 3:38

Sat 11

Call unto me, and I will answer thee. . . . —JEREMIAH 33:3

I dislike asking for help. Like a two-year-old child, I want to do it myself. Now in my seventies, I've remained stubborn.

Recently, my son Jeremy, who lives up the street, stopped by as I struggled furiously with the nozzle on a garden hose. He pulled his truck into the driveway, got out and informed me, "Mom, you're getting all wet. Let me help you."

"I can do it myself!" I snapped.

Gently, he took the hose from me. I didn't put up much of a fight, impatient, tired and damp. With one flick of his wrist, the water came out properly. He climbed back in his truck, "If there's anything you need, just call me."

I called him the next day. My twenty-nine-year-old electric typewriter was being repaired. (I don't use a computer.) I had a loaner, but it was in the trunk of my car and awfully heavy. Jeremy showed up the next morning, just as the sun was rising. Effortlessly, he carried the typewriter to my desk. "I can plug it in," I announced. Ignoring me, he crawled underneath my desk, connected it and then turned on the typewriter. It hummed to life, like me, eager to begin work. "Thank you, Jeremy," I smiled and gave him a hug.

"Remember, Mom, call me anytime." I walked to the back door with my son and waved good-bye. A thought drifted through my mind: *Call on Me, too, child... anytime.*

Hello, Father. Are You there?
—Marion Bond West

Digging Deeper: Ps. 62:6

Sun 12

Her children arise and call her blessed....
—Proverbs 31:28 (NIV)

Good morning, Little P!" my mom calls out. I welcome her in, ask her to help Prisca, my one-year-old, negotiate the half-banana she has decided to eat, and then busy myself pulling the blueberry torte from the oven.

When I turn, full plates in hand, I find my mom seated directly in front of Prisca's high chair, clutching the wee one's impossibly fat feet and chuckling over my daughter's guerrilla-style breakfast eating.

At this point, the typical Prisca/MiMi dynamic ensues: Mom makes a funny face and tells Prisca how adorable she is; Prisca reaches to touch Mom's crinkled-up nose; Mom pretends she is eating Prisca's pointer; Prisca falls apart in waves of elated squeals and snorts; Mom sits back in her chair, filled up with the good stuff, of life and love and joy.

"I love watching you love her," I say to my mom. Her capacity to delight herself in my daughter comes as no surprise to me. This is the woman who carried and birthed me, diapered and bathed me, fed and clothed me, held and consoled me, promised me everything would be all right.

As I grew, so did her capacity for motherhood. Sure, she taught me the functional tasks—how to drive a stick shift, write a proper thank-you note, conjugate a verb. But more significantly, all along the way, she modeled for me how to be a generous and grateful mom.

"Treasure every moment," she says with great frequency about the moments of Prisca's young and ever-changing life. But equally important to me is treasuring these glimpses of the woman I hope I'm becoming, the woman who raised her own daughter on grace so the daughter might pass grace along.

Father, what a magical thing it is when Your daughters carry grace to the world.
—ASHLEY WIERSMA

Digging Deeper: PROV. 14:1; PHIL. 1:2–3; 1 PET. 3:4

Mon 13

But let each one test his own work and then his reason to boast will be in himself alone and not in his neighbor.
—GALATIANS 6:4 (RSV)

Why so glum?" I asked my friend Shandra one day when we met for lunch.

"I got a promotion at work."

"Sounds great!" I commented, but I felt a twinge of jealousy. I'd been at my job longer and hadn't advanced.

"They usually promote just one person at a time and make a festival of it," Shandra continued. "You know, an announcement, a card, even a little ice cream. But this time they promoted three of us on the same day."

"So?"

"So it feels . . . less important."

"Same promotion, same pay raise, same honor . . . *Hmm*, this reminds me of my cats."

She looked at me as if I'd lost my mind. "My promotion reminds you of Prince and Junior?"

"Each day, as soon as I plop food into their bowls, they race over. But before Prince eats, he sizes up how much food I've given his brother, as if to say, 'I'm just making sure that Junior didn't get any more than I did.' And only then will he eat. The funniest part is, I've been giving them the exact same amount every day for two years and he still thinks I'm going to short him!"

"Okay, I get the point. It doesn't take away from my achievement if someone else achieves the same goal."

And I get the point, too, God, I said. But out loud I replied, "Now let's go have some ice cream to celebrate your promotion."

God, let me remember someone else's good fortune does not diminish my own. —LINDA NEUKRUG

Digging Deeper: DEUT. 8:2; Ps. 75:6–7; LUKE 14:7–11

Tue 14

Do not love the world or anything in the world. If anyone loves the world, love for the Father is not in them. For everything in the world—the lust of the flesh, the lust of the eyes, and the pride of life—comes not from the Father but from the world. The world and its desires pass away, but whoever does the will of God lives forever.
—1 JOHN 2:15–17 (NIV)

What are you doing?" I asked my little boy as he rummaged through my bag, which hung on the stroller.

"Animal crackers," he whined.

I gave him the small box, and he sat down content. I didn't realize he'd thrown my wallet onto the sidewalk, looking for his snack!

I strolled to the store, excited to buy something for myself. Now that I was working full time, it felt great to buy what I pleased. When I expressed my newfound financial freedom at work, a co-worker handed me a book about budgeting and godly stewardship.

Once at a shop, I picked out a much-needed pair of sneakers and a cute jacket that made me smile.

May

The smile went away when I got to the counter and discovered my wallet—with about two hundred dollars in cash—was gone. I ran with the stroller back home, hoping I'd find it there. It wasn't. I was breathless from running and began to cry in a panic. "What's wrong, Mami?" my son asked.

"What's wrong?" I shrieked. "My money! My money is gone!"

"My money"—the phrase brought me back to the book I'd read. Nothing is really yours, the book explained. Everything we think we own is really the Lord's, and He gives and takes away for His purpose.

As I meditated on those words, a peace came over me. God is my provider, not a paycheck. And it wasn't my money that was lost. It was God's money, to be used according to His will.

I praise You, Lord, because You are my provider. Everything I have comes from You. All the gifts You give, including my very life, are in Your hands.
—KAREN VALENTIN

Digging Deeper: DEUT. 10:14; PS. 24:1; MAL. 3:10

Wed 15

Wherefore they are no more twain, but one flesh. What therefore God hath joined together, let not man put asunder. —MATTHEW 19:6

For the last few weeks, I've been reading *The Lord of the Rings* to my seven-year-old son Stephen. Tonight we've reached the chapter in which Frodo and Sam, the hobbits who are taking the Ring (the foundation of the Dark Lord's power) back to the place it was forged in order to destroy it, meet Gollum, a twisted hobbitlike creature who is under the Ring's power and speaks of it in his hissing speech as "the Precious."

As I read to him, Stephen lights up; he loves to act out stories. "Give us the *Preciousss!*" he hisses in an almost uncannily Gollumlike voice. "We wants it."

"Stephen, don't jump on the bed."

Stephen leans over and grabs my left hand, his eye on my wedding ring. "Give us the *Preciousss!*"

When I've finished the night's reading, I point Stephen toward his toothbrush and head to the kitchen. As I begin washing the dinner dishes, my eye falls on my ring. I remember the day Julia and I went to buy it at a jewelry store on 47th Street—just that one, because the ring Julia wears was my mother's. I remember the jeweler engraving our wedding date, 5-15-93, inside it. I remember Julia putting it on my finger as we stood in the sanctuary and the promises we made to each other before God and the church. I think back over the years since then, our five children, our joys, our struggles.

Setting the plate in the dish rack, I send up a prayer that I may be worthy of this ring, truly a ring of power—and, oh, so precious.

Dear Lord, through better and worse, keep me faithful to those promises I made twenty years ago.
—ANDREW ATTAWAY

Digging Deeper: GEN. 2:18, 21–24; EPH. 5:23–32

THE GIFT OF TREES

Thu 16

After singing a hymn, they went out to the Mount of Olives.
—MATTHEW 26:30 (NAS)

From my childhood I have loved secret places. A corner in a house . . . a fork in a tree . . . a nook in the hedge . . . a tent. Jesus' favorite haven was an olive grove. Since the time of Noah when the dove returned with the olive leaf, this tree has symbolized peace.

The trees on the Mount of Olives were old. King David had climbed among them a thousand years earlier. Olives appear to live forever because as the central trunk decays, new shoots at the base grow more boles (stems). Some olive trees are two thousand years old!

They are cultivated for the rich oil extracted from their berries. God directed Moses to mix olive oil and other spices for a "holy anointing oil to Me" (Exodus 30:31).

The night before His Crucifixion, Jesus, the Christ (meaning "anointed one"), hiked to the olive grove once more. Falling to the ground, He cried, "My Father, if it is possible, let this cup pass from Me; yet not as I will, but as You will" (Matthew 26:39).

One time in California, I sat alone beneath my aunt's olive tree on the eve of Good Friday. I was transported in thought to Jesus in the olive garden. I wished in my life I'd chosen right every time. Only I hadn't. Most recently I'd disappointed practically everyone in my family.

But that's who Jesus reached out to—the ones who didn't get it right, who disappointed themselves and others. I felt filled with wonder at Jesus giving His own perfect life on the Cross to make a place for me in the family of God. Resting my hand on the olive's knobby trunk, I spoke out loud: "I think You are the 'O Live' tree."

Messiah... Christos... Anointed One, You are my sanctuary, my best secret place. —CAROL KNAPP

Digging Deeper: EXOD. 25:8; PSS. 52:8, 119:114

Fri 17

In the beginning was the Word....
—JOHN 1:1

We lost my mother-in-law last month. Though Edith was near eighty, her passing was sudden and shocking. No one thought she would ever die. She worked fifty-hour weeks as a newspaper editor until the very end. From her deathbed, she drew me close and whispered, "I need a story on recycling. About five hundred words. Get some good photos."

It was among her last messages to me, and it was appropriate. She was my first editor after college; I was part of a passel of young reporters at a small, suburban newspaper. Edith's style was legendary. She was copious and tenacious with her red pen, and not in a feel-good way. She'd often ask if we were simply bad writers or if we were stubbornly unteachable. (What's the right answer? Yes? No?)

It became an ongoing struggle: I'd submit something; she'd return a scathing request for revision, full of "suggestions." I began to feel as if I could never please her. Sometimes I'd get back a relatively uninjured article with those prized words *Good job*, but that was rare.

In her eulogy, my wife Sandee said that her mother had two great loves: God and newspapers. I'm not sure Edith made a distinction. To her, a well-written story was sacred ground. If a writer provided insight (quietly, unobtrusively) that made the reader more enlightened, then you were doing God's work.

Edith used to say the hardest part of the story was the lead paragraph; I'd tell her I thought it was the ending. Looking back on her life, I see why she wasn't worried about the ending. She knew her two great loves would see her through.

Lord, let Light Perpetual shine upon my mother-in-law. And when You see her, could You pass along this message: Good job, Edith. Good job.
—MARK COLLINS

Digging Deeper: MATT. 7:21, 25:21

Sat 18

You will keep in perfect peace those whose minds are steadfast, because they trust in you.
—ISAIAH 26:3 (NIV)

Recently, I read a report that stated that 30 percent of one's life is spent sleeping.

Not me! And according to the friends I've talked with lately, not them either. All of us seem to have trouble falling asleep most nights. Perhaps it's that time in our lives (we're all over fifty), or it could be the dire state of the world with all its assorted problems. In fact, it could be any number of things. Whatever the reason, sleep simply doesn't come as easily as it once did.

What I found amusing was the different techniques each of us has devised to help ease our way into slumber after a long day. Diane uses a machine with the sounds of ocean waves. Carrie takes half a prescribed sleeping pill. My own method is to work Sudoku puzzles or read until I'm ready to turn out the light.

Then I stumbled upon this Bible verse in Isaiah 26:3 ("He will keep us in perfect peace when our thoughts are fixed on Him"). Wow, now those are downright powerful words! For years I've written out a Bible verse each morning in my journal, and by the end of seven days I've got it pretty much memorized. Since this conversation about lack of sleep with my friends, I've added something extra to my nighttime ritual. I write out my weekly verse, place it inside my Sudoku puzzle book and meditate on it as I fall asleep. And you know what? I sleep like a baby.

Lord Jesus, may I fall asleep with my mind focused on You, knowing I will find perfect peace in Your loving arms. —DEBBIE MACOMBER

Digging Deeper: PS. 77:6; PROV. 3:24; JER. 31:26

Sun 19

Give thanks to the Lord....
—1 CHRONICLES 16:8 (RSV)

"Pops, I want a dad," my grandson Lil' Reggie said to me the other day.

Lil' Reggie is getting older—he's seven now—and noticing that all of his friends have fathers, so I didn't take this personally. I knew he was simply saying, "I want a dad too."

It was a heartbreaking reminder of what I can't forget at this time of year. Today, in 2004, our son Reggie was killed.

For a moment, I didn't know what to say. I have the same pain and questions about why we had to lose Reggie. *How can we be the best support system possible for Lil' Reggie? How can we let him know that he is incredibly loved?*

I remembered what David says in 1 Chronicles 16:8: "Give thanks to the Lord." I know that in all things I need to learn how to give thanks—not just for the good or easy things. The phrase "Pops, I want a dad" doesn't seem like something to thank God for, but I did.

And then I told Lil' Reggie, "I wish you still had your dad too. But God has given you Uncle Ryan and me. I will be your dad *and* your pops, and Ryan will be your dad *and* your uncle."

Lord, help me to always see things through Your eyes as I walk this journey. —DOLPHUS WEARY

Digging Deeper: LEV. 26:12; PS. 68:5; MATT. 6:26

Mon 20

The angel of the Lord encamps all around those who fear Him, And delivers them.
—PSALM 34:7 (NKJV)

I was heading to bed when the telephone rang. "Your son has been in a car accident. He's okay. He's being transported to the hospital," said my son's best friend's mother.

Paul had been at a birthday dinner party. The accident occurred afterward, less than a quarter mile from the restaurant. Yvette's words and demeanor on the telephone helped my wife Elba and me remain calm as we headed to the hospital.

At the emergency room, Paul was in a state of shock. He had blood stains on his right hand and leg and on the back of his head, and he wore a neck brace. We learned that the situation was worse than we had expected. Paul had fractured his neck and he was millimeters away from being paralyzed.

We were thankful that God spared our son, but soon after we learned about the death of the passenger of the other vehicle. Our hearts sank. Elba turned to me and said, "It could have been our son. Paul is going to have surgery in a few days for spinal stabilization and has a long recovery process, but someone died."

I knew deep within what she was feeling. Guilt and doubt plagued us. *How can we be thankful, Lord?* I asked. *What about the other family?*

Our torn feelings found comfort in the Scripture that reminds us that it is not about thanking *for* everything but *in* everything. Elba and I were thankful to God not for the loss but for His comfort and caring presence in the midst of difficult circumstances for all the families.

We look for Your comfort and caring presence, God, in the midst of difficult circumstances. —PABLO DIAZ

Digging Deeper: Ps. 106:1–2; COL. 3:15; 1 THESS. 5:16–18

Tue 21   *Love is patient, love is kind....*
—1 CORINTHIANS 13:4 (NIV)

"Julie, you're so stubborn," my husband Rick said. "You make life harder than it has to be. You're a lot like Clyde, you know."

May

"I can't believe you said that!" Clyde was our hard-headed seven-month-old Lab.

I'd added a few more items to Rick's to-do list: new light switch, organize carport, move wood-pile, fix clicking sound in the icemaker. I'd stuck a hardware store list in his lunch bag that morning: big nail to hang picture, florescent bulbs, weed killer.

I wanted my husband to do things my way. It had worked . . . for a few days. But now I could tell he was getting annoyed with me.

Close to 9:00 PM, I grabbed the flashlight and took Clyde outside for a walk. So far that day he'd chewed up part of the laundry, destroyed a basket of fresh flowers and refused to get off our bed. I decided to take him around the path through the woods to tire him out.

"Clyde, heel." Almost home again, I glanced down. No Clyde. My heart galloped as I whistled for him. "Clyde, come!" I said a quick prayer and back-tracked a few hundred feet. When he was good and ready, he came prancing toward me in the dark, carrying a giant pinecone in his mouth. I loved the dog, but lately, he'd worn me out.

Like you've been doing to Rick, God's gentle Spirit seemed to say. *Ease off.*

Later that night, we had a good talk. "I'm sorry for nagging. And for the lists."

He put his arm around me. "Not a problem. Let's try life a new way. Ask me to do something once, not so intently, and I'll start listening."

Lord, every time I see Clyde remind me not to nag.
—JULIE GARMON

Digging Deeper: PROV. 15:1; 1 COR. 13:4–5; EPH. 5:1

Wed 22

May the God who gives . . . encouragement give you the same attitude of mind toward each other. . . .
—ROMANS 15:5 (NIV)

Standing on the newly scalped road leading to our cabin, I was trying to escape the reality of the electric company's machinery. How could this be happening? The Queen Anne's lace, the blackberry bushes, even the wild persimmon and the sweet gum trees had been viciously mowed down under the guise of clearing space for power lines.

Ahead, on the other side of the causeway, the oak tree where I always stopped to talk to God was still standing. I considered the tree my "thin place," where I felt particularly close to "things not yet seen." Here, I had fervently prayed for our Aunt Kate in her last days. Here, I had asked God to take care of a dear friend, Frances, as she slowly drifted away.

Even now, the huge machine was headed in the direction of my tree. I gathered my courage, approached the monster and knocked on the door of its air-conditioned cab. The driver cut the engine and swung open the door. "Whataya want?" he snapped.

I felt hard, looking at him. Meeting my eyes, it was clear that he felt the same. I wanted to say mean things but out came words I didn't expect to say: "That tree, up ahead... the tallest one. Well, it's my... my praying place." His eyes softened, his expression changed. "I was just hoping," I finished, "that you might spare that tree."

The door closed, the engine restarted, and I hurried back to the cabin where my husband was waiting for a trip to town. Hours later, I squeezed my eyes tight as we approached the causeway. How could I bear seeing my tree twisted into splinters and sawdust?

"Pam," David said then, "what in the world happened? Your tree is still there, and it's the only one in sight!"

Father, through Your spirit of unity, my tree was saved. Thank You. —PAM KIDD

Digging Deeper: MATT. 7:7–11; JOHN 15:7

Thu 23

By day the Lord directs his love, at night his song is with me—a prayer to the God of my life.
—PSALM 42:8 (TNIV)

My husband and I were planning a small out-of-town trip for our wedding anniversary. We'd decided on Mendocino because it's not too far from our house in San Jose, it's not too expensive and it has nice parks and beaches where we can take our dog.

I thought about what we like to do together: eating, talking, watching movies. . . . We enjoy simply spending time together. We didn't need anything exciting to do. We found hotels that allow pets and tried to pick one. We looked at where each hotel was and the entertainments in the surrounding area.

"So what do you want to do in Mendocino?" my husband asked me.

I looked at him blankly. "Go to the beach?"

"Besides that."

We had thought about going on the trip but not about what we'd be doing. "I dunno."

I think that's how God enjoys spending time with us. I sometimes feel guilty if I don't learn something profound in my daily quiet time or if the church sermon doesn't particularly move me. But God is simply happy I'm there. He doesn't need excitement to enjoy the time I spend with Him.

Lord, thank You for this wonderful, quiet, comfortable, happy time I can spend with You. —CAMY TANG

Digging Deeper: Pss. 16:11, 95:2; ACTS 2:28

Fri 24

O Lord, You will hear the desire of the meek; You will strengthen their heart, You will incline Your ear.
—PSALM 10:17 (NRSV)

My friend Connie was born in China. She came to America at nineteen; English is her second language. She is a brilliant communicator. I've watched her smoothly run her restaurant filled with hungry crowds, soothe anxious customers, join in raucous birthday parties, joke with her staff (in Mandarin, Cantonese or English!) and patiently talk with older people. Color, gender, age, language—none of them seem to get in the way with Connie.

It took me a while, but by observing how she communicates with me I figured out how she does it. She listens. She listens attentively, with her whole body and face, particularly her eyes. Actually, she doesn't talk much at all. Even when I tell her something private or disturbing, she never reacts swiftly or attempts to interrupt with an opinion or advice. I always feel listened to—*heard*—when I am with her. I always feel better.

I was reminded of Connie's extraordinary gift a week or so ago. A friend who had been in rehab and alcohol-addiction programs for some time wanted to talk. We'd been friends for years, and I'd given her a lot of advice and support over that time. I had a stake in her. So when she told me about a recent escapade where she'd fallen rather spectacularly off the wagon, I didn't even stop to think. I exclaimed, "What were you thinking? Haven't you learned anything after all this time?"

Her face fell. I thought of Connie, and so did mine.

Compassionate Lord, teach me that good communication is a ministry I must practice, practice, practice. —MARCI ALBORGHETTI

Digging Deeper: EPH. 4:29; JAMES 1:19

Sat 25   *Blessed is the people that know the joyful sound: they shall walk, O Lord, in the light of thy countenance.*
—PSALM 89:15

I recall my pastor reminding us that our strengths are our weaknesses. I am focused and driven to see my visions come to pass. I work hard, but sometimes I forget to rejoice. Today, a memory made my pastor's saying clear to me.

When I was five, I was chosen to be a flower girl in my cousin Zella's wedding. I was excited at the prospect of the ceremony, my dress and the delightful food. I was determined to do a good job, to sprinkle just the right number of petals. At the rehearsal, I moved down the aisle at the perfect pace while sprinkling my imaginary flowers.

But on the wedding day, the velvety rose petals stuck to my hands. I had to shake most of them off, and they fell to the floor in clumps. To make matters worse, the ring bearer, Casterdaral, was dawdling and not moving down the aisle at the pace I thought suitable. I grabbed him to hurry him along and I was perplexed to hear the adults laughing. I was even more surprised when I realized they were laughing at me.

Looking back, I laugh at my little-girl anxiety. I don't remember the music, dancing, tasting wedding cake or even posing for photos. I missed the celebration, worrying that I would not get down the aisle perfectly.

Today, I hope that I recognize the humor in my stumbles. I hope that I enjoy the festivities even as I work to get things done.

Lord, help me to hear the music, taste the dessert and marvel over the gowns. —SHARON FOSTER

Digging Deeper: PROV. 24:16; EPH. 4:17–24

Sun 26

How sweet are your words to my taste, sweeter than honey to my mouth! —PSALM 119:103 (NRSV)

I'm a big fan of the Bible. It offers such reassuring promises, such straightforward—but never pat—answers to our most challenging questions.

As a writing teacher, I especially love the Bible's literariness. How recognizable the characters are, how gripping its stories! Unlike some faith-related writing, it is never sugary or trite. Like all great art, it perpetually surprises.

Consider the description of manna, which resembled frost, coriander seeds and resin—three substances nothing alike!—and tasted like "wafers made with honey" (Exodus 16:31, NRSV). So delightful sounding, yet the Israelites craved what they'd eaten as slaves. The Hebrew word *manna* itself thrills me, meaning not bread or food, as one might expect, but something like "What the heck is this crud?"

I love even the Bible's tough parts. In one disturbing story, Jephthah, an Old Testament warrior and judge highly praised in the New Testament, vows—in a murderous fit of hubris—to sacrifice as a burned offering "whoever comes out of the doors of my house to meet me, when I return victorious" (Judges 11:31, NRSV). His daughter emerges to welcome him "with timbrels and with dancing" (Judges 11:34, NRSV). Scholars disagree about whether Jephthah actually killed his daughter, although the text seems heartbreakingly clear to me.

Moses commands the Israelites to talk about Scripture "when you are at home and when you are away, when you lie down and when you rise" (Deuteronomy 6:7, NRSV). Surely this is a believer's most delightful assignment.

Father, thank You for the remarkable book of Your relationship with us. Inspire me to truly enjoy it and make it part of my daily conversation.
—PATTY KIRK

Digging Deeper: Ps. 18:30; Isa. 55:11; 2 Tim. 3:16

Mon 27 *Scatter the peoples who delight in war.* —PSALM 68:30 (RSV)

My brother Kevin takes great joy in exploiting my gullibility. (That's why God made older brothers.) Years ago, Kev and I were walking toward Soldiers and Sailors Memorial Hall on the University of Pittsburgh's campus. He pointed to a large white sculpture atop the building. "That's the Tomb of the Unknown Civil War Soldier," Kevin said solemnly. Of course, I believed him—much to his amusement.

Now I'm not so sure he was kidding. Soldiers and Sailors Hall carries the names of many honored dead from wars spanning a couple of centuries— and more honored dead are on the way, no doubt. "War is hell," Gen. William Sherman said. Worse, it's a special kind of hell: Its tentacles reach beyond the dead to the wounded, to the widows and orphans. So we the living build memorials and fold flags and play taps, hoping to bestow memory and meaning to young lives lost.

Ironically, I now have an office across the street from Soldiers and Sailors Hall, on the same campus where my father earned his engineering degree, thanks to World War II's GI Bill. Like many others, he faked his way into the US Navy (he memorized the eye test he couldn't have passed); like many others, he lost good friends and came home a different man. But he never took his service nor his country for granted.

Actually the quote from Sherman is incomplete. "I am tired and sick of war," he said. "Its glory is all moonshine. It is only those who have neither fired a shot nor heard the shrieks and groans of the wounded who cry aloud for blood, for vengeance. . . . War is hell."

Lord, remind the present generation—remind every present generation—to honor those who faced the fires for us. Amen. —MARK COLLINS

Digging Deeper: PS. 120; ECCLES. 9:17–18; ISA. 11:5–7

Tue 28

In the beginning God created the heavens and the earth.
—GENESIS 1:1 (NKJV)

When I was in my thirties, I enrolled in piano lessons under the watchful eye of Mrs. Love. I adored her instantly, especially when I learned that I would be the recipient of a present each week. Because I was an older student, I was her last class of the day. So each Monday evening at the close of my lesson, Mrs. Love wrapped the day's exquisite floral arrangement in a damp paper towel and sent it home with me.

Fast forward to last year. Many of the home-decorating magazines where I've worked as a stylist have folded due to the changing economy. The funds I earmarked for presents for people have decreased along with my beloved work. I enjoy giving gifts to my neighbors but had to come up with something that didn't cost a lot of money. That's when I remembered Mrs. Love and her bouquets.

I set about buying vases at yard sales and flea markets for a quarter or fifty cents. In April, I filled an ironstone milk pitcher with pristine white tulips from my garden. In May, it was a nosegay of delicate bleeding hearts in a rose-patterned shaving mug. In July, purple pansies blossomed out of a vintage medicine bottle. Come August, bountiful pink crape myrtle overflowed from a tole-painted candy tin—all for mere pennies.

There's something about receiving a gift borne out of recycling that seems to delight folks. Being short on money nudges us to think creatively as well. Is there something in your home that's waiting on a second chance at life? Your discards may pamper and please a dear one on your gift list . . . and be kind to your pocketbook.

I never feel more like You, dear Father, than when I create. Thank You for the opportunity to make something out of nothing. —ROBERTA MESSNER

Digging Deeper: JOHN 3:15–17; 2 COR. 9:7; HEB. 13:16

Wed 29

"I know that you can do all things; no purpose of yours can be thwarted." —JOB 42:2 (NIV)

Everything works together for good for those who love God. God's plans cannot be thwarted.

Sage words—straight from the Bible to my heart—yet today I'm struggling with them.

You see, last night a baby was born. A precious six-pound, ten-ounce bundle who was supposed to be my niece. A much-wanted, much-prayed-for, much-loved and much-anticipated addition to our family.

We cried when we got the call that the birth mother, who had so bravely chosen my sister and her husband to parent her daughter, was in labor. We laughed. We sang. We praised God in our gratefulness for this precious life.

Then, this morning, the birth mom changed her mind and decided to keep her baby—our baby. I confess, I'm struggling to see God's plan in this. We love the baby so much. And we wanted her so badly. I can't see how this is in God's plan.

But while I'm struggling with all of this, one thing keeps echoing in my mind: At least I have the comfort of knowing that God is in charge and that His plans cannot be thwarted.

Lord, I'm so grateful that the plans You have for my life are being woven together to form a picture that's much more beautiful than I can comprehend. Amen.
—Erin MacPherson

Digging Deeper: John 11; Rom. 8:28–30

Thu 30

These older women must train the younger women....
—Titus 2:4 (TLB)

My granddaughter Olivia often treats my husband and me to tasty cookies, muffins or pies. But she wasn't always so skillful. When she was twelve, she and her friend Megan decided to make a chocolate pie (including the crust) with *no help*. I was to stay out of the kitchen while they worked.

I answered the first four questions without leaving my office:

Olivia: "What is a pastry blender?"

Megan: "The crust fell apart. How do we fix it?"

Olivia: "How do we make a pretty edge?"

Megan: "When is the crust lightly browned?"

The fifth question, from both girls, sent me running: "Should flames be shooting out of the microwave?"

Definitely not! The pie was in the regular oven! But they'd set the microwave to Bake instead of Time and had cooked a sponge I'd sterilized and forgotten to remove. Fortunately I was able to extinguish the blaze with no harm done.

The finished pie tasted pretty good. While we ate, I said a silent prayer of thanks for my mother and grandma and all the women who forgave my messes and taught me cooking, along with other life lessons, including how to put out kitchen fires.

Thank You, Lord, for the wisdom passed down through generations. —PENNEY SCHWAB

Digging Deeper: RUTH 1:16–18; PROV. 2:6; JAMES 3:17

Fri 31

The Lord is my shepherd; I shall not want. —PSALM 23:1 (NKJV)

Nothing prepared me for my outhouse experiences in Alaska when I camped around that beautiful state last year. At every campground the first thing my sister-in-law Linda and I did was find the outhouse, count the steps from there to the van and camper, and wonder if we could get there and back at 3:00 AM without seeing a bear or a moose on the way.

Sometimes there was only one outhouse at least a football field away. Other times there were a few of them positioned every couple hundred feet from our camp. One had electric lights and an outlet in it, so we could charge up our digital cameras overnight. Imagine that. Another was dark, smelly and in the woods so deep that we opted to get in the van and drive all the way back to the campground entrance where they had more modern facilities available.

I survived those outhouses, and when I got home I made a beeline for my nice, comfy bathroom. And if you want to know the truth, I will be thanking God for indoor plumbing for the rest of my life.

Father, I know I take my conveniences for granted. Remind me to be truly thankful for every modern convenience and blessing that make my life easier.
—PATRICIA LORENZ

Digging Deeper: DAN. 4:28–37; EPH. 1:16; REV. 4:9

GIVING THANKS

1 _____
2 _____
3 _____
4 _____
5 _____
6 _____
7 _____
8 _____

May

9 _____

10 _____

11 _____

12 _____

13 _____

14 _____

15 _____

16 _____

17 _____

18 _____

19 _____

20 _____

21 _____

22 _____

23 _____

24 _____

25 _____

26 _____

27 _____

28 _____

29 _____

30 _____

31 _____

June

*Thanks be to God
for his inexpressible gift!*

—2 CORINTHIANS 9:15 (ESV)

OPERATION THANKFULNESS

Sat 1
When they came to the border of Mysia, they tried to enter Bithynia, but the Spirit of Jesus would not allow them to.
—ACTS 16:7 (NIV)

I was having a hard time dealing with people saying no when I asked them to help with a fundraising event for a good cause. Then a friend called me and told me that her daughter's car had been totaled by a careless driver. She was desperate for transportation to her entry-level job and didn't have any credit history to buy another one. "I'll pray that your daughter will find a reliable car," I told her.

A week later my friend excitedly told me that her daughter had qualified for a loan with a credit union and found a used car that seemed perfect! Two days later, my friend called back sounding defeated. "My daughter took the car title over to the credit union, and they denied her loan. They said the title search showed that the car was salvage because it had been totaled in an accident."

"Haven't we been praying for a dependable car? This is an answer to prayer," I found myself saying to my friend. "Thankfully, the title search turned up the truth. That car had problems that couldn't be seen on the outside."

As I hung up the phone, I realized that it's natural to feel disappointed and discouraged when we get "no" answers, especially when everything we see on the outside looks exactly like what we want and need.

I sat down and started listing names of other potential volunteers I could call to help with the fund-raiser, thankful that God in His infinite wisdom knows enough to sometimes say no.

Thank You, Father, that I can trust You to be with me, guiding and helping me as I continue to seek, ask, knock and trust. Amen. —KAREN BARBER

Digging Deeper: JOB 28:20–28; PS. 37; JER. 11:1–5

Sun 2

"Whoever has my commands and keeps them is the one who loves me. The one who loves me will be loved by my Father, and I too will love them and show myself to them."
—JOHN 14:21 (NIV)

Thankful? Me? Yes, all the time. Mostly for selfish reasons, because no man was ever blessed and graced more than me. And even my various back surgeries were gifts, I have begun to think, because there have been a few times I was so angry at my son I would have punched him and didn't.

So, for ten thousand days of back pain, I say, "Thank You, Coherent Mercy!" For children saved from rage and greed and pain, thank You! For children fed this evening, thank You. For children released from hospitals, thank You. For children who are allowed to be in the hospital, thank You. For children who are adopted, thank You. For children laughing hilariously from the bottom of their bones, thank You. For children smearing jelly on their heads, thank You. For the toddler I saw riding a large dog at the beach the other day, thank You.

For the day that will someday come when wars go out of business and children do not hide terrified in cellars, thank You. For the day that will someday come when we forget what fists are for, thank You. For the day that will come soon, I pray with all my might, the day that we suddenly get it that every child is our child, that every child is the most holy distilled essence of the Coherent Mercy, that every child is to be loved with joy and amazement and every ounce and iota of our energy, thank You, thank You, thank You.

Dear Lord, we say one thing about children but so often, so shamefully, we do another. Could You help us to remember to do what we know we must do to make the singing world? Please? —BRIAN DOYLE

Digging Deeper: EXOD. 34:6–7; PSS. 25:6, 127:3

Mon 3

Then Manoah prayed to the Lord: "Pardon your servant, Lord. I beg you to let the man of God you sent to us come again to teach us how to bring up the boy who is to be born."
—JUDGES 13:8 (TNIV)

My daughter Lulu just graduated from high school and spent the summer at home. As a professor, I'm home all summer, so Lulu and I spent the summer together.

The future troubled her. Despite impressive scholarships, her first-choice college was unaffordable. She also didn't know what to study.

She spent whole days out in the hammock or in her room, as miserable as Dustin Hoffman floating in that pool in *The Graduate*. She squelched her ennui with grand enterprises: learning linguistics, training to swim a mile. Nevertheless, her surly melancholy thickened till it coated us both and convinced me I was a parenting failure.

What do you do when your child is miserable and making you miserable? I wondered. *Can I do more than just suffer her unpleasantness and—like the prodigal son's dad—scan the horizon for the return of a more congenial Lulu?*

Friends I consulted seemed to think so. Indeed, some held me responsible for Lulu's surliness. I was too accepting. I needed to *make* her be agreeable.

In my prayers, I felt like Manoah and his wife, Samson's parents, who kept begging the angel to tell them how to raise their son, only to be offered the same advice: Avoid alcohol while pregnant; don't cut his hair. God's reluctance to offer useful tips for parenting was an unexpected comfort. Clearly, He trusted me to unravel it on my own.

As a friend once reassured me, God chose me as my daughter's mom. Hallelujah.

Thank You, Lord, for not loading me with burdens I can't carry and for trusting me to raise my daughters right. Please let me get the job done according to Your will!
—Patty Kirk

Digging Deeper: 1 Sam. 30:6; Luke 12:25; 2 Tim. 1:7

Tue 4

Jesus replied: "Love the Lord your God with all your heart and with all your soul and with all your mind."
—MATTHEW 22:37 (NIV)

Every night when I put Henry to bed, he touches my face and says, "I love you one." I think he first said it during an I-love-you-more tête-à-tête. "I love you one" was probably Henry's way to outdo me. To a five-year-old, nothing can ever beat being first. One is always best. Although now that I think about it, he could have been responding to my saying, "I love you too," which he heard as "I love you *two*."

This morning after the boys got on the school bus I started about my day, cleaning up the kitchen and putting in a load of laundry and Henry's bedtime ritual came to mind. I repeated the words *I love you one* in my head and thought about when Jesus is asked what is the most important commandment.

"The most important one," answered Jesus, "is this: 'Hear, O Israel, the Lord our God, the Lord is one. Love the Lord your God with all your heart and with all your soul and with all your mind and with all your strength'" (Mark 12:29–30, NIV).

It makes perfect sense. When God is first, everything else falls into place. And just as Henry shares his love for me every day, I, too, can add a daily prayer to my Eternal Parent.

Dear Lord, I love You one. —SABRA CIANCANELLI

Digging Deeper: EXOD. 20:1–17; Ps. 46:10

Wed 5

I am saying this for your own good, not to restrict you, but that you may live in a right way in undivided devotion to the Lord. —1 CORINTHIANS 7:35 (NIV)

My girlfriend and I were alone, driving down a dark and endless road, somewhere in the New Mexico desert. I kept checking to see if Emily was still asleep in the passenger seat. We had a long way yet to drive, but my mind was elsewhere, stuck on fears about how I'd make money now that I'd graduated from college and fantasies of writing my "great" novel.

Headlights appeared in the distance. Tired as I was, my eyes were out of focus, and the lights seemed to spread wide before me. I didn't realize it until the other car was almost on top of us; it was in our lane, headed straight for us. I didn't think to honk. I swerved away, but he swerved in the same direction. I turned more sharply. We just missed him, and our car came to a stop in time for me to see a truck pull back onto the road and drive away.

This near-crash opened my eyes. I saw that I had let this loss of focus pervade my life. I loved ethical philosophy but almost never did community service. I loved theology and God, but I often found excuses to skip church. I loved literature and wanted above all to be a writer, but I only strove for genuine human connection with a select few. I had turned my attention to ideas and lost track of the work needed to have real effects. I needed to turn my attention back to the world, to God's work, to the long road ahead.

Thank You, Lord, for when I waver, distracted from Your life, You always call me back. —SAM ADRIANCE

Digging Deeper: COL. 3:2; 1 PET. 1:13–16

Thu 6

But our citizenship is in heaven. And we eagerly await a Savior from there, the Lord Jesus Christ, who, by the power that enables him to bring everything under his control, will transform our lowly bodies so that they will be like his glorious body. —PHILIPPIANS 3:20–21 (NIV)

My great friend, mentor and boss Van Varner, longtime *Daily Guideposts* contributor, died in January 2008 of a stroke, just as he was about to embark on a globe-girdling ocean cruise. Van was an inveterate traveler, and my relationship with him was as much a journey as a friendship.

That winter passed in a fog of grief; Van had been part of my life for more than twenty years and his absence seemed to leave a hole that would never completely close. The world felt like a lonelier planet without him. Yet as time passed, that void diminished a bit. Then one spring morning my computer dinged: "Reminder for Van Varner's birthday on June 6. Check out our new e-cards today."

That ding dented my heart. I told myself I would have to remove the alert. There was no reason to be tortured like that. But I didn't. I forgot. And a year later the ding came again. "Don't forget Van's birthday!"

This time I smiled, remembering how completely delighted he was when he got his very first e-card from me. He was new to the computer, and no one had ever sent him an e-card before. He couldn't believe the animation. "How do they make the horses dance like that?" he asked through his laughter.

You know something? I never did remove the alert. Every spring I hear a ding and am reminded not to forget Van's birthday. But I am reminded of so much more: that love and friendship are gifts that never die.

Lord, Van is with You now, continuing his journey in heaven, where all the horses dance. Thank You for the time You gave me with him.
—EDWARD GRINNAN

Digging Deeper: 2 COR. 5:6–8; JAMES 2:23

Fri 7   *It is good for me that I have been afflicted....* —PSALM 119:71

Okay, guys," my eleven-year-old son Harrison hugged Corinne and me, "you better get on the road." His newfound independence at his first summer camp made us smile.

The next evening the phone rang. "Mr. Kidd, this is Betty from Camp Nacome. Harrison slipped off a rock ledge and broke his arm. We're on our way to the hospital."

When Corinne and I arrived at the emergency room, Harrison's first words were, "Dad, do I still get to go back to camp?"

"I'm sorry, son," the nurse said sympathetically. "You'll need to go home with your folks and take it easy."

Harrison's long-anticipated week at camp was over. On the way home, a very disappointed boy asked, "Why did God let this happen?"

Corinne, a real trouper in her new parenting role, cleared her throat. "I don't know, Harrison. But maybe God can use it for good."

As the days went by, Harrison managed to keep a great attitude. He especially enjoyed sporting the many signatures he had collected on his cast. One night at dinner he asked to do the prayer. "God, thank You for letting me break my arm. I don't know why You didn't want me to finish camp, but I'm awfully thankful for all the people who love me on my cast."

I smiled to Corinne as Harrison said, "Amen." As we dug into our homemade casserole, I was reminded to look for God's good in a recent disappointment in my own life.

Father, give us the wisdom to turn every affliction into something good. —Brock Kidd

Digging Deeper: Gen. 50; Prov. 3:5–6

Sat 8

We are saved by hope. . . .
—Romans 8:24

Nobody is ever supposed to remember what the speaker says at a graduation, but I still think about, and act on, something the speaker said at our son Tim's high school graduation not long ago.

Tina Fey, the actress and comedienne, gave the speech, thanks to some parent who happened to be the producer of her show, *30 Rock*, and Ms. Fey was touchingly, visibly nervous about addressing a bunch of seventeen- and eighteen-year-olds. She's a smart, funny woman, but she didn't hesitate to be boldly inspirational. Her advice to the kids was to use some of the rules for improvisational theater in life.

Among her many points was "Instead of saying 'Yes . . . but,' say 'Yes . . . and.' Think about it for a while." I did under the plane trees filtering dappled sun on a brilliant June day. Instead of saying "Yes, but I can't serve on that committee" or "Yes, but I can't bring snacks to church on Sunday" or "Yes, but I don't have time to pray for that worthy cause because my list is just too long already," why not say "Yes, and tell me what else I can do"? Instead of thinking "Yes, but your idea stinks," why not think "Yes, and that gives me this whole new idea"? Life is filled with a million opportunities. Why not say to them, "Yes . . . and"?

I've tried to do this since that graduation ceremony. I've ended up meeting people I wouldn't have met, taking on new responsibilities, writing things I didn't think I could write, saying prayers that stretched me. Yes . . . and there are times when my life gets too busy. Then I'll retreat into some prayer mode, ready to listen, waiting to respond. Some questions require a quick no ("Want to stay up all night partying?"). Far more are worthy of "Yes... and."

Let me be open to the possibilities, Lord, that You put in my way, waiting for me to say, "Yes... and."
—RICK HAMLIN

Digging Deeper: 1 SAM. 15:22; LUKE 6:46–49; JAMES 1:22

Sun 9

Approve the things that are excellent.... —ROMANS 2:18 (NKJV)

After twenty-five years, our pastor was retiring. On his last day, the parking lot was filled and the parish hall was overflowing. During his years of service, our pastor touched lives within our church, the community and the greater Boston area.

Weeks before the program, I was asked to say a few words at the farewell event. Other speakers would be the commissioner of the Massachusetts Retirement Board, the commanding officer of the Massachusetts National Guard and the mayor of our city. *What would I say?*

After much prayer, an idea popped into my mind. That Sunday afternoon, a hush fell over the hall as

I took the microphone and directed my gaze at the pastor's wife. "Diane, we thank you! We thank you for accepting the pesky telephone calls received both day and night. Thank you for sharing your husband as he counseled and comforted us during our times of crisis and heartbreak. Thank you for postponing Sunday dinner until Wednesday, for accepting loneliness, broken engagements, being taken for granted and often being ignored."

This experience made me reflect on the other areas of my life where recognition is needed. Is my mail carrier thanked at Christmas? When a delicious meal is served, do I show appreciation?

Heavenly Father, where I see good things in unexpected places, nudge me to give a word of thanks.
—OSCAR GREENE

Digging Deeper: ACTS 13:15; ROM. 1:8; 2 COR. 9:12–14

Mon 10

He put a new song in my mouth, a hymn of praise to our God....
—PSALM 40:3 (NIV)

I ce-cream soup...ice-cream soup...," I sang with my grandchildren as they sat at my kitchen counter one summer night after dinner. It's a totally silly ditty, but making ice-cream soup has become one of our favorite summer rituals. I drop generous scoops of vanilla ice cream into mugs, slide them across the counter, and then put out bowls of fresh fruit and whipped cream for them to add as they please. Then we all stir our ice cream until it's just the right, wonderful, soft, smooth consistency.

For them, this is just plain fun. For me, the meaning goes deeper. I used to love doing the very same thing as a child. But one day when my grandmother was taking care of me, I remember stirring my ice cream to just the right consistency when, to my bewilderment, she whisked away my bowl, scolding me for playing with my food. I have other better memories of my relationship with my grandmother, but I vividly remember my confusion and sadness about her response to making ice-cream soup.

Now, as I stir my ice cream with my grandchildren and watch them swoosh on globs of whipped cream, I realize the goodness of God Who gives us second chances to redo some of our memories. In giving my grandchildren what I didn't get from my grandmother, God heals the hurt of an old memory.

Lord, only You can transform an old wounding memory into a sweet new blessing.
—CAROL KUYKENDALL

Digging Deeper: PS. 103:2; ECCLES. 2:24; MATT. 18:3

Tue 11

Happy are those whose help is the God of Jacob, whose hope is in the Lord their God. . . .
—PSALM 146:5 (NRSV)

One of the most spectacular places I've ever been was the place I nearly missed. About a half-mile into a hike, there was a sign that said, "Caution: Creek May Flood." My friend and I kept going. A mile later, "Warning: Steep Terrain Ahead." We thought about that but kept going. And, finally, a sign that said, "Warning: Black Bears in the Area."

"If I had known at the beginning of the hike about all these warnings," I said, "I might not have come."

To which my friend replied, "Maybe it's a good thing that we don't always know what we're getting into, because we might never take the risk."

And then we rounded the next bend and stepped out from the trees into a wide meadow, alive with wildlife and exploding with wildflowers. It stretched out before us, stunning in its beauty.

I keep pictures of those warning signs to remind me: They can keep us from danger, but they also can make us fear the obstacles and undermine our ability to overcome them. *What if I don't have the right words for my grieving friend? Can I make that hard but ethical choice at work? Will I be able to accomplish that new assignment at church?* The sign says,

"Warning! Be Careful! Don't Go On!" And often I am tempted to play it safe, avoiding any risk.

But God hasn't placed those warning signs; my own fears have. If I'm brave enough to take the risk, to trust that God will be where He is calling me to go, I'll likely see things I never imagined.

Give me the courage, God, to follow Your desire for me so that I might see the glory of Your work.
—JEFFREY JAPINGA

Digging Deeper: EXOD. 19; LEV. 18:4; LUKE 4:9–11

Wed 12

From the end of the earth I will cry to You, When my heart is overwhelmed; Lead me to the rock that is higher than I.
—PSALM 61:2 (NKJV)

I was a gangly young ballet student, breaking in my new pointe shoes and sweating my way through a tough class. "To the corner." The teacher clapped her hands, and we all scurried like a bevy of quail. The pianist began sparkling music for turns, and in small groups we spun across the floor from upstage left to downstage right.

At least that was where our turns were supposed to take us. The reality wasn't quite as simple. We weaved dizzily through the studio, heading toward the mirror, the piano or the barres at the back of the room. "No, no!" the teacher shouted. "Don't forget to spot. Pick your focal point."

Sure enough, when I fixed my gaze at an eye-level object downstage right and snapped my head with each turn so my focus stayed fixed, my body followed. I moved toward whatever I focused on.

This morning, a TV news report pulled my attention to all that is worrisome in the world. Then a series of e-mails expanded my to-do list until I felt pulled in a zillion directions. Meanwhile, the glossy magazine on the coffee table pointed out all my inadequacies of fashion, hairstyles and home decorating.

As tension tightened my neck and shoulders, I remembered my long-ago ballet classes. I turned off the television, stepped away from the computer and tucked away the magazine. I curled up in my favorite chair and spent some time thinking about Jesus. When I fixed my gaze insistently on the beauty of God's grace and love for me, I stopped spinning in random directions.

Lord, help me lift my focus today and fix my eyes on You. Amen. —SHARON HINCK

Digging Deeper: MATT. 11:28; LUKE 12:6–7

Thu 13

A woman who fears the Lord is to be praised. —PROVERBS 31:30 (NIV)

Steak salad—that's all it took for me to spiral into a tailspin of guilt.

Let me make one thing clear: This wasn't some fancy steak salad with endive and heirloom tomatoes. This was something I threw together after looking in the fridge and finding only leftover steak, almost-wilted Romaine lettuce and a bottle of ranch dressing. Dinner is served. Not exactly something the Proverbs 31 woman would make for dinner, right?

I knew it wasn't my best dinnertime performance as soon as I made it—and the spiral of guilt started before I even set the table. Although I work part-time, I see my stay-at-home-mom gig as my most important responsibility. I take it seriously when it comes to taking care of our three children and the house. So you'd think I'd be able to make a decent dinner.

My husband walked in and kissed me on the cheek as I was slamming paper plates on the table.

Then came the question: "What's for dinner?"

"Umm, steak salad."

"Oh, looks good," he said without hesitation.

Turns out he thought my Tupperware concoction was good. Even more, as we ate, I saw that my husband didn't care what I had made for dinner.

And God doesn't care either. A woman who fears the Lord is to be praised—and feasting on Jesus was something I *could* do.

Jesus, help me to let go of my guilt so I can joyously join You at Your table. —ERIN MACPHERSON

Digging Deeper: LUKE 10:38–42; JOHN 21:17; 2 THESS. 3:10–13

Fri 14

You make the dawn and the sunset shout for joy. —PSALM 65:8 (NAS)

Why don't you leave Lolly at home?" my husband asked, loading our car for the airport. We were headed to visit friends in Cocoa Beach, Florida. "You'd have a better time without her."

Lolly is my laptop. I don't go *anywhere* without her.

"Probably, but I don't want to come home to a zillion e-mails. If I bring her, I won't have to dread catching up." I traced my fingertips across the black keyboard. Feeling a bit panicky, I decided to try and live more carefree, even if just for one weekend. I left Lolly behind.

My experiment seemed short-lived when I discovered my friend Lisa had a desktop in her condo. After hurriedly unpacking, I signed online but couldn't access my e-mails because of a server issue. The pinch of anxiety spread across my chest.

After dinner Saturday night, Lisa suggested we go out on her balcony overlooking the inlet waters. "Don't you love sunsets?" she asked. "I watch them every night."

Sure, the colors were gorgeous—violet and flaming orange surrounded by a coppery glow. "It's pretty, but I've always preferred sunrises. Sunsets mean the day is done, no more time to accomplish everything I should have handled today. Don't you ever feel that way?"

"No, never." Lisa looked at me with ocean-blue eyes. "I see sunsets as God smiling at me at the end of the day. Whatever I didn't get done, He's big enough to hold on to for me."

I hugged her. "You're so right. Thank you."

Oh, Father, I pray I never get too busy to miss Your unfailing splendor. —JULIE GARMON

Digging Deeper: Pss. 29:2, 96

THE GIFT OF TREES

Sat 15   *Nicodemus, who had first come to Him by night, also came, bringing a mixture of myrrh and aloes....* —JOHN 19:39 (NAS)

Camel caravans transported myrrh, an expensive aromatic oil, from the Arabian Peninsula to

Israel. Nicodemus, a Jewish ruler and secret follower of Jesus, carried nearly seven pounds of aloe
and myrrh mixture when he came to prepare Jesus'
body for burial.

Myrrh is a small thorny tree, not really anything
to tangle with. It produces a protective gum when
injured, which combats insects and bacteria. These
walnut-sized "tears" then harden and are harvested
for the musky oil they contain.

The myrrh doesn't release its perfume unless
it's hurt. The tree is gashed repeatedly to collect a harvest. Something precious from something
ugly.

My cousin and I stood once at the base of a
magnificent live oak tree in Southern California.
Its lower limbs had been chopped off years ago
by monks to fuel a kiln. The tree bore old scars.
On the inside, so did my cousin. Her past was
so painful to her that she actually changed her
name in an attempt to erase its power and move
forward.

She looked up at the monumental tree towering above us, and I will never forget her words:
"That's how I want to be—growing beyond my
scars."

Jesus didn't leave this earth without scars. None
of us does. But what Jesus did in rising above
His scars to new life gives us a chance to do
the same.

As I give each wound and scar to You, Lord, You alone can distill a fragrance pleasing to You and useful in the lives of others. —CAROL KNAPP

Digging Deeper: 1 COR. 3:7; GAL. 5:22

Sun 16 *The glory of sons is their fathers.* —PROVERBS 17:6 (NAS)

It was a very pleasant surprise when my father told me he was coming to New York City for my cousin Karen's wedding. He hadn't been away from Florida in years. "We're all getting older," he said—Dad was eighty-three—"and I don't know if the family will have another chance to be together."

I was especially happy that Dad was coming North because there was someone I wanted him to meet: Julia, a young woman I'd met at church. I'd been thinking more and more about her for a while, and two months earlier, I'd finally worked up the courage to ask her out. So when Dad was rested and settled in my tiny studio apartment in Brooklyn Heights, I phoned her and invited her to come over.

When she arrived, we sat down and began to talk—at least Dad began to talk. He talked about the family traditions, about his Grandfather Attaway whose name he bore (John Bunyan, after the author of *The Pilgrim's Progress*) and with whom he had lived as a boy, the way he was brought up, about the hymns he loved, and even (embarrassingly, though fortunately incompletely) about what I was like growing up. We talked until it was time for Dad and me to get ready for the wedding. The next day he joined us at church and then started back to Delray Beach.

We'd never have a conversation like that with him again. The night after we became engaged, a phone call from Florida told us that Dad had had a stroke. We brought him North for our wedding and kept him with us, but his thinking was rarely lucid.

I'm grateful that Julia had that one afternoon to get to know Dad as I remember him. I don't think she would have married me if she hadn't.

Lord, on this Father's Day, help me to be more like the father Dad was. —ANDREW ATTAWAY

Digging Deeper: Pss. 71:8–9, 103:13; Prov. 23:24

Mon 17

Pray for them which despitefully use you, and persecute you.
—MATTHEW 5:44

A friend confided that she was a victim of cyber-bullying. The harassers sent repeated texts, called work and home at all hours, and posted hurtful comments on social media sites. When she described a particularly cruel attack, I was so angry I couldn't sleep. Something needed to be done, but what? I prayed for my friend, but it didn't seem like nearly enough help.

The next morning I got up to find all the windows open and the heat turned on. "Are you crazy?" I asked my husband Don. "It's supposed to be 104 today! The air conditioner isn't working right, and the last thing we need is more heat!"

"Our geothermal heat pump heats and cools by circulating water through underground pipes," Don reminded me. "With this drought and string of one-hundred-degree-plus days, the water stays too warm. Turning on the heat actually cools the water, so the air conditioner will run properly when I turn it on again."

It didn't make sense, but it worked. For the first time in three weeks, the house stayed pleasant even when the outside temperature hit the century mark.

Jesus' words are counterintuitive too. Pray for your enemies? For people who try to ruin someone's life? It doesn't make sense. But when I started praying for the harassers, anger stopped ruling my thoughts so that I was able to support my friend while the appropriate people dealt with the situation.

*Lord, forgive me my sins as I forgive those who sin
against me or against those I love.*
—PENNEY SCHWAB

Digging Deeper: MATT. 5:10; 2 COR. 12:10

Tue 18

*"And the taskmasters hasted them,
saying, Fulfil your works...."*
—EXODUS 5:13

When my husband Keith and I moved into
our house in Bellingham, one of my tasks
was opening the thirty-five boxes of books we'd
brought with us from Los Angeles and shelving
them in our many bookcases.

Unpacking the boxes had the quality of meeting
old friends. The Grand Canyon picture books held
great beauty; my Medieval research books beckoned
with fascinating stories of the past; the books on
Judaism tempted me with new insights. If I would
only open them up and read, I could find treasures,
but I refused to allow distractions make me waste
time when I had a job to finish.

And then, at the bottom of a box I had almost
finished with, I found one of my old journals. I'd
kept it twenty-seven years earlier, the year before
I met Keith. All my stubborn resoluteness drained
away, and I sat down on the floor and started to
read.

Within the first few pages, I didn't even know who this person was. She'd been even more driven than I was presently trying to be, and she'd been sad and lonely, sometimes angry and bitter. I barely remembered the things she was devoting her time and energy to, but it was clear those things hadn't mattered.

Soon, I shelved the journal and left the remaining boxes unopened. Instead, I went to find Keith, who was putting dishes into the kitchen cabinets. He looked up in surprise. "Are you done already?" he asked.

"Not yet," I said. "I just wanted to tell you how much I love you."

Lord, You have the most interesting ways of showing me what's worth spending time on.
—RHODA BLECKER

Digging Deeper: LEV. 23:25; 2 KINGS 19:18

Wed 19

You have searched me, Lord, and you know me.
—PSALM 139:1 (NIV)

When I was five, I almost drowned. My uncle, who was supposed to be watching me, was distracted by friends. Always a daredevil, I had ventured alone, beyond the safety ropes. There, I found myself deep down in the murky lake, looking up at a bright light beyond the surface. How my uncle pulled me from the bottom and persuaded me not to tell my parents, I can't imagine. But sometime later, sitting in a theater, watching a newsreel play across the screen, frame by frame, I remembered being on the lake bottom and seeing the pictures of my tiny life flashing across some faraway stage: my mother cooking dinner; my brother helping me cut out paper dolls; my daddy carrying me on his shoulders.

My husband David tells me that some famous theologian once speculated that when we get to heaven, the first thing God says is, "Show me your slides."

I consider my present slide show, which grows longer and more complicated. I shudder at frames showing me rude, impatient, ungrateful, selfish. I'm not thrilled to include these in my unveiling, but nevertheless they are part of my reality. Next come faces of the elderly people we have helped, the strangers we have embraced, an African boy who looks to me for hope. I see the teacher I have defended, the laborer I have lifted.

Oh my goodness, what if we really are creating our own personal slide show, as we go through our days? Thinking this, my first inclination is to run straight to Jesus' teachings and rewrite my script: kindness, forgiveness, loving, serving.

If I start now, maybe my slide show will be a presentation that will make God laugh in great and lasting delight!

> *Father, let me please You with my life and delight You with my choices.* —PAM KIDD

> *Digging Deeper:* GAL. 2:20; EPH. 4:1–32; PHIL. 1:6

Thu 20

Each of you should give what you have decided in your heart to give, not reluctantly or under compulsion, for God loves a cheerful giver.
—2 CORINTHIANS 9:7 (NIV)

My one-year-old daughter Prisca recently established a love affair with Cheerios. After every meal, she thrusts her arms into the air, whoops out loud like an overzealous crane and pins me with a look that says, "You wouldn't dare disappoint someone this adorable, would you?"

Time and again, I step toward the pantry as the flailing and whooping intensifies, pull down the box that contains the sole source of her joy, give it a little shake for added excitement and then pour a dozen or so *O*s of delight onto her tray. As soon as the bits of sweetened grain reach her, she smiles and coos and promptly stuffs one into her mouth.

You can imagine my surprise, then, when after breakfast had come and gone, she didn't eat her beloved cereal. Not at first, anyway. We went through our usual routine, but after her chubby hand reached for that first *O*, it moved not toward her mouth but mine.

"You want me to eat it?" I asked my child who does not yet speak. The tiny fist clutching the cereal inched closer to my mouth. "Mommy gets your first *O*?" I said, even as I opened wide and accepted her selfless gift.

This same scene played out following all three of today's meals, and I'm wondering if we have a trend on our hands. I hadn't planned on teaching Prisca about giving of her first fruits until she could walk and talk and contribute to society in some meaningful way. As I reflect on the day's activity, it occurs to me that perhaps I was the one in need of this lesson instead.

God, whatever resources I find in my hands today, please show me how to use them to bless someone else's life. —ASHLEY WIERSMA

Digging Deeper: 1 CHRON. 29:14; ACTS 4:32–35; 2 COR. 9:6

June

Fri 21

I will lie down in peace and sleep, for though I am alone, O Lord, you will keep me safe. —PSALM 4:8 (TLB)

During my thirty-six summertime days in Alaska, I experienced more daylight than I ever imagined. For more than two weeks I slept in the back of my brother and sister-in-law's van while they slept in a tiny two-person camping trailer that we pulled.

After a fitful few hours of trying to sleep that first night, I was shocked to discover that at 3:00 AM it was light enough outside that I could see everything clearly as I made my way to the outhouse. I probably could have read a book in that daylight.

Back in the van I closed my eyes but couldn't sleep—too much light. The next morning when I was still yawning over my cup of tea, telling Joe and Linda of my middle-of-the-night daylight experience, Linda laughed. "Here, you need this." She handed me a soft cotton black eye-mask with elastic straps.

That mask made all the difference for the rest of the trip, and I made sure I hung it carefully over the seat's armrest each morning, so I could find it in the mess of stuff we three piled in that van. I grew to think of that mask as my best friend in Alaska . . . that is, if I wanted a good night's sleep. I laughed at the end of the trip when I realized how attached I was to it.

I know there are many things to be thankful for in this world, especially when I'm in a different state, experiencing all sorts of incredible scenery and adventures. But if you want the real truth, for me, that black eye-mask was one of my favorites.

Today, Lord, let me be thankful for the smallest things in my life and nudge me to thank those who made them possible. —PATRICIA LORENZ

Digging Deeper: JON. 4; JAMES 1:17, 4:17

Sat 22

Better is little with the fear of the Lord than great treasure and turmoil with it. —PROVERBS 15:16 (NAS)

Saturday morning, I was roaring around town in my copper-clad car, looking for rummage sales. On a side street, I saw two boys waving their arms and shouting, "Big sale, right here!" so I pulled over and parked.

Right away I could see that this was a poor family. They lived in a rickety little house, and the sale was set up in a dark garage with a dirt floor. Their offerings were meager, but everything was clean and neat, as if they were proud of what they did have. They were generous; everything was priced way too low. Among their things were an old family Bible and some framed pictures of biblical characters. These were people of faith.

One of the boys followed me around, pointing out bargains. "These lamps are a good deal. They're almost new." He was sweet, courteous, respectful.

The husband and wife joked around as they set up larger items in the yard: "Hon, please tell me you're not selling my favorite easy chair?" "Well, sweetheart, it's starting to smell." "Ugh, you are so right, hon. It smells like stale pepperoni and root beer."

I could feel the warmth of this close-knit family, and I shopped longer than I needed to, just basking in their glow, a bit envious of their joy. But I never found anything I needed or wanted.

Until I was driving down the street, and suddenly it occurred to me that this family had about everything I ever needed or wanted: faith, affection, contentment, happiness, generosity.

They made me more determined to pay less attention to my stuff and a lot more attention to what really matters.

Lord, You have "chosen the poor of this world, rich in faith" (James 2:5) as an example for all of us. Help me to be more like them. —Daniel Schantz

Digging Deeper: Eph. 5:21–6:9; Col. 3:14

Sun 23

*Draw near to God and He will
draw near to you.*
—JAMES 4:8 (NAS)

For the last several years, I've attended church
by myself and sat in the very back row of the
sanctuary. I liked it there. It felt far removed, but
distance gave me mental space in which to meditate
on my relationship with God.

About a month ago a friend started attending
with me, and she had no interest in my usual section. "Let's sit in the front row," she said. "I'd like
to be up close."

I'm a creature of habit and don't like disruption
to my routines. But I agreed, just once, to try the
front.

And you know what? I had no idea what I was
missing! Up close, you can see the passion on the
musicians' faces and feel their melodies resonating
in your chest. The pastor makes eye contact with
you during his sermon, and you feel like his message was written with your specific needs in mind.
Moving closer helped me feel more engaged during
the service.

This past Sunday, while sitting in the front row,
it hit me that I often do the same thing in my relationship with God. I have a tendency to let space
grow between us, not realizing what I'm missing
out on, what I could gain by drawing closer to

Him. The front row of a church service may not be for everyone, but in terms of our relationship with God, I believe it's where He most wants us to be.

God, help me to abide ever closer to Your Word, Your will and Your love. —JOSHUA SUNDQUIST

Digging Deeper: PHIL. 3:12–15; COL. 1:10; 1 PET. 2:2

Mon 24

Turn to the Lord, your God, with all your heart and with all your soul.
—DEUTERONOMY 30:10 (NIV)

Is it possible that I have a parakeet living in my backyard?" I asked the owner of the bird store as I placed a five-pound bag of birdseed on the counter. "I'm almost positive I saw a pretty green one perched on my bird feeder."

"Absolutely," he said. "It probably escaped its cage."

"How has it survived among doves, cardinals and blue jays in my oak tree?" I asked.

"It's adjusted," he said matter-of-factly as he handed me the receipt. "Most birds in that kind of situation don't make it simply because they fail to adapt."

I thought about my own struggle to handle some unanticipated changes at the university where I'm studying for my doctorate. My major professor retired unexpectedly, and I'd had some challenging requirements for course work unexpectedly assigned to me.

I grappled with the changes. "I've thought about going to the dean," I confided to a friend.

"Just remember," she said, "adapting successfully to change just depends on whether you turn toward God or away from Him."

So instead of complaining, I went to God in prayer. "Lord, when the known becomes the unknown and I lose sight of You, give me the faith to trust You even more."

Weeks later, I celebrated the end of the semester. My additional assignments had been turned in just fine. I spotted the parakeet fluttering through the oak tree. That little bird had learned to make the best of a challenging situation and taught me to do the same.

I turn to You, Lord, with love and belief in my heart.
—MELODY BONNETTE SWANG

Digging Deeper: GAL. 3:11–12; HEB. 11:1–39;
1 PET. 1:21

June

Tue 25

For I have learned, in whatever state I am, to be content.
—Philippians 4:11 (rsv)

Recently, I found myself on a whirlwind tour of business trips. Certainly, it was nothing I was complaining about. But by the fifth week of being on the road, I found myself longing for the familiar comfort of my own bed, the companionship of my husband, and the happy way I feel when I am greeted with a wiggling, wagging Nellie, our black Labrador retriever. *Lord, when could I take a deep breath and just be in one place again?*

So when I mentioned to a co-worker that I'd offered to make a cross-country drive with my son Sam, back from where he'd been residing in Texas to our family home in New Jersey, with a stop in Washington, DC, along the way to see my other son Ned, she asked if I'd gone a little crazy! In a quiet moment, I did wonder if I was really up for the three-day marathon car trip, which would come right on the heels of yet another business trip.

The day arrived, and I flew to Austin, helped Sam close up his sublet apartment and began our trek.

Mile after mile, Sam and I talked about all kinds of things, and at times we sat in happy quiet. I learned about little things he loved, and big things he was thinking about. We listened to music together, and I watched him sleep like I hadn't since he was a baby. With gratitude, I realized that life's travels have always brought me to exactly where I want to be.

Thank You, Lord, for guiding my path and providing me with loving companions wherever I journey in life.
—ANNE ADRIANCE

Digging Deeper: JOSH. 24:17; ECCLES. 4:10

Wed 26 *He turned the desert into pools of water and the parched ground into flowing springs.*
—PSALM 107:35 (NIV)

It was the first day the sprinklers came on in New York City's Central Park. Summer was finally here. I listened to the water splashing on the ground, watched my boys' faces as they ran under its cold stream, smelled the sunscreen still on my hands from slathering their arms and chubby bellies. I took in the moment with a breath, as if it were the first time I'd been able to breathe in a long time.

That winter had been the longest of my life. Just before the new year, my husband said we were on two different paths and he wanted a divorce. He left, the snow came, and every moment dragged like an eternity. All I wanted to do was curl up with this incredible pain and sob, yet as a mother I wasn't afforded that luxury. I still had diapers to change and sandwiches to make.

"How will I get through this month?" I asked my sister. I was on the verge of a nervous breakdown. "And if I get through January, I still have to live through February!"

I begged God to take away my pain, but I knew I'd have to face it each day and go through the process of mourning. Month by month, friends came over, church members watched my children, family prayed with me, music encouraged me, my boys made me laugh.

God didn't take away my heartache, but I felt His presence in each day and knew He was walking with me toward a brighter one. It was a long, painful road, but as I stood there with cool water under my bare feet, watching my kids enjoy the start of a long-awaited summer, I knew I was almost there.

Thank You, Lord, for walking with me through the seasons of my life. —KAREN VALENTIN

Digging Deeper: ECCLES. 3:1–22; ROM. 12:12; 1 PET. 5:10

Thu 27   *"For who has known the mind of the Lord so as to instruct Him?"* . . . —1 CORINTHIANS 2:16 (NRSV)

I have an extraordinary knack for accumulating pebbles, twigs and other annoying objects in my sneakers as I walk. How do I manage it so often? I lace my shoes tightly, wear thick socks, watch where I'm walking. Yet I stop frequently to pull out something that feels the size of a boulder or small sapling.

Lately, when it happens, I remind myself of a line from *Godspell*, the Broadway musical. The line refers to the singer deliberately putting a pebble in her shoe. I don't know precisely what the writers intended, but my sense was that the pebble was to be a reminder of Jesus, God-with-us. Now when I kick a pebble into my shoe, I try not to think of it as another clumsy misstep but as a reminder about God. I remember how Jesus suffered on the walk to Calvary, His feet bruised and bleeding. I use the pebble as a prompt to do something for someone in need, maybe something I've been putting off.

I wonder, sometimes, if I am like a pebble in God's shoes, except that God never bends down to pull me out and cast me onto the hard, cold street. God gives me chance after chance to smooth my rough edges, stop my cutting ways and join Him. No matter how hopeless I may be, God never loses hope in me. If only I could be as patient with the pebbles in my life as God is with me.

Lord, the next time a pebble finds its way into my shoe, give me a portion of Your patience.
—MARCI ALBORGHETTI

Digging Deeper: ROM. 8:16–17; HEB. 2:17–18

Fri 28   *For the servant does not know what his master is doing....*
—JOHN 15:15 (RSV)

When Mother Teresa died in 1997, the story of her consummate self-giving was everywhere on the news, making me aware of my own indulgent, self-centered life. What had I ever done to ease the world's suffering?

Then I had a letter. The name on the return address was unfamiliar; I couldn't think of anyone I knew in Indiana. "I'm writing to thank you," the letter began, "for what you did for me nearly twenty years ago.

"You and I," it continued, "were having coffee in your kitchen after fitting the new cover on your sofa." I remembered now: this was the lady who'd made the slipcovers for the living room. She'd been miserably unhappy in her marriage, she went on, and had started to tell me about it. I recalled now, too, being surprised at someone's pouring out her troubles to a total stranger.

"The phone rang," the letter continued, "but instead of picking it up to answer it, you *pulled out the cord!*"

I didn't remember doing that; it's the sort of automatic thing we all do. But apparently it had been a kind of watershed in this woman's life. "I mattered enough that someone would ignore the phone! I was important. I wasn't trash."

I sat marveling at how a routine action, which I probably wasn't aware of even at the time, could have carried such meaning for someone else. Apparently, God's healing work is done not just by saints like Mother Teresa, but by very ordinary people doing very ordinary things.

In what work of Yours, Father, will I
be an unknowing partner today?
—Elizabeth Sherrill

Digging Deeper: Prov. 14:31; Rom. 13:10;
Phil. 2:1–2

Sat 29

Do not forget to entertain strangers, for by so doing some have unwittingly entertained angels.
—Hebrews 13:2 (nkjv)

On the last evening of a youth mission trip in Jackson, Mississippi, we attended a community dinner. It was the last day of June, and, yes, late June in Jackson is hot and humid. Several young people were playing basketball or throwing a football in the evening sun, but I was doing what all the older adults were doing at the cookout—sitting in the shade and eating.

I sat next to a man who introduced himself as John Perkins. It seemed to me that we were very much alike. We both shared a belief that God changes our hearts if we let Him do so. I was referring to the fact that after forty years of cool Colorado weather, God had given me the strength to survive five days of a Jackson summer. Mr. Perkins didn't tell me to what extent God had changed his heart during his lifetime, but I found out later that he held his dying brother (a World War II hero) in his arms after a white sheriff's deputy shot him and was severely beaten himself and almost died at the hands of two patrolmen. Yet he returned to a state that only gave him an education through the third grade, earned seven doctorate degrees, authored nine books, went on to become an international speaker on race relations, and founded and is president of the John M. Perkins Foundation for Reconciliation and Development.

If only I had known, I would have... what? Been more in awe? Gawked? Asked for his autograph? Instead, I remembered that I had treated a stranger with respect and kindness, and he had done the same for me.

Dear God, thank You for people whose capacity to forgive and thrive is greater than we can imagine.
—TIM WILLIAMS

Digging Deeper: JOHN 3:16; ROM. 10:12; JAMES 2:1–13

Sun 30

These earthly bodies make us groan and sigh.... We want to slip into our new bodies so that these dying bodies will... be swallowed up by everlasting life.
—2 CORINTHIANS 5:4 (TLB)

It was one of those rare hot summer days in Vermont, and my husband Billy and I decided to take our daughter Brittany and our grandkids to the lake. As the grandchildren enjoyed the paddleboat we'd brought, I noticed a black Labrador retriever watching Billy. The Lab had a ball in his mouth, so it wasn't hard to figure out what was on his mind! Finally, the dog mustered up enough courage to come over and drop his ball into Billy's lap. Billy tossed the ball, and his new friend scurried to retrieve it. Again and again, Billy tossed the ball, and the Lab brought it back. All the while, Brittany watched from her adult stroller, closely following the interaction.

"Okay kids, time to go!" As I followed Billy toward the water, I turned to make sure that Brittany, just a short distance away, was all right. I stopped in my tracks as I saw Billy's new friend approach Brittany and toss the ball into her lap. Brittany, who cannot walk or talk and is unable to pick up balls, looked at the dog. Her eyes revealed her yearning to explain her situation to him. The dog sat in front of Brittany, patiently waiting. When she did not respond, he retrieved the ball gently and walked away. My heart filled with joy watching the tenderness of the interaction.

What a miraculous story I could have recounted if Brittany had picked up and thrown the ball. But I have come to learn that God's miracles are not always as grand as the parting of the Red Sea. Sometimes they are as simple as the eye contact Brittany had with her friend that day at the lake.

Lord, I am grateful for the presence of Brittany in my life and all that she teaches me.
—PATRICIA PUSEY

Digging Deeper: 2 SAM. 9; MARK 6:34

GIVING THANKS

1 _____

2 _____

3 _____

4 _____

5 _____

6 _____

7 _____

8 _____

9 _____

10 _____

11 _____

12 _____

13 _____

June

14 _____

15 _____

16 _____

17 _____

18 _____

19 _____

20 _____

21 _____

22 _____

23 _____

24 _____

25 _____

26 _____

27 _____

28 _____

29 _____

30 _____

July

*Devote yourselves to prayer,
being watchful and thankful.*

—Colossians 4:2 (NIV)

OPERATION THANKFULNESS

Mon 1   *But Moses said, "Pardon your servant, Lord. Please send someone else."* —Exodus 4:13 (NIV)

I got an idea about getting people to pray for the unemployed in our church and then immediately thought, *I can't do that. That's too big a job, and I don't have time.* Then I remembered another idea I had resisted because I thought I was too busy.

I was in the middle of five huge, time-consuming projects when our son Chris, who was deployed to Iraq, e-mailed me: "Mom, could you send me some prayers? I do a prayer with my guys before every mission and want to start using some."

I'd love to help, I thought, *but I don't have time, and what do I know about combat prayer?* Even though I had rejected the idea, the next day a detailed plan started rolling through my mind. *Why not have a Web site where people can post prayers for our soldiers?* Before I resisted again, the small inner voice asked, *How hard would it be to try?* I prayed, "God, please turn my can't-do attitude into a can-do one." To date, more than two thousand prayers for our troops have been posted by people all over the world on MilitaryPrayers.org.

Recalling those amazing results helped me apply a little can-do attitude to my idea about organizing prayers for the unemployed. Within a week, I created a simple binder that I put in the church prayer chapel. Those looking for jobs added their résumés to the notebook, and volunteers prayed over the résumés and wrote short personal notes of encouragement to the job-seekers. This almost didn't happen because of my can't-do attitude. Next time God gives me a good idea, I'll ask myself this simple question: "How hard would it be to try?"

Dear Father, thank You for sending me this idea. I'm really not sure I can handle it right now, but with Your help I'm willing to give it a try. Amen.
—KAREN BARBER

Digging Deeper: COL. 3:17, 23–24

Tue 2 *I will meditate on the glorious splendor of Your majesty, and on Your wondrous works.* —PSALM 145:5 (NKJV)

The setting sun threw pink and blue intermixed with shimmering gold highlights against the occasional cloud that dotted the sky. As the evening coolness pushed aside the lingering heat of summer, the ranch horses began to disperse from their afternoon knot under the shade of the juniper. They appeared calm and pastoral, but I knew they were all watching each other, tensing.

I waited breathlessly, not wanting to disturb them. It was the Appaloosa, Joseph, who started it. His head flew up and he snorted. Shaking his short mane, he squealed and crow-hopped once or twice before breaking into a canter, neck arched and nostrils flared. Fred followed suit and then Charlie Horse and then Bucko. Sonny and Jack held out the longest, but they, too, were soon swept up into the stampede. All six horses were running flat out, their tails streaming like banners behind them, kicking up a trail of dust that lingered in the air long after they had passed.

I could feel the ground rumbling beneath my feet as the *remuda* swept past me, each horse running out of sheer joy. Each race lasted for several minutes, culminating in a series of bucks and playful kicks before they took off again in a different direction. The finish line was arbitrary, and there were no clearly consistent winners. Each gelding seemed to celebrate his own victory by stamping up a circle of dust around himself wherever he stopped, rearing and snorting and lunging. Breathing hard but happy, the horses finally settled down to graze.

My heart soars whenever I can witness this nightly ritual, and even on days when I'm not there to see it, I smile when I hear their thundering hooves in the twilight.

> *Oh, Lord, thank You for letting me witness*
> *Your splendor in this spectacular world!*
> —ERIKA BENTSEN

Digging Deeper: REV. 19:11–16

Wed 3

My flesh and my heart fail; But God is the strength of my heart and my portion forever.
—PSALM 73:26 (NKJV)

Life is up in the air these days. We haven't found a therapeutic high school for John yet. Mary's ballet studio went through an acrimonious split, and she has to decide who to side with. Andrew's still job hunting. I'm not sure if we can afford to homeschool, and I just lost a freelance job. Yesterday, I spilled iced coffee on my laptop and damaged the keyboard.

I remind myself that things will work out somehow. We may have to move or make major adjustments to lifestyle. But swallowing those changes is more likely to be foul-tasting than fatal. When I force myself to look my fears in the face, I know the real problem: I don't want to be as strong as God is asking me to be. I wish His provision included a middle-class comfort clause. It doesn't.

So I breathe deeply, pulling the air God made into the lungs He crafted. I inhale a prayer and exhale another, calling out to the Comforter, absorbing Him into my body and soul. *Come, Holy Spirit, fill the heart of Your servant and kindle in me the fire of Your love.* Whatever changes are looming, the change in my heart has to come first.

> *Come, Lord, and deepen my desire to live in union with Your will.* —JULIA ATTAWAY

> *Digging Deeper:* ISA. 50:7–9, 51:1–3

Thu 4

There, in the presence of the Lord your God, you and your families shall eat and rejoice in everything you have put your hand to, because the Lord your God has blessed you.
—DEUTERONOMY 12:7 (NIV)

When my brother-in-law was a child, he always knew he was special. Every year on his birthday—the one he shared with the USA—the skies over the lake in the family's backyard would light up with explosions of fireworks, and the town would decorate itself and hold a parade. His older

brothers would play along as Justin eagerly anticipated "his" special celebration.

As Justin grew older, he realized that those fireworks weren't just for him. He could have let his
newfound knowledge cloud his childhood memories, but instead he celebrated the optimism of his
youth.

Justin's childlike outlook reminds me of the wonders God puts in the world. There are the rose
bushes in my backyard that greet me at breakfast,
the birds singing my way into work, and the amazing watermelon. True, God put those wonders on
earth for everyone, but I believe He also thought
specifically about me when He allowed the redbird
to nest in the tree beside my kitchen window.

Just as aspects of faith can be circular and mind-
boggling (remember when you first learned about
the Trinity?), I believe they can also be crystal-clear.
Of course those fireworks celebrated our country,
but they also celebrated Justin's existence. Take a
minute today to look at the wonders and blessings
that God has put in your path. It's okay to feel
spoiled in God's great love!

Lord, thank You for putting tiny pleasures like
fireworks and fireflies as reminders of Your presence
in our daily lives. —ASHLEY KAPPEL

Digging Deeper: DAN. 4:1–3

Fri 5

*Let your adornment be the inner self
with the lasting beauty of a gentle and
quiet spirit, which is very precious in
God's sight.* —1 PETER 3:4 (NRSV)

Mountain twilight. My friend Kevin and I stood at our campsite. A granite peak blazed with sunset pink. We were in Yosemite National Park. We'd hiked all day to reach this lake at tree line. It was just like I'd pictured all the months I'd looked forward to this trip. Four days in the wilderness; cares and worries left behind.

We stared at each other miserably. "These mosquitoes are eating me alive!" I cried.

"I can't take it!" cried Kevin. He dove into the tent. A few moments later I dove in with him. It had been a record snow year in the Sierra Nevada and now, in high summer, all that snow was melting, providing plenty of water for mosquitoes.

We spent the next ten minutes slapping mosquitoes that had accompanied us inside. Finally, the tent was clear. We sat catching our breath, watching the light deepen through the mesh tent walls. Wind stirred in the pines. Somewhere a stream murmured.

"You know," I said, "if we hadn't been driven in here, we'd probably be climbing up those rocks over there or rearranging our packs."

"It's easy to be busy," agreed Kevin.

We sat some more. The sunlight disappeared, and blue night hung over the lake. I thought of the very first words of Scripture, God's spirit hovering on the water. The mosquitoes still had us trapped, but I no longer cared. *It's easy to be busy,* I thought, *and much harder to sit, to listen, to give thanks.*

> *Today, God, I will slow down and savor Your creation.* —JIM HINCH

> *Digging Deeper:* 1 KINGS 19:4, 11–12

Sat 6   *The Lord says: "These people come near to me with their mouth and honor me with their lips, but their hearts are far from me. Their worship of me is based on merely human rules they have been taught."* —ISAIAH 29:13 (NIV)

Saturday was so hot, the birds had to use pot holders to fetch their worms. But that didn't deter me from combing the classifieds for estate sales. Anything to get my mind off yesterday.

A group of neighbors had been making fun of the new homeowner on the block. Instead of speaking up and saying how kind she'd been to me, I chuckled right along with them.

July

As soon as I entered the dining room at the estate sale, I spotted a charming vintage crystal chandelier. I've collected antiques since my teens—about thirty-five years now—and I pride myself on these things.

When I took it to a local shop that refurbishes old lamps, the proprietor swiped a thick coat of dust off it. My heart did a little victory dance as Jim confirmed my assessment. "The arms on this thing are absolutely mint," he pronounced. "There's ten of them and nary a nick anywhere. One thing's for sure, Roberta. You know your antiques."

Then Jim drew in a shaky breath. "Well, I never would've guessed." He dropped his eyes. "The arms on this thing are plastic."

I replayed Jim's praise in my mind. *One thing's for sure, Roberta. You know your antiques.* My purchase had fooled an expert on lamps, but in the end I'd been oh so wrong.

Then it hit me. When it comes to being a follower of Christ, am I always the real deal? Or am I sometimes a faux model, an inspired imposter, top quality plastic, even?

It was time to take a long look at the attributes of my heart. Perhaps I'd begin with pride.

Search me and know my thoughts, dear Father.
—Roberta Messner

Digging Deeper: Prov. 15:16, 33

Sun 7 *Your word I have hidden in my heart....* —PSALM 119:11 (NKJV)

My son has finally discovered the path that leads to God. Now, Jeremy and I are in the same Sunday school class, and when he walks through the door, I want to stand and say to everyone, "Look! My son who once was lost is found." But, of course, I restrain myself and only say, "Good morning, Jeremy."

Recently, our teacher posed a question about the letter of Paul to the Romans. Jeremy raised his hand and quoted, "What shall we say then? Shall we continue in sin, that grace may abound? God forbid. How shall we, that are dead to sin, live any longer there in?" (Romans 6:1–2).

He added matter-of-factly, "Mr. Bob Craig made us memorize almost all of the sixth chapter of Romans in high school. Even when I lived for years in rebellion, those words played over and over in my heart. Finally, I couldn't ignore them any longer."

We adjourned and moved into the sanctuary. The pastor announced that he'd be preaching from the sixth chapter of Romans. I looked toward the back for Jeremy. He, too, was searching for me. And when we connected, we gave each other a thumbs-up.

Most people in our small congregation understood and smiled, as did the pastor. I could even imagine God smiling and sticking His thumb up, celebrating Jeremy's rediscovered faith.

All those years, Father, when I thought You didn't hear my prayer, You were at work in Jeremy's heart.
—MARION BOND WEST

Digging Deeper: LUKE 15

Mon 8   *Be joyful at your festival....*
—DEUTERONOMY 16:14 (NIV)

Let's do a staycation," my daughter Kendall suggested when the usual family getaway of four families and eight children wasn't working out. "We'll all gather at the two closest houses over the Fourth of July weekend and plan some fun activities."

I have to admit I felt skeptical. *How will this be much fun, especially because our house is one of the host homes, and I'll probably be doing dishes and cleaning up most of the weekend?*

Over the next month, e-mails started circulating between the families, everybody offering to be in charge of one or two events. The idea was gaining momentum, but I mostly watched and read, still feeling skeptical.

Here's what happened: Everybody arrived with tents and sleeping bags and food and all the supplies for whatever their sponsored event required. One family created a red-white-and-blue balloon obstacle course in the front yard. Another family set up a craft project so that each person could make a tie-dye T-shirt. Still another family brought along a karaoke machine, an outdoor fire pit and plenty of sparklers.

What did I do? I mostly sat back and watched the staycation start to unfold all around me with this growing awareness that I didn't have to self-appoint myself as the sole hostess in charge.

I could pass out paper plates and provide a big trash bag and let the house and yard absorb the activity—and appreciate the gifts of God all around me. I could simply enter into the fun. So I picked six-year-old Genevieve as my partner in the three-legged race—and won! In more ways than one.

Lord, I can let many things steal my expectation of joy
and blind me to the goodness of Your gifts, or
I can remember to choose differently.
—CAROL KUYKENDALL

Digging Deeper: Pss. 38:9–11, 40:1–3

Tue 9

Giving thanks always for all things unto God and the Father in the name of our Lord Jesus Christ.
—EPHESIANS 5:20

My brother-in-law Mike was recovering in the burn unit when my sister Diane and her three daughters made a visit to the EMTs who had rescued him from the burning plane. I don't know quite where Diane found the wherewithal or strength to add one more thing to a busy schedule, going back and forth to the hospital twice a day and being the only parent, but it seemed important to her.

The visit proved to be a moving experience for everyone. The plane had crashed shortly after takeoff and the firefighters described the incredible chain of events that had made it possible for them to be at the plane within seconds. "If we'd been on the other side of the airport where we usually are," they said, "we would have had to wait to get clearance." Precious time would have been lost. "If we'd gotten there only thirty seconds later, your husband wouldn't have survived."

As it was, one responder had to use the "jaws of life," cutting through hot metal to reach Mike hunched over in the back of the plane. They rushed him to the ambulance and raced to the ER. These were the men who had saved Mike's life.

They talked for an hour and a half, and Diane let them know what a heroic recovery Mike was making, that the tests showed no lung damage, that the painful skin grafts were holding. "We usually don't get to hear what happens to the people we rescue," they said.

They found out because Diane wanted to say thanks. Two months later, Mike would visit them himself to say thanks. The photos of both tearful reunions fill me with gratitude. Mike's survival held many blessings. Here were more to add to the list, the blessings that came from saying thanks.

In thanking You, Lord, I will also thank those who have made a difference to me. —RICK HAMLIN

Digging Deeper: 2 COR. 1:9–11

Wed 10

All things were created through him and for him. . . . and in him all things hold together.
—COLOSSIANS 1:16–17 (RSV)

For almost a week now I've been nursing our pet dumbo rat back to health. Every few hours I put a syringe to Bill's furry mouth and watch as he grips the end of the plastic tip with his delicately small front foot. Bill looks at me with the deepest darkest eyes and takes a good drink.

Before Bill, I cared and prayed for Mr. Speckles, the goldfish. Mr. Speckles suffered from swim bladder disease and spent the better part of a year swimming upside down. Despite every medication and remedy on the Internet, including hand-feeding him frozen peas, Mr. Speckles never turned right-side-up.

Years ago when we excitedly went to the pet store and picked out our new furry and finned family members, I read about the many benefits of children having pets: lessons on love and responsibility, empathy and grief. I hadn't imagined I would be calling vets, desperately asking if they treated goldfish or rats, Googling odd symptoms and praying with all my heart that Mr. Speckles, the fish, would turn over and Bill, the dumbo rat, would enjoy solid food again.

My son comes over and leans his head on my arm. "I think he looks better, Mom," Solomon says. He watches Bill put his front foot up by his mouth and lick the drop at the end of the syringe.

"He knows, Mom," Solomon says.

I didn't understand. "He knows what?"

"Bill knows you love him."

Solomon ran downstairs, and I thought, *I hope so*. I suppose that's what God wants from all of us, for us to want His creatures to know our love.

*Dear God, when I show my love to Your creation,
I feel Your love back.*
—SABRA CIANCANELLI

Digging Deeper: GEN. 7:14–16

Thu 11

*Overlook my youthful sins, O Lord!
Look at me instead through eyes of
mercy and forgiveness, through eyes
of everlasting love and kindness.*
—PSALM 25:6–7 (TLB)

The older I get, the more lists I make: grocery lists, things to do, people to call, errands to run. Before Jack broke up with me in July 2010, I had even made a long list of reasons why I didn't want to marry him. He didn't exercise enough, watched too much sports on TV, didn't eat as healthily as I did, didn't read much except the daily newspaper. I thought I needed a man who was more like me, so I only gave him a portion of myself, always guarded lest he get too serious.

However, the break-up sent me reeling. First I was hurt, then angry, then hurt. I stayed that way for eleven months, not even speaking when I saw him. And since Jack lived only fifty-seven steps from me, in the same building, it was torture.

My friends talked me into visiting one of those online dating sites where I found eligible men, but they weren't Jack.

Finally, he approached me in the pool, asking if we could talk later at my place. He told me that he only felt complete and at home with me. In November 2011, he proposed and in June 2012, we got married.

I learned some important lessons. The biggest is that heart trumps brain. I also learned to stop making lists about matters of the heart. The only lists I make are fun things Jack and I can do together and ways I can show him every day how much I love him.

Lord, help me to be worthy of love and to show and share unconditional love to the man who has trumped my heart. —Patricia Lorenz

Digging Deeper: Prov. 31:10–31

Fri 12

Jesus asked, "Were not all ten cleansed? Where are the other nine?" —Luke 17:17 (NIV)

I went from Colorado to Mississippi in a van with one other adult and five youth members of our church. As the only man in the van—and as the only person who regularly receives mail from AARP—I soon felt out of place. I missed my home, I missed music that debuted on albums rather than iPods, and I missed my wife. After sleeping on a classroom floor with ten teenage boys for five nights at the mission camp, I couldn't wait to stay in a motel room by myself.

During that week, though, I witnessed the fine character of all the young men and women I worked with. Yes, I was the oldest adult leader at the mission site and, yes, I continued to feel out of place, but after seeing how the young people from Colorado, Pennsylvania and Washington impacted the people they met in Mississippi—and vice versa—I'm glad I was there.

I don't know if it will be a lifetime habit, but coming off that trip, I have been grateful every time our mountain evenings cool off after sunset. I'm grateful to God for the freedom of unscheduled hot showers. I'm grateful for beds and bathrooms and for privacy in each. I thank Jesus for kitchens and quiet drives and whole nights of not being stepped on by apologetic, but very heavy, high school boys....

Dear God, may we praise You for all Your blessings—large and small—all the time.
—TIM WILLIAMS

Digging Deeper: 1 TIM. 1:12, 4:12, 6:6, 18–19

Sat 13 *From this day will I bless you.*
—Haggai 2:19

A couple of years ago, I decided to keep a journal of what I was grateful for every day of the year. Sometimes the notations I made were big ("The mammogram was normal"), and sometimes they were small ("The cats didn't break anything today").

There were times when it was easy to think of something and other times when it was such a chore that I had to promise not to go to sleep at night until I'd made an entry. By the time we got to summer, if it had been a difficult day, I'd just write, "I'm grateful this day is over."

As autumn came, I really wasn't in the right spirit for the task I'd given myself. I hadn't meant to make being grateful as much work as paying the bills, but coming up with new things to record in the journal had become a bother. On December 31, I found myself writing, "I'm grateful I don't have to do this journal any longer."

Far into the next year, I felt guilty about it, disappointed in myself for not having done better. After all, I was happily married to a wonderful man, living in one of the most beautiful places in the world, aging not too uncomfortably. I had a great support system and was making a difference in my community.

Finally, it occurred to me that I didn't need to search for new and different things to be grateful for. I could simply recognize how blessed I was and repeatedly give heartfelt thanks for the very same things—no journal necessary.

Thank You, thank You, thank You, Lord, for helping me see that my everyday blessings are blessings every day. —RHODA BLECKER

Digging Deeper: DAN. 2:23

Sun 14

"God, have mercy on me, a sinner."
—LUKE 18:13 (NIV)

When setting up an informal supper, my guests and I had agreed on a few basics. Driving from a distance to get here, Norm and Mary had proposed a four o'clock arrival. But once on the road, they'd call and confirm, depending on traffic and who knew what else. "What can we bring?" they'd asked.

"Just a beverage," I said. "I'll take care of the food."

So last evening, about 4:00, I set the table, though Norm and Mary hadn't called. Nor by 5:00. About 5:30, I put the casserole in a warm oven. At 6:00, I paced. At 6:30, I called a friend to vent. At 6:45, the phone rang. "Hey, there. We're near you but lost—and have been for an hour." By 7:00, they knocked at my door, frustrated (no more than I), happy to see me, hungry. And . . . empty-handed. (*Wait! Hadn't this happened the last time they came?*)

Why hadn't they called earlier? They had excuses: They'd tried my disconnected cell phone. My landline number was buried in a suitcase in the trunk. They were hoping I'd call their cell phone.

They seemed to enjoy the thick soup and overcooked casserole. We caught up on one another's lives. As they left, they thanked me for my patience, but I sensed they were hardly aware of their rudeness.

At church this morning, the congregation asked our most merciful Father to forgive us our sins, known and unknown. I remembered my guests' shortcomings . . . and then my own. I silently opened my hands and accepted the possibility that they and I are one.

Lord, have mercy on us all. —EVELYN BENCE

Digging Deeper: PROV. 15:17–19

THE GIFT OF TREES

Mon 15 *"The fig tree has ripened its figs. . . ."*
—SONG OF SOLOMON 2:13 (NAS)

In the 1980s, when my husband wanted to move to Alaska, I was reluctant. I didn't tell him because he would have nixed his dream. So, in a daze, I went. Later, I wrote about the experience, which led to becoming published for the first time. Suddenly, in the middle of Terry's dream, I unexpectedly found myself in the middle of my dream.

I've learned since then, with deep lament, that daring to live an unselfish life is not natural for me. Even though I love and follow Jesus, I don't want to always cooperate with Him or others for the "greater good." I want my own good or, more truthfully, what I *think* is my own good.

The story of the fig tree is an interesting lesson in working together. Since the flowers are inside the fruit, they need the fig wasp to do the pollinating. The female wasp tunnels into the urnlike fruit of one kind of fig through a small hole in the top and lays her eggs in the flowers. As the wasps hatch and leave, they pick up pollen that they carry to a second kind of fig. This is the one that will produce seeds for new trees and grow delicious fruit.

The first fig can do nothing of itself; it is merely the host for the wasp. It's nicknamed the "goat tree" because only goats will try its puny inedible fruit. The second fig does everything but has to have a pollen delivery from the goat tree via the wasp. The fig tree, thriving for millennia, knows how to get along for the greater good.

God continually teaches me through His creation. I hope this pollen delivery sticks.

> *Jesus, You said that "apart from Me you can do nothing" (John 15:5). It's true.* —CAROL KNAPP

Digging Deeper: JOHN 5:29–31

Tue 16

I hasten and do not delay....
—PSALM 119:60 (RSV)

He's everyone's favorite handyman at our apartment complex. Jesse commutes to work on his Harley-Davidson, white hair worn in a long ponytail flapping below his helmet. Often during the day I'll pass him in a corridor, perched on a ladder, scraping plaster from the ceiling or kneeling to touch up chipped paint on a radiator.

Yesterday I came upon Jesse on my way back from the mailroom with a handful of letters to add to the stack on my desk. Unanswered mail is a perpetual source of guilt for me, not eased by the expedience of shoving it back behind the desk lamp. The bigger the pile grows, the more daunting the thought of tackling it, and the more reasons I can find for putting it off.

Jesse was sanding the arm of a bench in the corridor. Finding him at conversation level, I stopped to talk. When you can catch his attention, he often imparts nuggets of wisdom. I looked at the barely perceptible bubble of paint he was sanding down.

"You have sharp eyes!" I said. "No one would ever have noticed that little bump."

"No," he agreed, "but after a while it would have pulled away more paint." He ran a finger over the smoothed surface. "It's easier to keep up than to catch up."

The words echoed in my ears as I continued on to our apartment. I pulled the pile of mail from behind the lamp, switched on my computer and began answering letters.

Let me be prompt today, Father, to do the work
You set before me. —ELIZABETH SHERRILL

Digging Deeper: 2 PET. 1:3–6

Wed 17

For God knew his people in advance, and he chose them to become like his Son, so that his Son would be the firstborn among many brothers and sisters.
—ROMANS 8:29 (NLT)

I love ice cream—and by that I mean the real stuff, with chunks of strawberry or hunks of Oreo cookie or curlicues of caramel but, above all, fattening, rich, ridiculous cream. To me, it is undoubtedly one of the signs of God's sovereign provision that He empowered us to come up with such a miraculous culinary innovation as this.

Ice = unyielding, blah, cold. But ice *cream*? Transformed and transformative. And so I was delighted that for my birthday, I got an ice-cream maker.

There are, according to my scientific survey, about a gazillion ice-cream recipes on the Internet, and after reading two gazillion reviews, I settled on one somewhat laborious but appealing option. My first batch was a simple vanilla. For my second batch, I followed the same recipe but added some puree as well as some bits of peach to try to infuse the ice cream with one of the quintessential flavors of summer.

After the requisite time in the freezer, the texture of the vanilla seemed perfect. The peach? It was hard and difficult to scoop. As I was chipping away at it, I realized that the ice cream is, in many ways, not much different from us. For the most part, we are the same: flesh and bone, DNA and cells, heart and soul. But a slight shift in the ingredients—say, one precipitating event or experience—can transform the whole almost entirely.

A more experienced chef than I would know how to turn out a consistent and excellent ice cream, no matter the raw materials. And that is God. Even in our seemingly hardened states, God can take us, melt our hearts and make us better than we ever knew we could be.

Lord, I praise You for Your ongoing, transforming work in my heart and life. —Jeff Chu

Digging Deeper: Isa. 43:18–19

Thu 18 *In every thing give thanks. . . .*
—1 Thessalonians 5:18

You know what I am thankful for, this moist morning? All the things that are not gone as long as I remember them. I am a resurrection machine, a blow against dissolution, a thrust against rust, for I remember my grandmother's snicker in the clouds of flour in the kitchen, her firm amused voice as she informed the gaggle of grandsons that, no, the pie was not ready, and, no, we could not have just a sliver before the older kids gobbled it all. And, yes, she loved us better than the older kids, and, no, she would not tell that to the older kids, and, yes, she would pummel us with a broom if we told the older kids, and, no, we still could not have just a hint and suggestion of pie before dinner, and, yes, we could have one large cookie each.

And, no, she would not tell her daughter, our mother, even though she loved her daughter, our mother, very much indeed, but, yes, there were times—having to do generally with cookies and pies—when her daughter, our mother, need not be apprised of every blessed bite that went into the maws and gapes of her three little grandsons, on whom she daily prayed the blessings of the Lord of the Starfields.

This was how Gramma talked, and it is a blessing and miracle that she talks that way still in my heart, where she is not gone, even though she has returned to the Coherent Mercy.

What we remember, what we cherish, what we savor, what we love, does not die, not wholly, unless we forget. This is a miracle, and this morning I remind you of what you already know. Are we not blessed, brothers and sisters?

Dear Lord, You know, we never quite thank You enough for the unbelievable gift of memory. What a subtle bit of creation, that one—very well done! Deft. Totally cool work there. Thanks.
—BRIAN DOYLE

Digging Deeper: 2 TIM. 1:4–6

Fri 19   *Humble yourselves before the Lord, and he will lift you up.*
—JAMES 4:10 (NIV)

My days aren't exactly glamorous. I change diapers. I read stories. I wipe noses. I sing. I build Lego towers. I color. And I make some pretty delicious mac and cheese (from the box).

So when my husband Cameron came home from work, chatting excitedly about the problems he solved, the meetings he ran, the programs he started, my thoughts spun away from the conversation in prideful diversion. *I'm smart. I went to school. I should be solving problems and helping people and doing something bigger and better than changing diapers and reading nursery rhymes. Why isn't God using me to do big things? Why is my path so unglamorous?*

Then I got a call, asking me to speak at a local women's group. I smiled smugly and thought, *Finally, something glamorous!* I scrambled to find child care, spent hours writing my notes and preparing my speech and planned what to wear. And I even packed a real adult lunch with real adult food: iced tea and a turkey sandwich.

It was fun...but not as exciting as I had envisioned. Because deep inside I knew God didn't create me to be glamorous. God created me to fulfill His purposes, and right now His purposes are a bit humbling. They involve diapers, wipes and my delicious from-the-box mac and cheese.

Lord, take away my pride and help me to find joy
in the path You've created for me.
—ERIN MACPHERSON

Digging Deeper: GAL. 6:3–5, 9–10

Sat 20

"You are the light of the world. A city set on a hill cannot be hid."
—MATTHEW 5:14 (RSV)

I missed being with all my family together, so my husband, two sons Sam and Ned, and I arranged to meet up for a weekend in Washington, DC, where Ned was working for the summer.

As the time neared, more than the summer temperatures heated up. Political tensions reached a new level of rancor, and partisan vitriol seemed to have scorched the civility and underlying spirit of partnership in our nation's capital. I prayed that our family would spend our time enjoying one another and not be goaded by our surroundings to argue political positions, which we'd had occasion to do at times.

Our weekend arrived, and our day unfolded with all the joy and pleasure in being together that I had wished for. By afternoon, we'd decided on a visit to the Capitol. Working as an intern for a US senator, one of Ned's official duties was to lead tours, so we even had our very own personal guide to share the special highlights of the building.

Upon entering, we encountered a sea of hundreds of people filling the building. People patiently waiting in lines, people attentively following tours, people avidly listening to guides—folks who'd come from around the world to experience the seat of our democracy.

As our family stood there under the magnificent dome, surrounded by our fellow Americans and world citizens, there were no divisions. All I felt was extraordinary gratitude to live in freedom in this great nation, where my family can always come together in joy, where my sons can dream of serving through their work, and where we can abide in peace and community with our neighbors, endeavoring to ever-better serve one another and our world.

Oh, God, bless our nation and help us always to be a beacon of light for the world.
—ANNE ADRIANCE

Digging Deeper: GEN. 12–13

Sun 21   *I rejoice in following your statutes as one rejoices in great riches.*
—PSALM 119:14 (TNIV)

I used to think of Psalm 119 as just the longest chapter in the Bible, another psalm worshipping God. Then I took the challenge of reading the Bible in ninety days. It's not as crazy as it sounds. The upside is I got through Leviticus, Numbers and Deuteronomy in two days each! Thirty minutes of

Bible reading almost every day had me complete it in a little less than four months.

When reading through Psalms, suddenly the words seemed more intense, more powerful. What especially struck me was Psalm 119, where David seemed to absolutely love God's Word. I couldn't relate. Given a choice, I'd pick up a novel. I read my Bible because I knew it pleased God, not because I loved it.

I wanted to love God's Word. I wanted to look forward to reading it every day. I wanted it to fill my heart with the same joy King David had (Psalm 119:48, TNIV), but I also knew it couldn't happen because of anything I could do. A love for God's Word had to come from within.

So I started praying for God to teach me to love His Word. It is happening slowly, and I am learning to truly crave it every day.

Lord, thank You for the beauty of Your Word. Amen.
—CAMY TANG

Digging Deeper: 2 TIM. *3:14–17*

Mon 22 *Now choose life....*
—DEUTERONOMY 30:19 (NIV)

Going back for Harrison's program will cut our vacation in half," David said. Ever since Brock had called to let us know about the grandparents program at Harrison's school, we had been in a quandary. Leaving the cabin was never fun, but leaving early?

Just then, I heard a truck on the drive. "Must be the guy delivering gravel," I said. After the gravel was dumped, we asked the man to share a cup of coffee.

"Shur is a purty place, you have," he said.

"My daddy built it when I was young," I answered. "It was his favorite place in the world."

The man's eyes settled on the shimmering lake. "Me and my daddy weren't close when I was a kid," he reflected. "He was always gone, drivin' a truck. His boss would say, 'Git' and he'd be gone again. I played ball, but he never saw a game. Then I was a senior and it was homecomin', the biggest game of my life.

"That morning I said to Daddy, 'Couldn't you come just this once.' He looked real sad and shook his head, got in that truck and drove off.

"Later I heard how he went straight to his boss and asked him real nice if he would let him off for his boy's big game. When the bossman said, 'No,' Daddy took out the truck keys, laid them on his desk and said, 'I quit.'

"He set off walkin'. We didn't have no car. It was fourteen miles to the school, but he got there

July

in time for my game." He paused, wiped away the hint of a tear and held up his hand, his first and middle fingers entwined. "We've been this close ever since."

My eyes met David's. I knew we would be packing soon to go home for Harrison's program.

Father, I long to see Your face reflected in my choices. Thank You for the gravel man who showed me Your way. —PAM KIDD

Digging Deeper: DEUT. 30:18–20

Tue 23

Do not merely listen to the word, and so deceive yourselves. Do what it says. Anyone who listens to the word but does not do what it says is like someone who looks at his face in a mirror and, after looking at himself, goes away and immediately forgets what he looks like.
—JAMES 1:22–24 (NIV)

A cute joke gave me a much-needed reminder that expressing Christianity involves a lot more than opening my mouth. A preacher is new in town and looking for the post office. He walks around, searching, and sees a small boy. He asks the child for directions to the post office, and the child gives them. The preacher, seeing an opportunity for a little free advertising, thanks him and says, "If you come to my church on Sunday and bring your family, I'll tell you how to get to heaven." "Mister," the boy replies, "you don't even know how to get to the post office. How're you going to show us the way to heaven?"

We imagine, with a little undeniable satisfaction, the preacher getting his comeuppance. Yet after the chuckles fade, we can see something in here for more than just preachers and clerics. It's an echo of Jesus' words to all of us when He tells His disciples to remove the planks from their own eyes before they try to remove the sliver from their neighbor's eye. I like to think I know the way to God. But some days I can barely manage to be loving to my husband, tolerant of my noisy neighbors or patient with the problems of my friends.

Finding the way to heaven, I am reminded by this anecdote, is not a matter of talking about it with arrogant certainty. It is a matter of searching quietly, acting humbly and serving gracefully. Most of all, it is a matter of accepting my own flaws before I go searching for the limitations of others.

Father, teach me the right path to You, and then let me show others in how I live my life.
—MARCI ALBORGHETTI

Digging Deeper: 1 PET. 1:14–17

Wed 24

*And I caused it to rain upon one city, and caused it not to rain upon another city. . . . —*Amos 4:7

Everyone *around* us was getting rain. We'd hear, "We got nearly three inches. Y'all get any?" Our answer was always "no."

Often my husband Gene stood on the front porch, looking at distant clouds. "It's going to go around us again."

I recalled days as a child when I awakened hearing rain pounding on the roof, and it continued all day long. Often I could smell rain on its way. A fragrance much like perfume preceded it.

Day after day now, the temperature hovered around one hundred degrees. One scorching day, I heard welcome thunder. It came very close then moved on. An old hymn, "Pass Me Not, O Gentle Savior" by Fannie Crosby, touched my heart.

Thinking I couldn't bear the rain passing us again, I sang to myself, "Pass me not, oh, gentle rain, hear my humble cry. While on others thou are falling, do not pass me by."

Without really expecting it, faith ignited in my heart, and I believed God for rain. A terrible, wonderful clap of thunder sounded and lightning struck close by. Then it came: the gentle rain. I hurried out on the porch to marvel.

Father, I'm singing in the rain, but I'm praising You.
—MARION BOND WEST

Digging Deeper: GEN. 2:1–6; JOB 37:5–6

Thu 25

"The Lord your God wins victory after victory and is always with you. He celebrates and sings because of you, and he will refresh your life with his love."
—ZEPHANIAH 3:17 (CEV)

It's fair to say I am fanatical when it comes to the TV show *So You Think You Can Dance.* Each week, male and female performers from a variety of disciplines—contemporary, jazz, ballet, tap, ballroom, hip-hop, and more—compete against each other for the end-of-season prize of $250,000, not to mention the title of "America's Favorite Dancer." And each week for two full hours, I sit transfixed by their every move.

I watched my favorite contestant Melanie stand before the judges following her flawless routine. It occurred to me that while I'll never dance on the show, I know precisely how Melanie feels. She had performed to the best of her ability and now stood there shakily, reflexively wringing her hands. Had she gotten all the steps right? Had each move flowed into the next? Were the judges pleased by her stage presence? Would their reaction spear her or make her soar? She eyed the panel expectantly, sweaty-palmed as they sealed her fate. And all I could think was *I've been there. I've performed in hopes of finding acceptance and then worried that what I'd done was not enough.*

When I was a new believer, I'd memorize my routines, wring my hands and present my best work to God. Despite all that I had heard of grace, my heart just couldn't believe. Wide-open acceptance awaited, even as I stayed caged by my fear of misstep. Had my best efforts been good enough? Was God pleased with how I'd performed?

Oh, the sweaty-palmed hours I wasted, viewing God as a punishing brute. I couldn't get that it was about *relationship,* not about rules.

Lord, I'm indeed amazed by You and by how You love me so lavishly today. —ASHLEY WIERSMA

Digging Deeper: Ps. 149:1–5

Fri 26

I will give you the treasures of darkness, riches stored in secret places, so that you may know that I am the Lord, the God of Israel, who summons you by name.
—ISAIAH 45:3 (TNIV)

This summer we suffered a long, scorching drought here in eastern Oklahoma. Ponds everywhere dried up, the grass disappeared and, during one whole week, temperatures rose steadily past one hundred.

By midsummer, trees were turning brown. And, although few birds normally visit my feeders in summer when they can find lots of seeds and berries to eat, this year they flocked to the backyard for water. They gathered around the dogs' water dishes in gaudy clumps: cardinals, indigo buntings, goldfinches, cowbirds, jays.

I was watching them through my kitchen window one particularly merciless morning. A mockingbird on a branch near me breathed heavily through its wide-open beak. At first I thought it might be sick, but then I noticed that all the birds had their beaks open.

I rigged a hose with a sprayer nozzle onto the edge of the dogs' dish and turned the water on just enough to mist outward a few feet. The birds were so tamed by thirst, they didn't fly away as I worked.

By the time I returned to my window to see what would happen, the backyard was clotted with birds—not just the birds I saw routinely, but groups of painted buntings, which I'd only ever seen singly and fleetingly, and yellow-billed cuckoos, which I had long since decided had been listed in my field guide by mistake. Also vireos, parulas and warblers, which I had no hope of seeing without camping out in the ticky woods.

The awful heat wore on, and we all thought the summer would never end, but seeing those new birds was a singular treat. Surely there are, as the Lord promises, treasures in darkness!

How often You bring new delights out of what seems so irretrievably awful, O God! Thank You!
—PATTY KIRK

Digging Deeper: ISA. 58:10–12

Sat 27

Teach us to number our days that we may get a heart of wisdom.
—PSALM 90:12 (ESV)

If I could be a young mother again, I'd slow down, enjoy the little things.

Last summer, we took our first family vacation since our three children were young. Reminiscing before we left, I studied old photos—Thomas lining Matchbox cars in the sand, Katie wearing her red sunhat and Jamie gathering seashells with her daddy. Back then, I hurried through my days, assuming I'd always be driving carpools and making lunches.

God, I want a chance to recreate those sweet moments. But how? It's too late. A ridiculous idea skipped across my heart. *Get vacation goody bags again.*

I headed to the toy aisle at the grocery store. Thomas' girlfriend Brittany would be joining us, so I'd make one for her too. The kitten coloring book was perfect for Jamie. Katie and Brittany were dog-lovers, so I grabbed two puppy coloring books and three packs of crayons. *Thomas?* Grape sports drinks for when he fishes. I also gathered handfuls of candy.

Would my adult children laugh at me? Ignore my attempts to connect us? I felt a little foolish.

However, as soon as we arrived at the beach, I handed out their bags, explaining nervously, "Don't get too excited. It's nothing—"

"Wow! Thanks, Mom." Thomas opened a box of candy.

"Coloring books and crayons—cool," Katie murmured.

"How'd you remember how much I love to color?" Jamie's blue eyes met mine.

I smiled. *How could I forget?*

We held coloring contests every night. I never won, but there was no greater prize than togetherness and laughter with my children.

Lord, show me what matters most—every day of my life. —Julie Garmon

Digging Deeper: Prov. 31:27–29

July

Sun 28

"It is not good that the man should be alone...."
—GENESIS 2:18 (NRSV)

Right after my graduation from college in Santa Fe, New Mexico, I went with my brother and parents on a family vacation to the Grand Canyon.

It was a long stretch over desolate desert roads, where you can drive seventy-five miles without seeing a gas station and marked by the absence of humanity. There were towering black mountains and empty sand, abandoned shacks and blowing dust. I looked at it all in awe, thinking this is the world God made.

In the midst of all this, however, was a peculiar tourist attraction called the Four Corners, the spot where Utah, New Mexico, Arizona and Colorado meet in a single point. When we saw the sign, we had to stop.

I was skeptical before we arrived and became only more so as we stepped out of our car. The monument was surrounded by stands selling fry bread and knickknacks, and I felt like I was walking into the world's smallest and worst state fair. *Why should I care about this monument, built not to the majesty of the earth or to any intrinsically valuable achievement, but to the arbitrary placement of state lines by some human hand?*

As I was thinking all this, I saw my brother go up to one of the souvenir stands and buy a T-shirt.

"Why would you possibly want that?" I asked.

Ned shook his head at me. "This is that guy's livelihood. This is how he eats."

He was right, of course. While that vast, uninhabited stretch of road had been a testament to the majesty of God's creation, the real heart of God's teaching is always to be found in the presence of others.

Thank You, Lord, for the majesty of all Your creation—nature and humanity alike.
—SAM ADRIANCE

Digging Deeper: HEB. 13:1, 16, 21

Mon 29

For God is not a god of disorder but of peace. . . .
—I CORINTHIANS 14:33 (NIV)

Living in a two-room apartment is sometimes stressful and much more so when one of the two occupants is hard-core messy. I tried everything I could think of: piling things in the middle of the floor, sulking, pleading, sneaking to the trash room. Nothing worked. My husband really thought he was improving. So one day I took a deep breath, picked up the phone and did the unthinkable: I called a professional organizer!

She came to evaluate with a little camera, taking pictures of the bulging closets and the piles on the floor. "I can transform your apartment," she said. "You have lots of space." I could not have been more skeptical but maybe, I thought, she's a magician. Willing to try anything, I hired her.

Total chaos ensued. Cupboards unexcavated in fifteen years were turned out. Many trips were made to the store for plastic boxes, slim velvet coat-hangers, even a small steel desk instead of my wooden monster. I had to admit, some of the clutter was mine. She rearranged the bookshelves and pried volumes from my husband.

On the last day, as I looked around and saw the neat rows in my closet, the computer wires all untangled and labeled, the floor visible, I felt lightness in my soul. "Bless you," I said to the organizer. "Even my husband is pleased."

Weeks later, the basic order is still in place. Blessings, it turns out, are sometimes young and smiling and willing to tackle any mess.

We give thanks, Lord, for the unexpected and the amazing and for help sent when it is most needed.
—Brigitte Weeks

Digging Deeper: Col. 2:5–7

Tue 30

"I do not pray for these alone, but also for those who will believe in Me through their word; that they all may be one, as You, Father, are in Me, and I in You; that they also may be one in Us, that the world may believe that You sent Me. . . . and that the world may know that You have sent Me, and have loved them as You have loved Me."
—JOHN 17:20–23 (NKJV)

No, no! Right! Pull right!" my husband said, a little out of breath and uncharacteristically exasperated.

I glared back over my shoulder. "I *am* going right."

Both our paddles splashed an impressive amount of water, but our two-person kayak swung slowly to face upstream again—the opposite way we wanted to go.

Downstream, a beautiful secluded river invited us to explore. The other kayaking teams disappeared around a bend. My husband and I kept going in circles. The river was peaceful. We had no white water to blame, no trouble with equipment. We just weren't coordinating our strokes.

How often has God desired to steer me in a new direction, toward something beautiful? Yet my frantic efforts kept me paddling in circles, often rowing against His strength. During times when Christ has asked me to head in a new direction, I've read the verse above and thought that His yoke feels far from light. Maybe that's because I was pulling in the wrong direction. Oh, I expend a lot of energy. But just like on the river that day, my arms tire and my kayak makes no progress.

Once my husband and I were in sync, the current became our friend and the work of pulling the kayak through the water felt effortless. When I allow God to steer the direction of my life instead of stubbornly setting my own course, I'm able to feel the power of His arms doing the hard work.

Lord, where are You steering me today? Teach me to spend my effort rowing in the same direction, instead of pushing against Your will. —SHARON HINCK

Digging Deeper: Ps. 25:4–6

Wed 31

Commit to the Lord whatever you do, and he will establish your plans.
—PROVERBS 16:3 (NIV)

I was on my way into the office; several matters weighed heavily on my mind. I was behind on a deadline and needed to write several pages if I was going to turn in the manuscript on time. In addition, I had a meeting scheduled that afternoon with my accountant and a lunch appointment as well. The two appointments meant I'd be staying late at the office, which would cut into my family time that evening. Worrying about time constraints and other commitments wasn't the way I wanted to start my day.

As is my habit, I pulled into a drive-through coffee shop, and when my turn came, I gave the barista my order for a skinny vanilla latté. I didn't bother to fiddle with digging into my purse for money because I pay ahead. A couple of times a month I give the barista money, which she keeps track of on a card. It's simply more convenient that way.

It came to me as I waited for my order that I needed to do the same thing with the matters of each day. Instead of paying ahead, I needed to be *praying* ahead. If I prayed ahead, I could relieve myself of dread and worry, knowing that the matters I had placed in God's hands were automatically covered.

Since then, praying ahead has become a wonderful practice. Just like that latté, praying ahead has made my days go much easier.

Lord, thank You for the simple reminder that what works well at a latté stand can work just as well with the rest of my life. —DEBBIE MACOMBER

Digging Deeper: MAL. 2:6; LUKE 11:1–3

GIVING THANKS

1 _____

2 _____

3 _____

4 _____

5 _____

6 _____

7 _____

8 _____

9 _____

10 _____

11 _____

12 _____

13 _____

14 _____

15 _____

16 _____

17 _____

18 _____

19 _____

20 _____

21 _____

22 _____

23 _____

24 _____

25 _____

26 _____

27 _____

28 _____

29 _____

30 _____

31 _____

August

For everything God created is good,
and nothing is to be rejected if it is received
with thanksgiving, because it is consecrated
by the word of God and prayer.

—1 TIMOTHY 4:4–5 (NIV)

OPERATION THANKFULNESS

Thu 1   *Pray that you will not fall into
temptation.* —LUKE 22:40 (NIV)

I was meeting a friend for lunch to talk over our new nonprofit ministry. I hadn't seen her for four years, and I got to thinking about all of the negative things she didn't know about that had gone on at our church since she left. "Lord, please keep me from gossiping," I prayed. "And help me to actually want this prayer to work!"

As I waited at the restaurant, I was surprised when someone who went to our church walked in. The door opened again. Another church member! Before long three church members were there. Finally, my friend arrived, and I told her about my prayer not to gossip and how church members kept mysteriously coming through the door. Then who walks in, but the choir director!

It's a big noisy restaurant, I thought as we followed our hostess to a table. *Maybe I can sneak in one or two juicy stories.* You guessed it. The hostess seated us right across from the table full of church members! I looked at my friend, and we both broke out in grins. There was no need to gossip. We'd just been given an answer to prayer well worth repeating.

> *Jesus, help me to really want this prayer to work.*
> *Amen.* —KAREN BARBER

> *Digging Deeper:* PHIL. 4

Fri 2   *Fix your thoughts on what is true and good and right. . . .*
—PHILIPPIANS 4:8 (TLB)

Among my favorite things to read are the one-line descriptions of movies found in the newspaper. One sentence, never more than ten or twelve words, that sums up the movie perfectly. "Cloned dinosaurs run amok at an island-jungle theme park." What else but *Jurassic Park*? One of my recent favorites is "A woman falls for an artist aboard an ill-fated ship." I'm impressed that a writer could summarize the three-hour-plus epic that is *Titanic* in just ten words. The movie is about a bit more than just a woman falling for an artist, but that one sentence certainly tells a lot about what gives the story its power.

So that got me thinking: What one-sentence description could I give my life on any given day? "Woman tries to juggle job and family—and fails." Or "Life's everyday problems overwhelm tired mother and wife." Some days, those are the messages I tell myself. Even though I know God's spirit within me gives me strength during the tough days and makes the small victories possible, it's hard not to focus on the struggles when an especially frustrating workday makes me snap at my husband or daughter.

What would happen if I saw the one-line summary of my life differently? "Mom helps teenage daughter overcome difficult problem" or "School employee encourages co-workers." My heart tells me I'd have better days if I focused on the gem hidden inside each one and gave the power to the story line authored by the spirit of God.

Lord, focus my mind on the power You have given me, every day, to see the good things in my life.
—GINA BRIDGEMAN

Digging Deeper: 1 PET. 5:2–4

Sat 3   *Precious shall their blood be in his sight.*
—PSALM 72:14

My church's Health and Wellness Committee has sponsored quarterly blood drives for years, but I didn't participate until I retired. My first attempt was nearly the last. I fainted and had to be driven home, and my blood was discarded. The next few attempts were successful, but I had to answer the same questions each time I donated, the process took more than an hour, and my arm almost always bruised. Worse, I was exhausted and drained of energy for hours afterward. My doctor assured me the symptoms were because I'm on the thin side. It was perfectly safe to give, but I decided it wasn't worth the effort.

Then Jonathan, a nineteen-year-old who sometimes attends our church, had a terrible accident. Saving his life took more than seventy units of whole blood and plasma. A few months later my neighbor needed blood plasma, but it was in such short supply the hospital had to have it brought in from another part of the state.

I signed up again and have now given more than two gallons. It still takes its toll on me, but the close-to-home needs helped me understand that a little time and discomfort are a small price to pay for a gift that can save a friend or a stranger.

Thank You, Jesus, for the privilege of taking part in a church project that helps restore health and wellness to those who are ill or injured.
—PENNEY SCHWAB

Digging Deeper: LUKE 10

Sun 4

If you are going to be used by God, he will take you through a multitude of experiences that are not meant for you at all; they are meant to make you useful in his hands.
—OSWALD CHAMBERS

When I placed this quote above my computer several years ago, I wanted a reminder that God intended to bring some good out of my Stage 4 ovarian cancer diagnosis. I had no idea then how meaningful those words would become for me now.

When first diagnosed, I was given a two-year life expectancy. Instead of fighting that prediction, I let it shape my life purpose: to do what mattered most in the days I had and to trust God to give me exactly what I needed every step of this new journey, even if it included dying much sooner than I expected.

But I didn't die, and when I passed the five-year anniversary of my diagnosis, I wondered if I could find a new life purpose about being a survivor.

Soon, my phone started ringing and people identified themselves as recently diagnosed cancer patients. "How have you survived cancer?" I was asked again and again. I felt a bit baffled. I didn't have any nice neat list of do's and don'ts about not eating sugar or eating only raw vegetables.

"My survival is far more about what God has done than what I have done," I replied, and went on to relate my story about the ways God prepared and equipped me for my journey.

In these conversations, I keep discovering how life-giving and hope-bringing our personal stories can be, especially when they are shared with a person walking the same challenging path that God has walked with us. That's sacred ground. And I've discovered a new life purpose.

Lord, I hope that I am useful in Your hands when I tell and retell my stories about Your faithfulness.
—CAROL KUYKENDALL

Digging Deeper: 2 SAM. 22:33–34; PSS. 10:17, 16:9

Mon 5

"Is not life more than food...? Consider the lilies of the field, how they grow; they neither toil nor spin.... Therefore do not be anxious about tomorrow...."
—MATTHEW 6:25, 28, 34 (RSV)

I was feeling burned out from long days of driving tour coaches in Skagway, Alaska. I decided to take advantage of an adventure, one of many available to us for free. I decided to float down the Taiya River.

Can a day be lovelier? Summer. A lazy river. Salmon spawning. Eagles soaring; bears looking up from the shoreline. Sun looping through a cerulean sky; hang gliders adding color to a glacier glinting off the horizon. Everywhere I looked, the raw wilderness spread forever, untouched and pristine as the day God made it, gently lifting me into a place of peace and rejuvenation.

"Hey! Anyone lose ten dollars?" Our guide Jake pointed to a bill floating on the river's surface.

We laughed heartily at ourselves as we all made a reach for the greenback bobbing along like so much flotsam. Jake had the advantage though. His paddle. Neatly, he snagged the ten bucks, and we all laughed some more as he shook it out and made a show of giving the money to the dog.

Rest. Renewal. Abundance for the taking. I got the message.

Lord, instead of fretting and working myself to the bone, I will instead take time to enjoy the gifts You offer here and now. —BRENDA WILBEE

Digging Deeper: Ps. 91

Tue 6

If that is how God clothes the grass of the field, which is here today and tomorrow is thrown into the fire, will he not much more clothe you—you of little faith? —MATTHEW 6:30 (NIV)

As an amputee who does not wear an artificial leg, whenever I buy a new pair of sneakers I end up with an unused left shoe. My first inclination used to be to simply throw it away, but my mother insisted that I hold onto it in case I someday met an amputee who was missing the opposite leg but had the same shoe size.

"Mom," I told her. "It's extremely unlikely I'd ever find a person like that. And even if I did, what are the chances he would have the same fashion sense?"

Nevertheless, I took her advice and let my extra left shoes accumulate in a storage box for many years. Then one day I received an e-mail from a young man who had seen one of my videos on the Internet.

"I noticed you are missing your left leg," he wrote. "I am missing my right."

As it turns out, we had the same size shoe, he lives nearby, and we even like the same type of sneakers! Like me, he had been saving his extras, so we exchanged boxes of brand-new single shoes. Now, whenever one of us buys a new pair, we give the other person the unused one.

In thinking about finding this "sole mate," it occurred to me that if God cares enough to connect me with a person with whom I can exchange surplus shoes, how much more can I trust Him in more significant searches, such as finding a wife, a fulfilling career or anything else I need on my journey through life?

Lord, help me trust that You will always clothe me, that You will always provide for me.
—JOSHUA SUNDQUIST

Digging Deeper: Ps. 136

Wed 7 *In the shadow of thy wings will I make my refuge....* —PSALM 57:1

I was on a crowded plane about to take off in a raging thunderstorm. As we cruised down the runway, a bolt of lightning lit up the darkness, shining on the plane's silver wing and on a memory from another trip.

Whitney and I were on a second honeymoon to Bermuda. On Sunday, we went to a small church near our motel. During the service, the minister introduced his mother who'd recently moved from the United States to live with him. He invited her to come forward and say a few words and sing a special song.

An elderly woman, frail and stooped, made her way slowly to the pulpit. I strained to hear her. "I'd never flown before I came here a few weeks ago," she said in a thin, reedy voice. "But it was the only way I could be with my son and his family. When I boarded the plane, the kind stewardess helped buckle me into my seat. My heart pounded like it would burst. But then I looked out the window and saw this big silver wing. It called up the words of an old hymn, reminding me under Whose protection I was kept."

And now, on this dark and stormy flight, with the plane feeling as fragile as a toy, I remembered:

*Under His wings I am safely abiding. Though the night deepens and tempests are wild,
still I will trust Him; I know He will keep me.
He has redeemed me and I am His child.
Under His wings, under His wings, who from His love can sever?
Under His wings, my soul shall abide, safely abide forever.*

Almighty God, as I lift my eyes to You, I soar above the storm. —SHARI SMYTH

Digging Deeper: Ps. 4:6–8

Thu 8 *Wisdom belongs to the aged, and understanding to the old.*
—JOB 12:12 (NLT)

My eighty-nine-year-old father and I have an interesting relationship. (*Interesting* is a wonderful word that covers so much ground.) We love each other very much but sometimes seem to talk past each other rather than to each other.

A while ago, he asked about my high school experience, a question that took me back thirty-plus years. Like many teenagers, I had a difficult time—which was doubly tough on my parents, scraping together their shekels for my private school education while paying for my brother and sister in college.

"In retrospect," I said, "I'm glad I went to Central Catholic."

"Well," my father said, "I wish you would have told your mother when she was still alive."

I don't know if he knew how much he stung me; I'm sure that wasn't his intent. My father doesn't suffer from a lack of candor, but that's not to say he's mean. He was simply reporting what he saw—and, worse for me, he was correct. I should have. It would have meant a lot to her.

"You're right, Dad," I finally said, "but I can't apologize now for being young and stupid then. I had a lot to learn."

"The opposite of a fact is falsehood," physicist Niels Bohr said, "but the opposite of one profound truth may very well be another profound truth." Despite our differences, my father and I seek the same sacred end: understanding. It's not always a smooth investigation . . . then again, neither is that whole love-your-neighbor thing.

Lord, help me realize that my father and I are two sides of the same coin. To paraphrase writer Lewis Grizzard, my daddy is a pistol and I'm a son of a gun.
—MARK COLLINS

Digging Deeper: JAMES 1

Fri 9 *The night cometh, when no man can work.* —JOHN 9:4

In August 1959, we had one of those life-changing moments. John and I and our three children, ages three, five and eight, were on a small boat en route from Seattle to the brand-new state of Alaska, looking for stories of pioneering families.

Trouble was, we were exhausted. We'd been on this trip since school let out, zigzagging five thousand miles across the country. "Perhaps we'd better not try any more long trips," I said to John as we settled the kids into their bunks, "until they're older."

"*Much* older," John agreed.

Our family occupied five of the six berths. The other passenger was an older man who, happily, enjoyed children. He was taking the trip, he told us, to fulfill a long-cherished dream of his and his wife's. For many years he'd worked at a bank, every month setting aside money for the travel they'd never done.

"'As soon as I retire,' we told each other." Two months before that day, his wife died. "I have to take the trip for us both."

I met John's eyes and knew at that instant that any time a chance to travel came, we'd go. Our three are traveling with their own kids now, and "going" remains John's and my way of life. All because one night a man told us, "We waited too long."

Make me alert to Your timing, Father, neither running ahead nor lagging behind.
—ELIZABETH SHERRILL

Digging Deeper: PROV. 9:1–10

Sat 10

My son, do not despise the Lord's discipline, and do not resent his rebuke, because the Lord disciplines those he loves, as a father the son he delights in. —PROVERBS 3:11–12 (TNIV)

I need to tell you something." The wary tone of my friend's voice on the phone made dread pool in my stomach.

"What is it?" I asked.

"You said something really bossy a few weeks ago. I mentioned liking a particular toy store we were walking past, but you immediately said you didn't want to go inside."

At first I was defensive. "I don't even remember saying that."

"I was annoyed because I hadn't said I wanted to go inside," she continued. "I just mentioned I liked it."

I had to respect her for having the courage to tell me I had upset her. "I'm sorry I annoyed you," I said rather hopelessly.

Most of the time, I don't even realize I'm being bossy and I don't know how to fix that part of myself. But I don't want to hurt my friends and family.

The next day I started reading the book of Proverbs, and I think God orchestrated it because He knew exactly what I needed. Verses 11–12 of chapter 3 reminded me to listen to this rebuke because it was not only from my friend but also from God. My friend and God love me deeply and will teach me and help me to become a better person.

Lord, thank You for my friend's and Your deep love for me. Please help me to become the person You want me to be. Amen. —CAMY TANG

Digging Deeper: JOB 6:23–25

Sun 11

For God hath not given us the spirit of fear; but of power, and of love.... —2 TIMOTHY 1:7

I don't even know how I signed up. Coercion by the clever Sunday school coordinator, I guess. They desperately needed teachers, and I was available. But I hadn't entered a classroom in decades. My Sunday school training was lacking, to say the least. I shook my head and thought of the scarcity on any spiritual table I might prepare for children.

The next Sunday, I entered the classroom, bright and early, and faced the children's hostile stares. "Are we gonna have to read any boring books?" snarled a little fellow. One girl squealed, "Last year, four teachers quit. One lasted a whole month!" "I hate school and I *hate* Sunday school," growled another boy. Inside, I died a little, but I remained silent.

Teaching was difficult. Yet, week after week, we met. We used a drawing to show being and thinking differently was not being wrong. We stacked alphabet blocks to show how important love, home and family were. We used toy cars to show no one wins a head-on quarrel.

One Sunday a father visited and said, "I don't know what you're teaching, but my son refuses to miss Sunday school."

His words startled me. *What was I teaching?* Only lessons straight from the Bible.

On the final day, the boy who had snarled said, "Mr. Greene, you taught me to love the church." The little girl who had squealed told me, "We like you, Mr. Greene, because you listen." Then the boy who hated school and Sunday school leaped into my arms, kissed me and ran from the room, sobbing.

I blushed and felt I finally knew what I could give the children. I could trust their love, pressed down and overflowing.

Heavenly Father, now I understand Your way of teaching comes through serving. —OSCAR GREENE

Digging Deeper: MARK 10:13–15

Mon 12

He told them this parable: "No one tears a piece out of a new garment to patch an old one. Otherwise, they will have torn the new garment, and the patch from the new will not match the old."
—LUKE 5:36 (NIV)

As part of a weeklong cruise, I was in Guatemala for a day packed with adventures, including swimming in hot springs, tasting tea made from some kind of tree bark, and taking a high-speed boat ride into the Rio Dulce (Sweet River) that sashays in and out of the rain forest.

When I climbed into the boat, I met Jeanne, a blind woman. I sat next to her, struck up a conversation, then held her hand as we bounced along.

Mostly that day I was fascinated by all the things Jeanne could do. I guided her down some steep steps into the hot springs where we splashed around with glee and were the only two from our boat who ventured in.

Later, I followed a Guatemalan boy into a cave for a short tour. He had one small flashlight, and all I could think as we inched our way down steep, wet stone steps was *What if his batteries go out?*

"Look over there," the guide whispered as he pointed his light toward the biggest cockroach I'd ever seen, at least five inches long. Around the next corner the teen pointed his flashlight up on a small ledge about shoulder high where a baseball-sized spider was enjoying the cool darkness. Terror punctuated my every cell. I took a deep breath, closed my eyes and prayed, "Lord, get me out of here soon!"

I thought of Jeanne and understood that her life is like being in a dark cave all the time. She never really knows what's going to dart out in front of her. Then I thought about her spunk and willingness to try new things and how her spirit had grown out of her lifelong faith that basically all is right with the world, if she just uses common sense and proceeds with a bit of caution.

Lord, let me be more like Jeanne, always willing to try something new, even if it is dark, scary, fast or bumpy.
—PATRICIA LORENZ

Digging Deeper: LUKE 1:78–80

Tue 13   *"I will heal them. . . ."*
—JEREMIAH 33:6 (RSV)

I live on a remote cattle ranch in Oregon. I don't own a television, so when I climb in the pickup after irrigating or chasing cattle or feeding hay, the radio is always on, to keep me company if nothing else. Today I caught Dr. Dean Edell's "Medical Minutes." Instead of hopping out right away to close the gate I'd just driven through, I sat still with the door half opened, riveted to the broadcast. His topic was the healing benefits of spirituality.

According to medical reports, folks who have a deep, abiding faith suffer from less stress than the faithless person. Stress causes depression, hinders healing and can shorten the human life span. The doctor's conclusion was further research studying spirituality as a stress reducer could be a great advantage to the health and well-being of Americans, who are ranked the highest users of antistress/antidepressant medication in the world.

I've already seen this in my own life. The more I turn my troubles over to God, the less I worry. The less burden I have to bear, the freer I am. I'm healthier, happier and more energetic. God isn't there to keep me *from* trouble in this world; God's there to help me when I'm *in* trouble. God's a shoulder to lean on when I'm in a jam. And believe me, in ranching, I'm up to my eyeballs in jams.

I hope Dr. Edell can stir up interest in a study pertaining to the healing benefits of spirituality. Wouldn't it be great to hear our doctor tell us, "Say two prayers and call me in the morning"?

As long as You have my back, Lord, what on earth can trouble me? —ERIKA BENTSEN

Digging Deeper: Ps. 57:5

Wed 14   *And I am but a little child....*
—I KINGS 3:7

A letter from a childhood friend ignited sweet memories of playhouses we'd created together under shade trees. Nostalgic longings tugged at me just as I was feeling old and dull. Then a birthday card arrived from a new dear friend. Melba had enclosed a check with stern instructions: "Shop for something you wouldn't ordinarily buy."

All I could think about were those long-ago playhouses my girlfriends and I would make. We'd lugged old crate boxes, dolls and Mason jars filled with wildflowers to our cherished spot in the red Georgia clay.

Remembering ignited a wild kind of excitement. *Lord, guide me to all I need.*

My first find was the red-and-white-checked oilcloth for the neglected wrought-iron table on our back porch. Next, I spotted colorful cushions for the four chairs—all on sale. It seemed God led me right to a huge, half-dead geranium for less than half price. I adored the big red pot. Fertilizer for my neglected hanging ferns completed my shopping.

My treasures fit nicely in the trunk of my car, except for the rescued geranium in the passenger seat. At red lights, I smiled over at it.

Now each morning when I settle down in my playhouse, joy finds me and lingers. My heart feels childlike as I begin my prayer time.

Father, thank You—and Melba—for satisfying the little girl in me. —MARION BOND WEST

Digging Deeper: PROV. 16:24, 17:17, 18:24

THE GIFT OF TREES

Thu 15

Abraham planted a tamarisk tree at Beersheba, and there he called on the name of the Lord, the Everlasting God. —GENESIS 21:33 (NAS)

Trees, the largest plants on earth, have been worshiped since ancient times as manifestations of gods and goddesses. But for the prophet Isaiah something didn't add up. He tells of a man who plants an evergreen, later cutting it to warm himself beside a fire and bake his bread. With half the tree, he carves an idol, praying to it and saying, "Deliver me, for you are my god" (Isaiah 44:17). Isaiah questions why the man doesn't remember it is "just a block of wood" (44:19).

I'm glad Isaiah's not watching me. Because I have my "blocks of wood" when disillusionment sets in . . . or sadness . . . or frustration. I lose myself in a novel, or reach in the drawer for chocolate, or head for the theater or discount stores. It's not the doing of these things, it's the *why*. Inside myself, I know I'm seeking false deliverance.

Abraham didn't mistake where the real power lies. He didn't worship the tree. He *planted* the tamarisk and called there upon the Everlasting God. Tamarisks are an ornamental tree, blooming in pale pink and white flowers. At night, they release salt crystals to their branchlets. The evening moisture clings to these crystals, condensing to droplets. The rising sun slowly evaporates the beads, cooling the feathery branches, making them an exceptionally refreshing desert shade tree.

Tamarisks still flourish in Israel. I'd love to see them... to reflect in their shade on the refreshing presence of the Everlasting God Who created them.

Wonderful Counselor, Mighty God, Eternal Father, Prince of Peace, forgive me my imposters. You alone deliver. —CAROL KNAPP

Digging Deeper: Ps. 96:11–13

Fri 16

"And surely I am with you always, to the very end of the age." —MATTHEW 28:20 (NIV)

A dear friend left a message saying it looked like the adoption she and her husband were pursuing—not one child, but three—was going to be approved. I returned the call, simply to join in their excitement and congratulate her on expanding their family in such a meaningful way, but something else was on her mind.

The sibling group that soon will be part of my friend's family is being adopted out of the foster-care system. They are young, but they have suffered more in their short lifetimes than most people four times their age. Instability. Neglect. Lack of caring parents. Lack of appropriate physical touch. With each entry on the troubling list, my friend's heart plummeted.

"I know that God is sovereign," she said, her voice sure and strong, "but where was He when these kids' mother was making so many devastating decisions in a row?"

Practically, I knew where she was coming from. If God is mighty and powerful and all-knowing . . . if He cares like He says He cares . . . then couldn't He have prevented that mom from entangling herself in multiple relationships with men who had no intentions of sticking around? Couldn't He have compelled her to chase after purity instead?

I absorbed my friend's heartfelt questions and then offered my honest reply. "God was right there," I said. During the one-night stands and the pregnancy tests and the ultrasounds and the groans and cries of delivering those babies into life, God's presence never once wiggled or waned. "Equally true," I continued, "is God is here—right here, right now."

God remains present and accounted for today as three young souls prepare to set foot in their new home: a place of refuge, a place of peace, a place—at last—to belong.

Father, please make Your nearness known
to my friend's new family today.
—ASHLEY WIERSMA

Digging Deeper: Ps. 46:7–11

Sat 17

Thy statutes have been my songs in the house of my pilgrimage.
—PSALM 119:54 (RSV)

Walking a hundred miles in rural France and Spain would be a challenge, but I was thrilled at the idea of following the path of St. Jacques de Compostelle, in the footsteps of pilgrims who had walked this trail since the eleventh century. Then I tore a muscle in my knee.

"Please, doctor, tell me what I must do," I almost whined.

"Walk with two poles. One pole, and you'll stay home," he said firmly.

The two long poles became my best friends. *Thud, thud*—they hit the earth as we passed the different crosses that marked the route, with stones heaped around them by walkers before us. *What is a pilgrim?* I wondered as my poles and I followed the paths that for centuries had drawn God's people.

I didn't feel holy, but I did feel as if I were walking supervised by the grace of God. The poles were an outward and visible sign of His inward and spiritual grace. They got me across a stream and up some steep hills. I felt close to the faithful Christians who had walked before me, sustained by the same grace. The destination—if they survived robbers, weather and lack of food—remains unchanged: the cathedral in Santiago, Spain, with the tomb where (at least in legend) St. James, the apostle, is buried.

As they had for hundreds of years, the villagers welcomed us as pilgrims. They showed us where to find fresh water and offered coffee and cookies. Travel can be difficult and often scary in these tempestuous times, but this trail felt warm and supported. With my trusty poles and the grace of God, I learned how to be a twenty-first-century pilgrim.

Lord, bless all pilgrims, near and far, as we seek solace from those who have gone before us.
—Brigitte Weeks

Digging Deeper: Ps. 84:4–7

Sun 18 *"So in everything, do to others what you would have them do to you...."*
—Matthew 7:12 (NIV)

Our friends Kip and Laura missed Bible study for two weeks when they went to a family reunion. Their former exchange student Tong stayed at their house to care for their gardens and all their ornamental hanging plants.

Kip and Laura have welcomed exchange students into their home for the past eight years. When Tong lived with them, he spent much of the first few weeks with his host family having extensive dental care, because he had never been to a dentist. Each week at church we would see his painful smile and ask, "What did the dentist do to you this time?"

My wife and I checked on Tong twice while Kip and Laura were gone. Tong was treating their plants with near-reverence, watering often to prevent the desert sun from damaging them. I tried to thank Tong for doing so much work for our friends, but he interrupted me. "Is all right," he said in broken English. "They already do so much to me."

Tong may not distinguish between *to* and *for* but I think it is my English that is broken. The next time someone does something *to* me—even if it's a dentist doing something painful to my teeth—I will think of Tong's now beautiful smile and be grateful.

Dear God, thank You for the good things You do to us every day. —TIM WILLIAMS

Digging Deeper: Ps. 92:1–4

Mon 19

Do you not know that your bodies are temples...?
—1 CORINTHIANS 6:19 (NIV)

Oh no, my earth suit is melting!" I tease my granddaughter Abby as she gently pinches the loose skin of my upper arm. That elicits a giggle, and we go on playing. But it's the truth: My earth suit is melting.

The way I see it, we first try on our earth suits somewhere around the time our first breath is breathed. Then our suit grows with us until the fit is right. With the proper maintenance, we can use it as a fine-tuned vehicle to carry us through life. We can diligently care for it, or we can abuse it until we reach a place where dragging it around makes our days difficult and the weight of neglect holds us back from the full life we were meant to have.

Here we all are, God's children, gathered on this one planet. Spirits wearing earth suits. Some mesh perfectly with society's formula of perfect: tall, dark, handsome. Small, blonde, blue-eyed. And then there's the rest of us. All sizes, shapes, nationalities and faiths. Some of us are beautiful; others not so much. I like to think that in God's eyes we are all beyond gorgeous.

Herein lies a challenge: to look past the wrappings and recognize all human beings as sisters and brothers in God's great family.

Someday, when the time is right, I'll breathe my last breath and leave it all behind, earth suit included. Until that time, I promise to take care of it so that I can see out as clearly as God sees in.

Father, help me make the most of this mysterious earth suit that You have assigned to me. —PAM KIDD

Digging Deeper: ROM. 12

Tue 20

He bindeth the floods from overflowing; and the thing that is hid bringeth he forth to light.
—JOB 28:11

I'd been noticing little grains of grit on the toothbrush holder in our bathroom. A few months later, a damp spot appeared on the ceiling and we called the super. Then one evening, while I was trying to get some work done—

Boom!

I rushed into the hallway. A cloud of dust was wafting out of the bathroom doorway. Inside, chunks of plaster and cement were everywhere, and over all was a dusting of little (and not so little) grains of grit. Eventually a pipe was replaced in the apartment above us, and the hole in our ceiling was plastered and painted. But a few days later, there was another damp spot.

For the next few weeks, a parade of visitors marched to and from our bathroom—the building manager, the super, the plumber. It took a lot of rummaging under our upstairs neighbors' floorboards, but finally the source of the leak was located and the ceiling was closed and plastered again.

I think I got something valuable out of the Case of the Collapsing Ceiling. When I stumble in my walk, I can see that there were little grains of grit— an unkind word here, a missed prayer time there— to warn me of where I was headed. And after I've ignored them and the crash has come, it's all too easy to patch things up, slap on a coat of paint and pretend that all's well. But unless I dig down deep and find the real cause of my problem, I'm only storing up trouble to come, grain by grain.

Lord, give me the insight to see my faults and the courage to face them. —ANDREW ATTAWAY

Digging Deeper: 2 COR. 7:9–12

Wed 21

Give thanks to the Lord, for he is good; his love endures forever.
—PSALM 118:1 (NIV)

I got to talking to a shy, quiet emergency room doctor the other night, in a corner of a seething bubbling event, and he told me a story I cannot forget. So I tell it to you because you won't be able to forget it either, and I think that will be a prayer.

"One time very early in the morning, I opened the chest of a nine-year-old girl, he said quietly. It was a desperate last try at saving her. She had been in the river a long time. She had a ponytail. But it was too late. She was gone, and I could do nothing.

"I am sorry to say that I have had many deceased children laid out under my hands. But I tell you this story for another reason. Her mother did not stop kissing her baby girl. She kissed her feet and her hands and her cheeks, and kept kissing and kissing her baby girl.

"People came to take the girl's body away, but I told them to wait. The mother wasn't screaming or wailing. She knew that her daughter was dead. But she kept kissing her baby's feet and hands.

"She was praying with her hands and lips, I think. She was saying things we don't have any words for. We think that words have weight, but so often they are just shadows of what they mean. I think that mother was saying *thank you* and *I love you* and *I will always love you* and *I will see you again* and *I loved the gift of you*. She kissed her girl for a very long time.

"I made everyone wait until she was ready to wrap her baby in a blanket. She wrapped her so tenderly. I'll always remember that."

I don't think we say thank you enough. Sometimes I think we hardly say thank you at all. If we were wise, we would just say thank you all day long and that would be the best prayer ever.

> *Dear Lord, oh, with humility and ashes in my mouth for the careless ways I have taken Your stunning gifts of love and pain and light and song for granted, thank You. Thank You. Thank You. And then again thank You.* —BRIAN DOYLE

Digging Deeper: LUKE 7:36–50

Thu 22

The angel of the Lord asked [Balaam], "Why have you beaten your donkey these three times? I have come here to oppose you because your path is a reckless one before me."
—NUMBERS 22:32 (NIV)

Balaam was barreling toward a lucrative opportunity when his donkey balked. An angel stood in the road to give a clear reminder that Balaam should speak only what God told him to in the upcoming encounter.

But why did Balaam take it out on his donkey? Verse 29 reveals the crux of Balaam's response to an obstacle: "You have made a fool of me!" *Pride.* It didn't look good for the sought-after oracle to be seen in a mundane struggle with a donkey that wouldn't move.

I'll be honest: There are times God stands in my path, and I don't see Him. All I see is that things are going wrong and I'm looking like an idiot and it makes me grumpy.

I once directed an arts ministry, and after several years, major difficulties arose: conflicting goals, dwindling resources, obstacles as frustrating and inexplicable as Balaam's balking donkey. I stubbornly pushed ahead, trying to force success, until I became so exhausted I stopped to listen. God made it clear that it was time for me to serve Him in new ways.

When pride snarls around my heart, my path becomes a reckless one. I'm so glad God stands in the way, confronts my motives and prepares me before allowing me to continue.

Lord, next time I face an obstacle, help me leap off the donkey, fall to my knees and listen to Your words. And help me never, ever, beat the donkey You are using to get my attention. —SHARON HINCK

Digging Deeper: PROV. 13

Fri 23

Incline your ear, and come unto me: hear, and your soul shall live....
—Isaiah 55:3

I click on the computer and log on. A long lattice of unanswered messages unfurls. I groan inside at the number and scroll down. "Yes...no...let me see...that might work...I can do that...," I respond, ever efficient. Some messages get saved; others get deleted.

But then there will be something a loved one sends, a link to an article, a video, a humorous blog. "I really loved this," they say. I sigh. *How long will it take to read the article? How long will the video run? I would gladly read what they write, but must I read what they liked?*

Then I recall what goes through my mind when I forward that arresting blog, send along that moving picture, link to that charming video. I'm sharing a part of me. I'm saying, "This made me laugh/cry/think/smile. I hope it does for you too." I'm opening my heart in hopes that what touches it will touch yours.

Spiritual growth comes from different sources. Yes, God speaks to me through Scripture and through prayer and through the drop-dead view of the sunset over the river. But doesn't God also speak to me through the people I love, and then sometimes, through the seemingly mundane things they love?

When my son slips the ear bud into my ear and urges me, "Dad, you've got to listen to this song," I listen. It's not my music, but it's his and he's letting me know what makes him tick. No, I probably won't download it myself, but he's just given me a chance to download a part of him.

At home, when I have more computer time, I look at the links that come from those I love. I remember how lucky I am that I have people looking out for me, helping me expand my world. A link to a link to the heart can always expand the soul.

Give me the ears, Lord, to listen closely to those I love.
—RICK HAMLIN

Digging Deeper: ROM. 12:9–18

Sat 24

Religion that God our Father accepts as pure and faultless is this: to look after orphans and widows in their distress.... —JAMES 1:27 (NIV)

B ut what about Star Wars toys?" Joey asked. "No, Joey, people need food and water and blankets, not toys," I responded quickly and walked to the front of the store, anxious to get my fussy son out of the store and to the relief station to donate supplies to those who had lost everything in the massive wildfires that destroyed more than fifteen hundred homes in Austin, Texas.

Joey was persistent. "But, *Mommy*, there are little boys who lost all of their Star Wars toys. We have to help them."

I hesitated. People desperately needed food and water and blankets, but would it really hurt to throw in a few Star Wars toys as well?

We went to the toy section, where Joey carefully selected several toys. At the relief station, I sheepishly watched as Joey handed the workers a Yoda figurine, a light saber and a small spaceship.

Later that night, I watched a news clip of supplies being handed out to children in temporary shelters—and watched their faces light up joyfully when they were handed small toys, stuffed animals and books.

As God's people, we are called to show God's love to the poor, the oppressed, the orphaned and the widowed—but showing God's love doesn't simply mean providing for their physical needs. It means much more. It means showing them the hope and *joy* we have in Christ.

As Joey so wisely pointed out, for a child who has lost everything, joy may come in the form of a new Star Wars toy.

Lord, give me opportunities to share Your love with those in need in the way they need it most. Amen.
—ERIN MACPHERSON

Digging Deeper: MATT. 10:5–8

Sun 25

Let us therefore no longer pass judgment on one another. . . .
—ROMANS 14:13 (NRSV)

Friends of mine were talking about the joys and aggravations of our families. Abruptly one said, "Sometimes I feel so isolated, even within my family. Maybe that's just the way life is these days— people feel alone."

The lighthearted banter stopped cold. It wasn't that we pitied her; it was that, at some level, each of us understood exactly what she meant. She recalled how she and her brother had tried family therapy. She'd always thought he was perfect, with no problems. And during the sessions, he spoke about his terrific life, his perfect wife, children, job, bank account. My friend had felt inadequate. At their last session, she believed the therapy had been a waste of time. On their way to the parking lot, her brother grew quiet and then said, "I never feel like I'm really part of things. I feel like I've always been alone."

How easily we misperceive others, especially those close to us. For decades, my friend had considered her brother too high and mighty to bother with her, much less to have the same problems she had. I do the same thing. I consider my husband too affable and well adjusted to ever be hurt until I say something careless to him. I think of my neighbor as the perfect Christian and then she tells me she's stopped going to church. I label my friend Jeff as the world's most solicitous son, only to have him confess he's not speaking to his parents.

Maybe we do live in lonely, isolating times, but perhaps that is less a matter of the times than of our unwillingness to try to understand the person standing right beside us.

Holy Spirit, imbue me with a desire to learn about those around me. —MARCI ALBORGHETTI

Digging Deeper: ROM. 15:1–6

Mon 26

Lo, children are an heritage of the Lord. . . . Happy is the man that hath his quiver full of them. . . . —PSALM 127:3, 5

It's the first day of college for my daughter Hope, and we're unpacking her stuff (apparently everything she's ever owned) in her dorm room. Check that: My wife and Hope are unpacking; I am untangling. In her haste, Hope threw all of her necklaces and earrings into one small box, and the chains have become hopelessly intertwined. I am (not so) patiently sorting through the mess, separating the silver heart from the friendship chain, the faux-diamond earring from the necklace with the cross.

This is not the first time I have untangled things for Hope. It started young, with the long, thick hair she refused to comb. It continued into grade school, where Hope often twisted her homework assignments, turning in some early and others not at all. And it was still an issue in high school, with all the typically tangled relationships. (I may never know why Brian took Missy to the prom, and I may never care.)

I finally realize the way out of this matted mess: If I focus on the cross, the chains will fall away. Sure enough it works, and everything is straightened out. The last piece to fall into place is Hope's heart.

Well, not quite the last thing. The last thing I need to do is share this story with Hope, sparing the obvious parable. She's a college student now—she can figure out her own metaphors, she can figure out her own focus, she can figure out her own heart.

Lord, most of life's tangled messes are our own creation. When Hope needs You, help her see her way out of the dark thicket and into the light. Amen.
—MARK COLLINS

Digging Deeper: ISA. 40:3–5

Tue 27

As Jesus looked up, he saw the rich putting their gifts into the temple treasury. He also saw a poor widow put in two very small copper coins. "Truly I tell you," he said, "this poor widow has put in more than all the others." —LUKE 21:1–3 (NIV)

The flood of e-mails that day told a story of overwhelming human need: a devastating famine in Africa; severe flooding in one part of the United States and a drought in another; two local schoolchildren murdered; unemployment up, poverty up, hunger up. Just reciting the mournful list to a friend left me exhausted and, worse, feeling helpless to make any difference.

"I wish I could do something about all this," I said. "But I'd need ten million dollars to have an impact, and I don't have ten million dollars."

"Do you have ten minutes?" she replied.

"Well, of course. But for what?"

"To write a card to someone grieving. To make a small donation to an organization that can help someone. To pray for those on the front lines." She paused. "I don't have ten million dollars either, and I know I can't solve all the big problems of the world alone. But I can do something today, in just ten minutes, to answer one specific need. And if we all answered one need..."

My friend was right. Too often I've fallen prey to the idea that only lots of money can make a big difference in a troubled world, and so I've done nothing. Now, instead of my ten-million-dollar lament, I try to live by her ten-minute rule.

How about you? Could you give ten minutes today? And tomorrow? And the next day?

You have blessed me with much, God. Help me to give back today and every day. Amen. —JEFFREY JAPINGA

Digging Deeper: 1 JOHN 1:5–8

Wed 28

The Lord will work out his plans for my life....
—PSALM 138:8 (NLT)

On my way out of the library, I ran into Denise, a former co-worker who a few months earlier decided to make a career change from technology to teaching. I asked her how things were going. Denise's face lit up and enthusiastically she shared. "I'm teaching seventh grade in a New York City public school in a low-income community. I love it. I am getting up at 4:00 AM and getting to bed late, but I feel excited about my job."

I was energized by her mission to teach and help inner-city children get an education that would allow them to rise above poverty. Her mission resonated with me. I was once one of those kids.

I knew firsthand the power and positive influence of having a competent and caring teacher in my life. I told her how Mrs. Kelly, my seventh-grade teacher, had a profound impact upon my education. She encouraged me to excel in my school work so I said to Denise, "You will always be remembered by your kids. Teachers live forever in our memories, especially the ones who make an impact upon us."

As I walked back to my car, Denise continued on her way to the library, on a mission. When I was younger, a pastor told me, "Do what makes you come alive." It is exciting to know that God has called each of us to a mission greater than ourselves that makes us come alive.

God, I thank You for the special callings You've given each of us that make us come alive. —PABLO DIAZ

Digging Deeper: 1 COR. 12

Thu 29

"Neither do people pour new wine into old wineskins. If they do, the skins will burst; the wine will run out and the wineskins will be ruined. No, they pour new wine into new wineskins, and both are preserved."
—MATTHEW 9:17 (NIV)

I traveled thousands of miles following my college graduation. Starting in Santa Fe, New Mexico,

I drove to Arizona to see the Grand Canyon, then Austin, Texas to live for a few months. Later, my mom rode with me as I drove from Austin to New Jersey, passing through cities like Dallas, Memphis and Washington, DC. From there, after taking less than a day to savor being back at my childhood home, I made the ten-hour trip to Maine and then the six-hour trip back down to Providence, Rhode Island, where I was ultimately moving.

As the end of summer approached and the miles added up, I felt very stressed. I was so used to being comfortable and settled in a place I could call *home*. Now, as I drove a moving truck through the night, the rule of my life seemed to be constant change, constant transition. I would have to find a new job, a new church, new friends... a new life. I knew God was always there, never changing, but it was hard for me to accept His comfort. Nothing was simple any longer. My old life seemed to be falling further and further back in my rearview mirror.

The next day, my parents came to Providence to help me move into my apartment. My dad and I carried the furniture up the winding stairs, struggling the whole way. The project took all morning. When we were finished, both of us breathing a little heavily, he put his hand on my shoulder and asked, "So, does it feel like home?"

"No," I said, shaking my head. "Nowhere feels like home anymore."

"Well," he said, "that's how you know you're growing up."

Thank You, Lord, for reminding me that there is no growth without change. —SAM ADRIANCE

Digging Deeper: Ps. 86:8–13

Fri 30   *I thank my God upon every remembrance of you.*
—PHILIPPIANS 1:3

This evening, I ran into a person from my past, Pattie Garrett Walker. Pattie's wedding in 1964 was the first one I ever attended at my home church of Seventh Avenue Baptist. I was just ten years old. Back then, my world was intact for my mother hadn't yet had the terrible head injury that changed everything. It was before her thinking and actions became impaired. Before words like *dementia* were spoken in hushed tones.

"Did you know, I still have the gift your wonderful mother gave us?" Pattie said to me, smiling. "It's a yellow mixer, and I use it to make a favorite icing."

July 1964: I remember Mother taking us three sisters to the S&H Green Stamps Redemption Center. Rachael and Rebekkah were only six. "What do you want to get Pattie for her wedding?" Mother asked. "We could find her a new iron to press her husband Tom's shirts, a percolator to make coffee, or a mixer to whip up a batch of cupcakes."

An iron sounded like work. We didn't like the taste of coffee. But cupcakes were fun, fun, fun! We went with the mixer.

As Mother pointed out that day, "Pattie is getting married forever and ever." It turns out that the mixer and the marriage have lasted quite a long time. Pattie is just as radiant today as when she was a brand-new bride with a brand-new mixer.

Today, I'm filling in the blanks for my sisters who don't remember much of Mother before the brain injury. And because of Pattie, I'm thanking God for the girlhood memory of my mother.

Thank You, Lord Jesus, for memories and memory-makers. Amen. —Roberta Messner

Digging Deeper: John 19:23–27

Sat 31

"Do not lay up for yourselves treasures on earth, where moth and rust destroy . . . but lay up for yourselves treasures in heaven. . . . For where you treasure is, there your heart will be also." —Matthew 6:19–21 (nkjv)

Fourteen inches of rain in twenty-four hours had left our basement—and everything in it—awash in water. As I viewed all my stuff floating in the muck, I realized that my years of hoarding had finally caught up with me.

I am a clutter bug. Everything I own seems to have some emotional connection, so I have a hard time discarding or donating things that people have given me. My attic, my basement, my cabinets and even my inbox overflow with clutter. Every once in a while I go on a tear, thinking, *My children will hate me when I die and leave this mess for them!* But just as quickly another thought pops in about whatever it is I'm trying to throw out: *Wait . . . this was given to me by my niece, and if I give it away she may think I don't value her.*

I know there are people who could really use my things, but still I hold on tight. The flood in the basement made the decision for me: Everything had to go. And later, when it was all gone, I thought about how other stuff—unforgiveness, bad habits, impatience with my husband, jealousy toward a friend—clutters up my spiritual life and keeps me from focusing on the blessings God has for me now.

If I am busy holding on to all of my stuff, then I am not looking at the glorious and free present and future God has for me.

Lord, show me what it is that is hidden, which You desire for me to discard, so that I can be out in the open, sharing with all. —PATRICIA PUSEY

Digging Deeper: PHIL. 4:11–13

GIVING THANKS

1 _____

2 _____

3 _____

4 _____

5 _____

6 _____

7 _____

8 _____

9 _____

10 _____

11 _____

12 _____

13 _____

14 _____

15 _____

16 _____

17 _____

18 _____

19 _____

20 _____

21 _____

22 _____

23 _____

24 _____

25 _____

26 _____

27 _____

28 _____

29 _____

30 _____

31 _____

September

But thanks be to God, who gives us the victory through our Lord Jesus Christ.

—1 Corinthians 15:57 (esv)

OPERATION THANKFULNESS

Sun 1   *"Praise be to the Lord, to God our
Savior, who daily bears our burdens."*
—PSALM 68:19 (NIV)

The weekend before our son Chris deployed to
Iraq, our whole family pitched in to clear everything out of his three-bedroom house, so it could be
rented while he was off to a war zone. The job was
huge. Yet it was nothing compared to the impossible task of making it through the next year under
the daily stress of knowing that Chris could be in
mortal danger. *How on earth am I going to make it
through his deployment?* I wondered.

I carried a bucket of heavy-duty cleaning supplies into the bathroom. The walls and floor of the
shower were caked with a thick layer of grayish soap
film. *An impossible job!* I thought.

I pulled on rubber gloves and sprayed cleanser on
the shower wall until it dripped down the drain. I
took a sponge and made a swipe. The gray yuck
didn't budge. I picked up a scrub brush and leaned
my whole weight against it. Nothing. Then I repeated the process. Spray. Scrub. Lean. Spray....
In a few minutes a clean patch of white shower
wall emerged. Encouraged that the job really wasn't
impossible, I kept at it. An hour later I stiffly

stood and looked with satisfaction at the now white shower.

Cleaning the shower showed me how to get through a huge life challenge like being a mom of a soldier in a war zone. Don't try to handle the whole overwhelming job at once. Just finish up one small part at a time until the long difficult task is done.

Father, what I'm facing feels impossible but with Your help, I will make a little progress each day.
—KAREN BARBER

Digging Deeper: MATT. 11:28–30

Mon 2 *We have different gifts, according to the grace given to each of us....*
—ROMANS 12:6 (NIV)

I was at one of those large gatherings, in a room filled with people you know only by their name tags. When I asked a woman I'd just met one of the typical questions we all ask in settings like that—"What do you do?"—I expected a typical response in return.

But that's not what I got.

She smiled and said quietly, "I bring hope to people who are hurting."

With a little more digging, I got the answer I had originally expected: She was a clerk in a local grocery store. But she didn't see her job simply as a job. It was also a way to use the gifts of hospitality and love God had given her to help make the world a better place. And so, she said, she especially paid attention to people who looked sad or careworn, and intentionally offered them a simple word of kindness. "I think it makes a difference," she concluded.

What do I do? I'm a seminary dean, and with the academic year just starting, I've got a to-do list the length of my arm. If we met today, I could tell you all about that, and you could tell me your job title and functions too.

But because someone recently gave me an answer I didn't expect, it's helped me see my work in a whole new way. *What do I do?* I use my gifts of administration and teaching to help prepare people for ministry and build up the kingdom of God. It doesn't make my to-do list any shorter, but it does make it more compelling.

This Labor Day, why not ask yourself: What larger work has God called me to do? Then look for it.

Bless the work of our hands, Lord, that it may always bring glory to You. —JEFFREY JAPINGA

Digging Deeper: 1 COR. 1:26–31

Tue 3

For you have been my hope, Sovereign Lord, my confidence since my youth.
—PSALM 71:5 (NIV)

The utterly terrifying instructions for kindergarten drop-off came in the mail: I was supposed to drop my son Joey off in front of the school and let him walk into the cafeteria to meet his teacher by himself—alone.

I panicked. *What if Joey got lost? What if some big fifth-grader picked on him? What if . . . ?*

We practiced. We rehearsed. We prayed. But as we pulled up to the school on the first day, Joey looked at me with big terrified eyes as he hopped out of the car. Then he froze. He stood on the sidewalk, looking at me, then at the school, and then back at me. I saw the tears start to flow.

I wanted to help him, to grab him by the hand and show him the way. But I couldn't. Doing that would only show him that I didn't have confidence in him, that I didn't trust him to stand on his own two feet. So I put on a smile and waved. I yelled, "You got this, buddy! You know what to do!"

As I pulled away, crying, I took a deep breath and reminded myself that while sometimes the path God created for us is frightening, I can have confidence that He has given me every tool I need to walk down the path set before me. Even if that path crosses through a crowd of tough-looking fifth-graders.

Lord, thank You for giving me every tool I need to walk through life and to do so confidently.
—ERIN MACPHERSON

Digging Deeper: JUDE 1:5, 20–21, 24–25

Wed 4   If we say that we have no sin, we are only fooling ourselves, and refusing to accept the truth. But if we confess our sins to him, he can be depended on to forgive us and to cleanse us from every wrong.... —1 JOHN 1:8–9 (TLB)

One day before we were married, I was at Jack's condo, fifty-seven steps from mine, making homemade soup for dinner that night. Before chopping up the broccoli stems, I peeled the tough woody outer layer and stuffed it into the garbage disposal.

When I turned it on, it groaned and gurgled. Finally, water began to rise in the sink. I'd clogged it. Jack, who was about to walk out the door to go golfing, calmly went to his tool closet, found a brand-new plunger and worked silently to fix the mess I'd made.

Just as he was about to say something, which I knew would be a plea to not stuff such tough vegetable parts down the drain, I smiled and said, "May I say something first?"

He looked at me, grinned and said, "Go ahead."

"Do you know one reason why I love you so much?"

"Why?" he asked.

"Because you never get angry. You never shout. I know I screwed up. I'm really sorry. I messed up your garbage disposal one other time a few years ago, and you did the same thing. You fixed it without getting mad at me. I love that about you."

Jack smiled, shook his head and said, "Okay, fine. But please, no more tough vegetable peels in here, okay?"

"I promise." And at that moment I experienced what makes a relationship work: patience, kindness, being slow to anger and learning to say, "I'm sorry."

Lord, continue to teach me lessons about how to make my relationships work. Keep my eyes and ears open and a few "I'm sorrys" at the tip of my tongue.
—Patricia Lorenz

Digging Deeper: Lam. 3:40–41

Thu 5

This is the day which the Lord hath made; we will rejoice and be glad in it.
—PSALM 118:24

The last fall and winter of his life my dad spent in a nursing facility near his home in California. Once a month I flew out to visit. The place had lovely gardens with paths winding through citrus trees, roses, jasmine, exotic bird-of-paradise—especially welcome to me, coming from the frigid East Coast. But I always felt pressed, wanting to make the most of this precious time. Did Dad have any last words of wisdom? Were there any important stories he wanted to pass on?

One day I drove his old white Chrysler convertible to the nursing facility and pushed his wheelchair out into the brilliant sunshine. We sat on a bench near his car, the top down, and I put on his favorite hat. "Remember how you used to wear this hat when you drove your car, Dad?" I asked, hoping to jog his memory.

But Dad didn't feel like reminiscing about the past or giving me wisdom on the future. His mind was focused on the day. He looked to the driveway. "There's a truck unloading," he observed. He stared at the oak tree. "No breeze today. Those leaves aren't moving." He pointed to a statue of Jesus on the path. "I like that," he said. It reminded me of sitting with my boys when they were toddlers, watching a dump truck or catching a ladybug. All that mattered was the moment we were in.

This is why I'm here, I thought. *Not to give my time to Dad but to get his quiet sense of time.* The hardest thing in the world—and maybe the easiest—is to be present where you are. That's exactly what Dad was offering.

"The sun is nice," he said.

"It is." I tossed the hat back into the open convertible.

Lord, let me enjoy this day, this moment, to the fullest.
—RICK HAMLIN

Digging Deeper: ROM. 15:32–33

Fri 6

We are confident, yes, well pleased rather to be absent from the body and to be present with the Lord.
—2 CORINTHIANS 5:8 (NKJV)

The sun was streaming through the dining room window as I was putting the finishing touches on getting Miss Brittany, our handicapped daughter, ready for church. If all went well, we would actually be on time for a change.

Then the phone rang. Billy looked at me with a question in his eyes that said, "Should I answer it?" at the same time as he picked up the receiver. I couldn't hear him speaking, but I saw that he had sagged against the wall, with his head nestled on his forearm. I immediately went to his side as he mouthed, "Pick up the phone."

At first, I couldn't recognize the voice of the person at the other end; she was sobbing. As I listened, the horrible truth became clear. It was Billy's younger sister Rose, and the news she shared was devastating. The night before, her youngest son Caleb, only twenty-six years old, was found lying dead by his bed. We listened and tried our best to comfort her, even though our own hearts ached and we couldn't make sense of what had happened any more than she could.

In that moment, we were a small congregation of souls and our "church" was right there where we stood.

Lord, I know that I am Your vessel and that through me, prayers of need, praise and petition can be channeled to Your hands for healing, helping and rejoicing. —PATRICIA PUSEY

Digging Deeper: EPH. 2:19–22

Sat 7   *Rejoice in the Lord always. Again I will say, rejoice!* —PHILIPPIANS 4:4 (NKJV)

My son Solomon is going through a massive growth spurt. The pants we bought just two months ago are already too short. It's not just his body that's growing in leaps and bounds. It's his wants too.

Out of nowhere he's developing new interests. His latest passions are chess and the trumpet. This morning, even though it's Saturday, he woke up at dawn and paced the living room, listing things he wanted to do.

"Solomon, relax," I said.

"But I want to do stuff," he said.

"Go ahead. Today is a free day. We don't have any plans. You can do anything you want."

Solomon groaned. "But I don't want to do what I want to do."

I tried not to smile. "Come here," I said and gave him a big hug.

We sat together in the dining room. I drank my coffee, and he stared at his bowl of cereal. I'm often faced with the exact same problem; I want to do something and yet options paralyze me. I gave him the advice I give myself: "Sometimes when you feel overwhelmed by what to do, the best thing to do is just start something. Begin."

Solomon looked down at his bowl of cereal, and I didn't know if he'd heard me. I got up and started the morning dishes. In minutes, the booming sound of Solomon's trumpet filled the room.

*Dear God, help me to remember choices are a blessing.
Help me to enjoy every moment, especially when I'm
doing what I want to do.* —SABRA CIANCANELLI

Digging Deeper: Ps. 98:4–6

Sun 8

*"Can any of you by worrying add a
single hour to his span of life?"*
—MATTHEW 6:27 (NRSV)

The view from the car window was breathtaking,
but I didn't notice. Kate and I were driving
down from the mountains, returning from a four-
day backpacking trip. We'd left the kids with my
mom at our house. We'd been out of cell phone
range, deep in the backcountry. My mother had
sworn the children would be fine, but by now all
I could think about was how everyone was doing.
Kate glanced at her phone. "No signal yet," she said.

I'd imagined all sorts of mishaps. Benjamin, not
yet two, falling into the pool at the neighborhood
swim center. Frances, almost five, tumbling off the
jungle gym from a daredevil height. What if someone choked on a carrot? Fell off a highchair? My
mom is fit and active and raised her own kids just
fine. But she didn't know our neighborhood well—
we'd only recently moved there. What would she
do in an emergency?

"I have a signal," Kate said. She dialed our number. "Hi, Robin!" I glanced over. Lots of smiling and "Oh, good!" and "What fun!" Kate hung up. "They had a wonderful time. Frances even had a bad dream one night and crawled into bed with your mom. She kept thanking me and said if it wasn't for trips like this, she wouldn't get as much special time with the kids."

I looked out the window. Around us rose the beauty of the Sierra Nevada. I thought of the peaks Kate and I had seen, the lonely mountain passes we'd crossed, the lakes where we'd camped. We'd found precious time together. And my mom and the kids had found their own precious time. No mishaps. But more than that, we'd all been nourished exactly as we needed. Nothing to worry about, indeed.

Lord, help me to trust You always.
—Jim Hinch

Digging Deeper: Ps. 90

Mon 9

They sent a letter unto him. . . . —Ezra 5:7

The first scene in the second act of the play I was stage-managing hinged on the placement of a letter—where it was onstage, which actor grabbed it and moved it, who found it, and what they ulti-mately read in it.

Just after the curtain went up, the props master ran to me in a panic, waving the letter, which he hadn't yet put in place. There was no way to get the crucial prop to the actors, and I couldn't bring the curtain down again. I felt helpless, convinced that there was nothing anyone could do to save the show.

Don, the actor who was to find the letter on the mantelpiece, crossed to his position and, his back to the audience, registered the fact that the letter wasn't there. I saw one moment of confusion on his face and then it was replaced by resolution. He reached out, took hold of nothing at all, turned and kept playing the scene.

The other actors took their cues from him; every-one performed as if the letter was there. I peered around the curtain at the audience to see if anyone was frowning or bewildered, but all the spectators seemed to be involved in the action onstage.

After the lights went down at the end of the first scene, the prop master scurried onstage to set the letter and I called Don over. "How did you do that?" I asked him.

He grinned at me. "I just told myself to believe it was there all along," he said.

How powerful simple belief can be! And acting on it can change the perceptions of everyone around us.

*You teach us belief in small ways as well as big ones,
Lord. Thank You for the gentleness of Your lessons.*
—RHODA BLECKER

Digging Deeper: 1 SAM. 12:24

DIVINE ABUNDANCE

Tue 10

*"What is it?" For they did not know
what it was. And Moses said to
them, "This is the bread which the
Lord has given you to eat."*
—EXODUS 16:15 (NKJV)

How could my children eat so much? Yes, they were healthy, but the weeks that I needed extra cash for a kid repair (broken arm), a car repair (transmission), or clothing replacement ("You *lost* your new winter coat?"), I could barely squeeze out the groceries. I needed a miracle, just as God had provided manna for the Israelites in the desert.

Perhaps it was my complaining about making ends meet that prompted my friend Grandma Margaret to give me the gallon-sized jar of dried pinto beans.

Later that fall, a neighbor cleaned her freezer to prepare for a one-hundred-pound side of beef that she had ordered. She phoned to offer me ten to fifteen pounds of leftover stew meat. "It's still good, but I don't have room. It's great for soups. Come get it if you want it." I went.

Not too long after that, my social worker friend arrived with a crate of cucumbers and another of tomatoes grown at the low-security prison where he worked.

Beans. Meat. Tomatoes. Those seemingly random windfalls enabled me to fill my freezer with cartons of chili, each a hearty family meal. As for the cucumbers? Well, they turned into pickles, thanks to a prison garden and a providential God.

Lord, we thank You for the unexpected ways You nourish us. —GAIL THORELL SCHILLING

Digging Deeper: LUKE 9:10–17

Wed 11

Pray for each other so that you may be healed. . . . —JAMES 5:16 (NIV)

A haunted day, September 11, here in the States that are still United in the wild idea that interindependence is possible and glorious. A shivering day. It always will be. I pray it never becomes a mere anniversary, an event only to remember murder and terror and fire and fear—or even worse, a day only to celebrate vengeance.

No, I pray it becomes a day to remember courage and grace and love. I pray that will someday be the story of September 11.

To remember right is to pray right, says my dad, and he knows about murderous souls; he fought against Hitler. He says to remember the roaring courage of the people who rushed to help, and the people who helped others out of the fire and ash, and the people who used their last minutes on earth to call their families and say, "I love you. I love you. I will love you forever," is to pray for them and us and even for the poor silly murderers, themselves just lanky, frightened boys, in the end, bloody boys terrified of a free world.

He says to remember the firemen who ran up, knowing they would never come down, the passengers storming the cockpit, the sergeant who ran out of the Pentagon to catch women leaping from high windows is the way to erase the name of the chief murderer.

He says that if we remember right, if we pray with our hearts in our mouths, maybe someday no one will remember the architect of ruin, but everyone will remember a day when the courage and mercy and glory of human beings rose to such a tide that no one will ever forget.

That could happen, says my dad, and who will gainsay my dad? Not I.

Dear Lord, for the murdered, our prayers. For the murderers, our prayers. For us, frightened and muddled, prayers. For the courage to remember right, to witness and sing grace under duress, to someday find the country of forgiveness, prayers.
—BRIAN DOYLE

Digging Deeper: MATT. 5:38–48

Thu 12

The righteous care for the needs of their animals. . . .
—PROVERBS 12:10 (NIV)

Meow! Meow! Meow!
My husband and I exchanged glances to be sure we'd both heard it. The kitty was back.

She'd appear on the back porch of our apartment and whine until we came out. Then she'd rub against our ankles and climb into our laps, eager for a scratch behind the ears or a thorough belly rub.

As the weeks went on, we named her Olivia and took to bringing her dishes of warm milk before bed. As a "dog person," I was surprised at my growing love for this kitty. "This must be what new parents feel like," I found myself saying to Brian. "How can I be totally in love with this kitten I don't even know?"

Fall quickly turned into winter and, even in Florida, it was too cold for a tiny kitty. Our only option, it seemed, was to call the local animal patrol. It broke my heart to think of Olivia mewing all alone at night!

Our landlord, who felt her own fondness for Olivia, called a few nights later and said she'd found a home for our kitty with a good family who had long wished for a pet. They came for Olivia that night.

Brian and I were heartbroken. "She's so much happier sleeping in a big bed with her new family," he said. I knew he was right.

Still, I felt that I was getting a lesson straight from God's book of love. He, too, had loved and lost in order to allow much greater things to happen. *If I can feel this way about a cat*, I thought, *then I can only imagine the depth and strength of God's love for each of us.*

Thank You, Lord, for friends and family, both human and those of the fur-covered variety. Experiencing their love allows us a glimpse into the abundance that awaits us in heaven. —ASHLEY KAPPEL

Digging Deeper: 1 COR. 2:9–11

Fri 13

*See what great love the Father has lavished on us, that we should be called children of God! And that is what we are!... —*1 JOHN 3:1 (TNIV)

Your girls always seem so perfect!" one friend recently told me.

They are, alas, far from perfect. True, they've outgrown their childhood rivalries and are now good friends. And they work hard in school. In fact, in public they seem nice enough.

But I'm no stranger to their malice or to the baffling rages and malevolent silences of teenagerdom. Almost daily, they reveal my failures as a parent, and I find myself regretting the spared rod, the indulgence with which I have placated them, the robe and ring I proffer after one of their temporary returns to civility.

In my own childhood, I think, *I'd never have gotten away with such behavior.*

But I remember, with the clarity of my present shame, an afternoon from my last year of high school. I sat at the game table in the family room with my mom, sharing a salad, and can still feel the hatred heave within me, like nausea. If hatred really is, as the Apostle John suggests, tantamount to murder, I murdered my mother in that moment. Her crime? Chewing too loudly.

Scripture reveals a divine parent who suffers our meannesses just as we do our own children's. The Father of creation, like the father in Jesus' story of two sons—one a squanderer, the other a complainer—suffers on our behalf. That's the God I go to when my children plague me: the God Who knows our worst crimes and loves us still.

Holy Father, help me forgive and love and grow those in my charge, just as You forgive and love and grow me daily. —Patty Kirk

Digging Deeper: 1 John 4:7–11, 17–21

Sat 14

The heavens are telling the glory of God; and the firmament proclaims his handiwork. —Psalm 19:1

"If any of you wakes up and sees the aurora borealis, give me a poke," I ordered, climbing into my sleeping bag.

Eight of us had decided to take the ferry out of Skagway, Alaska, our summer employment over and all of us going our separate ways once we hit Bellingham, Washington. We'd taken the chaise lounges and lined them up next to each other in the solarium where we'd sleep, under the heat lamps and looking out over the ship's open stern. The *Columbia* pulled out at 7:45 PM and after setting up our bags, we cozied into our row of chairs, watching our happy home of five months disappear into the distance.

"I haven't seen the lights all summer," I told my best friend as I zipped in.

"I'll wake you," Nick promised.

Next thing I knew, he was jostling me. There they were. Circling the sky, silhouetting the shoreline, reflecting in dimpled light off the ocean. I stumbled to my feet, shivering, and headed for the rail. All of us stood in the magic light dancing silently in the heavens.

There are no words to define the swirling, twisting light that overtakes a starry night. Awe took our breath, closed our throats; we could not speak in the sacred. My friends, I knew, had all grown disenchanted with God—some more than others—yet here was heaven declaring God's glory, speaking to me and, in some mysterious way, to them.

I went to bed thrilled, the heavens silent with the voice of God.

Truly, heaven declares Your glory, God—silent declaration that speaks to me, my friends and the world. —BRENDA WILBEE

Digging Deeper: Ps. 8

Sun 15

Do not move an ancient boundary stone....
—PROVERBS 23:10 (NIV)

We are gathered around the cooking hut fire on a rural Zimbabwe farm. In the circle are men, women and many children, all a part of the Village Hope family. We have come on our yearly visit to enjoy the progress that's taking place in the community. Paddington, the father of Village Hope, is talking earnestly to the children about their "golden opportunities," as he calls them. "You must focus on your studies and set boundaries around your schoolwork."

Some days later, before heading back to the United States, my husband David and I stop off at Victoria Falls, one of the seven natural wonders of the world. Lying along Zimbabwe's northern border, the falls are the largest in the world. We are transfixed by the constant mist that creates a lush rainforest at the top of the falls and then by the constant roar that grows louder and louder, leaving no doubt as to the reason the Shona people call it the "water that thunders."

Though I'm a fairly fearless person, I am terrified to discover the dangers that lurk around the falls. In a place that lacks government regulations, there are few guard rails and other safety precautions to ensure security. We learn that each year many people, mesmerized by the grandeur of the scene, step too close to the edge and fall to their deaths.

I am reminded of Paddington's constant encouragement to the Village Hope children. His words become stellar advice for us all.

We look to You, Father. Make Your loving boundaries ever clear. —PAM KIDD

Digging Deeper: JOHN 14:15–24

THE GIFT OF TREES

Mon 16   *The word of the Lord came to me saying, "What do you see, Jeremiah?" And I said, "I see a rod of an almond tree."*
—JEREMIAH 1:11 (NAS)

The poetic Hebrew name for the almond tree is Awakening One. It is the first tree to flower, in late January or early February. White blossoms, tinted pink, cover branches still bare from winter.

You wouldn't think anything could flower on a bare branch. Perhaps such a miraculous sight is why God included the almond motif in His instructions to Moses for making the tabernacle's golden lampstand. Its cups were opened almond blossoms hammered in gold.

God sent me a flowering almond branch once when I struggled with a costly decision. In California, after Sunday worship in a large cathedral, I sat alone and bereft, head bowed. I felt a hand on my shoulder and heard a woman say, "I don't know what it is, but I'm praying for you."

I invited her to sit with me. She listened and offered comforting words. When she stood to leave I asked her name. "Carol," she answered. Startled, I asked her middle name. "Anne," she replied.

"Does it have an *e*?" I continued.

"Yes," she said.

When the Lord showed Jeremiah the almond branch, He said to him, "You have seen well, for I am watching over My word to perform it" (Jeremiah 1:12).

I believe it. God sent an older, wiser Carol Anne to this Carol Anne, to show me I could get it right.

Heavenly Father, Who watches over me, truly there is flowering on a bare branch and in a barren heart.
—CAROL KNAPP

Digging Deeper: ISA. 40

LISTENING TO MY LIFE

Tue 17

"To everything there is a season, and a time and a purpose under heaven."
—ECCLESIASTES 3:1

DAY I: A NEW SEASON

It was near midnight in central Texas as September merged into October. The sky was infinite black, yet glowing with stars, as I looked for my lost and comforting friend, the constellation Orion. This great hunter in the sky slips beyond sight in spring but always returns in fall as frost covers prairie land. Since childhood, Orion has been my symbol of the faithful presence of God amidst the change of seasons.

After nearly forty years of being a pastor, I sensed that a new season was approaching in my life and that I would soon shepherd sheep in a far different pasture. I slipped into dialogue with one of my mentors, Dr. Daniel Levinson, who wrote *The Seasons of a Man's Life.* Levinson taught me that our lives naturally flow through four major seasons: "birth through adolescence," "young adulthood," "middle adulthood" and "late adulthood." As we transition between these seasons, we are often challenged to make significant adjustments in our personal, professional and spiritual lives.

My wife Beth and I knew we wanted to spend our remaining professional years on a university campus, helping young adults discover their sense of purpose and vocational dreams. We did not know how we would get there. It often seemed like a far-fetched dream. But we did know that our Good Shepherd, Who created Orion, would guide us into the joy and promise of the beckoning unknown.

Dear Father, when in the midst of change and new directions, may I fear no evil for You are with me. Amen. —SCOTT WALKER

Digging Deeper: Ps. 23

LISTENING TO MY LIFE

Wed 18

Listen to Me . . . And pay attention. . . .
—ISAIAH 49:1 (NAS)

DAY 2: HEARING THE VOICE OF GOD

As I struggled for vocational and spiritual direction, a friend placed a small book in my hands that spoke with the quiet voice of seasoned wisdom. In *Let Your Life Speak: Listening for the Voice of Vocation*, Parker Palmer writes: "Before you tell your life what you intend to do with it, listen for what it intends to do with you."

At age fifty-seven, I was listening to a heavy voice that droned, "You have been a pastor for more than thirty years and you will finish the course to retirement!" However, another voice was shouting, "Listen, Scott! The most important thing to do in the years ahead is to help university students dream dreams and see visions."

Ironically, our church was located several blocks from Baylor University. The pastoral demands of a large church greatly limited my time with students, so to remedy this situation, my wife Beth and I started a Bible study for them, which met in our home each Wednesday night. Soon dozens of students were dropping by for coffee, dessert, friendship and Bible study. I was finally engaging them in a way that was meaningful, enjoyable and effective.

Wednesday nights were the most pleasurable hours of my week, and I now had to ask, "What is my life saying to me? What is God saying to me? Why do I feel so fulfilled now?"

Father, help me to listen to my life and pay attention. Amen. —Scott Walker

Digging Deeper: Jer. 29:11–13

LISTENING TO MY LIFE

Thu 19

"For the eyes of the Lord range throughout the earth to strengthen those whose hearts are fully committed to him. . . ."
—2 Chronicles 16:9 (NIV)

DAY 3: DISCOVERING GREAT GLADNESS

One day while writing a sermon, I stumbled across the words of a favorite author and minister, Frederick Buechner. In reflecting on his long life of seeking God's leadership, Buechner writes in *Wishful Thinking: A Theological ABC*, "The place God calls you to be is the place where your deep gladness and the world's great hunger meet."

This short sentence grasped me and set me free. At age fifty-seven, I knew that my deep gladness was working with young adults. I also sensed that the world's greatest hunger is for an emerging generation to live with passion, purpose and vision. In the convergence of these forces, I sensed I would discover "the place God calls you to."

The most wonderful thing about Buechner's words, however, was a spiritual invitation that exulted, "Don't be compelled to do what you should do, ought to do, must do, have to do, don't want to do. Rather, get in touch with your great gladness and be free to go do it."

It was hard for me to believe that our loving God wanted me to focus my life on what brings me the greatest joy, but I was certain this is what it means "to be about my Father's business."

Dear Father, put me in touch with my great gladness. And may I have the courage to embrace joy. Amen.
—Scott Walker

Digging Deeper: Ps. 16

LISTENING TO MY LIFE

Fri 20

Where there is no vision, the people perish.... —PROVERBS 29:18

DAY 4: WRITING MY DREAMS

It is one thing to decide that you are going to change directions and move into a new chapter of life. It is quite another thing to discern how to make such a transition. As I anxiously paced the floor of my church office, I recalled a book I read shortly before college graduation when I was a nervous young man seeking a job. Written by Richard Bolles, *What Color Is Your Parachute?* is now a classic work.

Bolles posits that when you decide to alter your vocation, the last thing you should do is search the want ads. Rather, you should take a good look at yourself, define what brings you great gladness, and write your own proposal and job description. Then, go find someone who needs your skills and believes in your dream.

Based on Bolles' thesis, I wrote a proposal for what I termed an Institute of Life Purpose to be located on a university campus. The institute would offer academic courses, seminars, counseling and international service experiences to help young adults clarify their talents and life-dreams.

I made appointments with two universities, and my alma mater, Mercer University in Macon, Georgia, expressed interest. If I could raise the funds to start the institute, they would invite the Institute of Life Purpose to be part of the university. Taking a deep breath, I accepted the challenge.

Father, may bright hope overcome deep fear. Amen.
—SCOTT WALKER

Digging Deeper: JOEL 2:27–29

LISTENING TO MY LIFE

Sat 21

"He who loves his life loses it, and he who hates his life in this world will keep it to life eternal."
—JOHN 12:25 (NAS)

DAY 5: STEPPING OUT IN FAITH

I resigned as pastor of First Baptist Church of Waco, Texas, on my fifteenth anniversary. As I stood to read my letter of resignation and preach my final sermon, I scanned the familiar faces across the congregation. So many memories converged at once: marriages, funerals, counseling sessions, baby dedications, baptisms and all of the things involved in a pastor's life.

For a moment, things seemed surreal. Then I remembered the words of the young Danish philosopher Soren Kierkegaard: "During periods of a man's life, the greatest danger is not to take the risk." Despite fear and anxiety, I knew it was time to make my decision public, to pass the point of no return.

Many times it is best to choose caution over risk. There is real danger in the world, and to throw stability and practicality to the wind is frequently foolish. However, there are rare moments when wisdom and faith demand risk. In these times we must hope and love and put our trust in the goodness of life and the faithfulness of God.

> *Father, help me to know when to be cautious and when to take risk. Amen.*
> —SCOTT WALKER

Digging Deeper: Ps. 37:3–5, 23–26

LISTENING TO MY LIFE

Sun 22   *And Moses said... "Gather of it every man as much as he should eat.... Let no man leave any of it until morning."*
—EXODUS 16:15–16, 19 (NAS)

DAY 6: GOD'S GRACIOUS PROVISION

The day after I resigned as pastor, I woke up early in a cold panic. My next task was to raise funds to start the Institute of Life Purpose!

As I squirmed and pondered my dilemma, the phone rang. It was a friend calling to invite me to lunch. He had no idea that I had resigned, and when I told him, he nearly dropped the phone. "Well, you've done it now! What in the world are you going to do?" So I told him my story and shared my dream. He listened and said, "That sounds like a worthy cause and a wonderful idea. I would like to help you do this."

I was awestruck! I had nothing to do with the phone ringing that morning. I never would have initiated the conversation. But God had a way of saying, "You can do this! I am working with you."

It has now been more than three years since that phone call. There have been moments when finances have grown low and I have doubted God's sustaining ability. However, like the Hebrew children crossing the Sinai desert toward a promised land, I have learned that God gives manna only one day at a time. And when I grumble and demand long-term security, I lose vitality and spirit. God leads in the present moment, and God's way is the only way to escape slavery and discover freedom.

Father, thank You for giving food for this day. May I not doubt Your provision for tomorrow. Amen.
—Scott Walker

Digging Deeper: Heb. 11

LISTENING TO MY LIFE

Mon 23

"Lord, make me to know . . . the measure of my days. . . . "
—Psalm 39:4

DAY 7: LIFE TO THE FULL

I am increasingly aware of how fast the years are passing. Just last week, while sitting with my family around the dinner table, we celebrated my mother's ninetieth birthday and I turned sixty-one. We smiled at each other, eyes moist, grateful for the years shared together. And yet, I was keenly aware we will not live forever.

In my current freshman class at Mercer University titled "Composing the Self," my students spend a semester reviewing the first eighteen years of their lives. Yesterday, we read a poem by Mary Oliver, "The Summer Day," which depicts a young woman resting in a lush green pasture as she encounters a small grasshopper attached to her sweater. Holding the small insect tenderly in her hand, she gazes into its "enormous and complicated eyes" and realizes that the insect will live only a few more weeks until summer turns to fall. As the grasshopper snaps her wings and floats away, the girl whispers, "Doesn't everything die at last, and too soon? Tell me, what is it you plan to do with your one wild and precious life?"

This is the most important question for us all: my ninety-year-old mother, her sixty-one-year-old son, my twenty-three-year-old daughter, my college freshman students.

Sometimes a singer has only one song, a preacher one sermon, a writer one book and a prophet one vision. Life is drawn into narrow and intense focus. Now I know that my one question for each person I meet is "What is your dream for your one precious life?" Each answer will shape the course of history.

Father, inspire me to know how to live the years that are before me. Amen.
—SCOTT WALKER

Digging Deeper: JOHN 12:27–36

LISTENING TO MY LIFE

Tue 24   *By love serve one another.*
—GALATIANS 5:13

DAY 8: WORKING FOR GOODNESS AND JUSTICE

Yesterday, I woke up on the wrong side of the bed, and as I walked to meet a recent Mercer University graduate for lunch, I asked God for the gift of encouragement.

Alicia is a brilliant young woman who attended law school for several semesters. However, she increasingly felt that this course of study was not joining her unique talents to the world's greatest need. Perplexed and discouraged, she read about a new program started by the Institute of Life Purpose called Service First, which connects Mercer's graduates to international service projects for one year.

Alicia applied to Service First and was sent to teach English as a second language to elementary and high school students in Thailand. For nine months, she lived in Bangkok and experienced a world she had not known. She soon realized that her deepest desire was to help political refugees, women abused by sex trafficking, and those who are most marginalized and helpless.

As Alicia talked about this new clarification of her life-dream, I felt my mood lift. My spirit and Alicia's spirit and God's Spirit were working together. I saw how the opportunity to spend one year beyond college discovering "the world's greatest hunger" was empowering a young woman to work for goodness and justice long after my life is a dim memory.

This morning, as I wrote a letter of recommendation for Alicia to attend a graduate school specializing in international aid and human rights issues, I smiled. God did grant my prayer for encouragement, and I was the one most uplifted.

> *Father, may we believe that all things work together for good. Amen.* —SCOTT WALKER

> *Digging Deeper:* I COR. 15:58, 16:13–14

Wed 25

Be transformed by the renewing of your mind....
—ROMANS 12:2 (NIV)

I had a disagreement with a friend several weeks ago. Since then, God has been nudging me to have a healing, eye-to-eye conversation with her, and I've resisted, filled with all sorts of excuses about why I don't need to. After all, time heals all wounds, right?

But God wouldn't let my rebellion win, so I finally asked my friend to join me for coffee and she agreed.

So here we are today at the coffee shop, seated across from each other at a little round table. It's cold and blustery outside, but the coffee cup is warm in my hands. We sit and sip, and at first our conversation feels a bit awkward. Gradually, we go back to that time and place and start to untangle parts of it. I try to explain myself and apologize for getting emotional. We agree that we don't want to get stuck in this broken place; we want to move forward. Eventually, we're even able to laugh at our fallibilities, which we often try to hide. Finally, we pray, hug and head for home.

I sit still behind the steering wheel for a few moments, wondering why I resisted God's nudges so long, because being on the other side of this kind of open-hearted conversation not only humbles me, but also brings me freedom and hope and the potential for a more meaningful friendship.

Lord, even though Your way may not always feel like the easy way, it is the right way and makes me both a receiver and giver of Your grace.
—CAROL KUYKENDALL

Digging Deeper: MATT. 5:21–26

Thu 26

I am the Lord. . . . I am with you and will watch over you wherever you go. . . .
—GENESIS 28:13, 15 (NIV)

I'd just checked into a small guesthouse in Chicago, where I was attending a retreat and was eager to catch my first-ever glimpse of Lake

September

Michigan. Impulsively, I set out on my own, knowing I had to get back soon. It was an easy five-block walk, and there was the lake stretching as far as the eye could see.

On my way back to the retreat center, I saw what I took to be a parallel street to mine. For a while I enjoyed the scenery, counting the blocks that, in my mind, would connect with the street I wanted. But when I turned left, I couldn't find it. I turned this way and that, and in my fear and confusion, I couldn't remember the address of the guesthouse. I had no purse, no money, no identification. Exhausted and fighting tears, I sat on a bench. "Lord, help me," I prayed.

Go back to the lake, I plainly heard.

But I must be miles away, I thought.

And yet, when I asked someone how to get to Lake Michigan, she told me I was very close. "These streets can be disorienting," she said.

Sure enough, I followed her directions and was soon at the lake. A short block away was the street from which I'd come. I walked to the end of the pier. Waves slapped; fish jumped; sailboats glided. *Thank You for bringing me back*, I whispered.

Just minutes ago I'd felt hopelessly lost. But here, in the immensity of sky and water, surrounded by the largesse of the Creator, I felt the security of knowing that no matter how far I roam, I could never be lost from God.

Father, when I lose my way, You are there!
—SHARI SMYTH

Digging Deeper: Ps. 31:21–24

Fri 27

Blessed is the man who listens to me, watching daily at my gates, waiting at the posts of my doors.
—PROVERBS 8:34 (NKJV)

Thanks to my work as a journalist, I've logged hundreds of miles on America's roads in recent months. I've driven across century-old wooden covered bridges in Vermont, gazed at white-laced mountains in Colorado, and skirted fields abundant with amber waves of grain in Iowa. Months after I visited Cape Cod in Massachusetts, I'm still finding grains of sand in my car.

One of my favorite parts of the landscape is the church sign. Some stick to the basics; I've seen lots that say, "God Loves You!" Many cite Scripture; John 3:16 is popular everywhere. The best ones are both witty and provocative. When I drove past Victory Rock Church in Warsaw, Indiana, theirs read: "Your Sanctuary? The Local Church or the Town Bar?"

The most memorable I've seen was at Greenwood Baptist Church in Valdosta, Georgia, which decided to tackle a modern addiction: social media. The sign declared, "Get Off of Facebook and into My Book."

Now, I have something of a Facebook habit. The Web site has quickly become a modern-day meeting place where I can reconnect with people from various stages of my life. In many ways, it's a terrific thing—a twenty-first-century way of cultivating community.

But am I investing a commensurate amount of time in my relationship with God? I can spend hours looking at photos from someone else's family reunion or Facebook messages, but how much time am I spending with a more time-honored message—the one God gives through Scripture? Yes, the sign is a vital reminder for an online junkie like me: I ought to log in where it really matters.

God, I know You're there, waiting to hear from me.
Help me to think of You—not updating my
Facebook status—first.—Jeff Chu

Digging Deeper: Ps. 119:9–16

Sat 28

"Heaven and earth will pass away,
but my words will never pass away."
—Matthew 24:35 (niv)

I was slightly out of breath, having come up a long winding path, then climbed the eighty marble steps to the top of the Acropolis in Athens. Now I gazed in awe at the central votive monument, the Parthenon, a Doric masterpiece, temple of Athena, the patron goddess of the ancient city, and certainly one of the most recognizable buildings in all the world.

We had spent the last two days of this Guideposts Holy Lands Tour tracing the path of the Apostle Paul. In Ephesus, Turkey, I viewed the massive amphitheatre where he preached after being banned from the Jewish temple. In Corinth, we toured the ruins of the marketplace where again Paul had shared the story of Jesus.

I knew the story of Paul, itinerant tent-maker. But until I walked in his footsteps and understood the distances he traveled and the unforgiving terrain, the danger and the hardships, I did not truly apprehend the fire that blazed in his soul.

Our guide now pointed to a spot in front of the Parthenon. "It would be logical that Paul preached from this location, directly before the temple entrance."

I let my gaze drift high above me, above the iconic colonnade, to the crumbling remnants of the once magnificent frieze. Even now the Parthenon was imposing. Imagine how impressive it must have been in all its glory to this simple tent-maker. What faith it must have taken to mount the steps of these perfect edifices and tell a strange new story of resurrection and redemption, about humankind's relationship to a singular and all-loving God. It took more than faith and bravery, it took a divine imagination.

Yes, the ruins of the Parthenon still stand; the tents Paul sewed have long crumbled to dust. But the words he preached still change the world.

Lord, You ask us to carry Your message of salvation and eternal life. Make me worthy to bear Your word.
—EDWARD GRINNAN

Digging Deeper: EPH. 1–6

Sun 29

And He sat down, called the twelve, and said to them, "If anyone desires to be first, he shall be last of all and servant of all."—MARK 9:35 (NKJV)

I stared at the blank document on my computer. *I've done it again. I've overextended myself.* I certainly didn't have to accept the chairmanship of a nonprofit board, but I had.

Growing up I had often heard about the Martha O'Bryan Center; it had been serving the less fortunate of our community for more than 120 years.

They don't really need me, I argued with myself. With a great staff and strong supporters, it would continue to prosper. The chunk of time required of me wouldn't make a huge difference in its operation. *Why do I feel called?*

These thoughts ran through my mind as I prepared a talk for the board's annual retreat. I was missing work, my wife Corinne was joyously pregnant, and my son Harrison was scheduled for his first touch-football practice. *What have I gotten myself into?*

In desperation, I called Christine, a staff member at Martha O'Bryan. "What message would you like for me to stress?" I asked.

"Brock, if the board members knew what was here *for them*, they would run to it."

For them? I thought, leaning back in my chair. *For me? What did a charitable organization have to give me and the other board members?* We were prominent folks with big houses, fancy cars and impressive ZIP codes.

I felt a bit of shame then. Happiness isn't a natural byproduct of wealth or prominence. Happiness comes with serving others. Of course, in God's clever way, the chairmanship was a gift. God was giving me the opportunity to serve or, as the Bible so aptly points out, to be happy.

Father, help me step past my smaller self and run to the joys of serving Your children. —BROCK KIDD

Digging Deeper: GEN. 33:4–6

September

Mon 30

"If you then, being evil, know how to give good gifts to your children, how much more will your Father who is in heaven give good things to those who ask Him!"
—MATTHEW 7:11 (NKJV)

L ast month my entire family—my parents, two brothers, sister, and I—went on vacation to Alaska. My mother planned all the details of our itinerary, and towards the end of the week she informed us that our last day would be spent driving through a national park. On a school bus. On a gravel road. For fourteen hours.

Mind you, it was a round trip; we were going to be dropped off at the same place we were picked up. There was no destination. We would just be looking out the windows at passing mountains and wildlife.

Don't get me wrong: Alaska is beautiful. We were fortunate to be there. But fourteen hours on a school bus?

As a person who reads a lot of devotional stories, at this point you're probably expecting me to tell you that we went on the trip and I saw God's creation and it was the best fourteen hours of my life. Well, yes. But maybe not for the reasons you'd expect. The mountains were amazing, certainly, but after about eight hours they all start to look the same.

What made the day fun and special was that the whole family was there, crammed into three benches on the back of the bus. We talked. We laughed. We were together.

God's most beautiful creation, as it turns out, is a loving family.

Lord, thank You for creating my family.
—Joshua Sundquist

Digging Deeper: 1 Pet. 3:8–12

GIVING THANKS

1 _____

2 _____

3 _____

4 _____

5 _____

6 _____

7 _____

8 _____

9 _____

10 _____

11 _____

September

12 _____

13 _____

14 _____

15 _____

16 _____

17 _____

18 _____

19 _____

20 _____

21 _____

22 _____

23 _____

24 _____

25 _____

26 _____

27 _____

28 _____

29 _____

30 _____

October

Jesus then took the loaves,
and when he had given thanks,
he distributed them to those who were seated.
So also the fish, as much as they wanted.

—JOHN 6:11 (ESV)

OPERATION THANKFULNESS

Tue 1   *Blessed are all who take refuge in him.*
—PSALM 2:12 (NIV)

When my sister Susan and I dropped by to see Aunt Josie at her assisted-living center, we found her room locked. "She's been transferred to a nursing home to get over a serious lung infection," the attendant told us. When we got to Aunt Josie's temporary home, it was absolutely dismal. Because of her hasty transfer, the bare room didn't have a single decoration—not a get-well card, not even a TV! There was exactly one personal item on top of the utilitarian dresser: Aunt Josie's Bible, which she'd had for decades, looking much the worse for wear in its limp white-eyelet cover edged in lace.

We bent down and hugged Aunt Josie as she lay in bed in the empty, cheerless room. Then the room fell silent. "Would you like for me to read some Scriptures?" I asked. Aunt Josie nodded.

As I opened her Bible to the Psalms, my eyes fell on large-print words lined with yellow highlighter Aunt Josie had added over the years to emphasize her favorite passages. I proceeded to read only the verses she had highlighted, and as I did, the linoleum floors echoed an incredibly beautiful collection of cleansing confession, glorious promises and beautiful praise. My spirits lifted as the words from Aunt Josie's marvelous, personalized treasury of grace filled the room.

As we hugged and kissed her good-bye and walked out the door, I knew we weren't leaving Aunt Josie alone. I was thankful that the Bible can turn even the most bare, utilitarian place into a beautiful haven of peace and comfort.

Father, thank You for Your living words in the Bible that fill even the emptiest of places with Your comforting presence. Amen.
—KAREN BARBER

Digging Deeper: LUKE 11:28; REV. 1:2–3

Wed 2

"The Lord is my helper; I will not be afraid. . . ."
—HEBREWS 13:6 (NRSV)

A rustle in the brush. I jumped. My heart raced. I was taking a chance, running in the hills near our house where more than one person had warned me mountain lions prowl in the early morning. I was here, hoping the beauty might calm my anxieties about the day. Work, kids, life—always something to worry about.

And now mountain lions. I froze. About twenty feet ahead the grass shook and then a small fawn poked its head out and stepped gingerly across the trail. Mama deer followed; three more fawns waited to cross the trail. Suddenly, the deer realized I was there. Five tawny heads turned and stared. Mama deer stared hardest. Three of her babies were behind her across the trail. What should she do? Go back for them, abandoning the fawn beside her?

For a full minute, we all looked at one another. The morning light grew and the breeze stirred. Mama deer's eyes met mine, and in that instant I knew exactly how she felt. What parent doesn't know those times of utter helplessness, when you realize you are no match for the big world your children are heading into?

"Go on," I said out loud, hoping to startle the three fawns into action. For a few seconds they remained motionless. Then with fluid leaps they bounded across the road. The moment they landed, mama deer led them bolting down the hillside. They disappeared into the brush. I resumed running. My own kids would probably be awake when I got home. Another day was beginning. *Go on*, I seemed to hear God say, *I'm here.*

God, help me live without fear. —JIM HINCH

Digging Deeper: Ps. 18:30–36

Thu 3

Thou preparest a table before me in the presence of mine enemies....
—Psalm 23:5

"T hese potatoes are awful!" I complained about our college cafeteria food, but one of my farm-grown students called me out.

"You should spend a summer on the farm," he said. "Then you would see food in a new light."

"Oh, how's that?" I reached for my glass of milk.

"Well, take that milk you are drinking. I have to get up at 4:00 AM to milk the cows and go out again at 4:00 PM, every day of the week."

I took a bite out of my hamburger.

"You should witness a butchering, and see what goes into making one hamburger." He scooped up a forkful of corn. "And these veggies? The deer and the raccoons can clean out an entire stand of corn in one night." He reached for the green beans. "And the bean beetles can reduce an entire row of beans to stems in twenty-four hours."

"Wow, that must be discouraging."

"There's more. The blight usually gets the tomatoes in August, and the rabbits eat the peas as fast as they ripen. Not to mention a dozen evil weeds that choke out everything. And you can spend days just reading all the government regulations on raising food to sell."

The girl sitting beside me chimed in. "I work in food preparation. It's the hardest job I have ever had. I wish every student had to work in the kitchen for one week."

They were ganging up on me! "So you're telling me that a plate of food is a rather amazing thing, is that it?"

"Pretty close to a miracle," the boy concluded.

I reached for the saltshaker. "You know, I think these potatoes just need a little seasoning."

Lord, forgive me for complaining about the flavor of Your miracles. —DANIEL SCHANTZ

Digging Deeper: GEN. 41

Fri 4

"You are worthy, O Lord, To receive glory and honor and power; For You created all things, And by Your will they exist and were created."
—REVELATION 4:11 (NKJV)

The first Friday in October was always special for me. I left my office early, with a spring in my step, headed for the annual Boston Globe Book Festival at the John B. Hynes Auditorium. I crept through the rush-hour traffic, concerned I might miss an outstanding speaker. I had to find a parking space, grab a bite to eat and get to the auditorium.

One evening I saw Archibald MacLeish, who possessed forty-six years of poetic creativity, and his dear friend Ogden Nash, the famed humor writer. MacLeisch conducted the introduction, and Nash read his rollicking poetry and even confessed he had a tooth extracted hours before. Being there and listening to side-splitting poetry about people, insects and situations lifted my spirits and inspired me for days.

But the festivals are no more. Mounting costs, dwindling parking spaces and scheduling problems ended this wonderful event. I will always be grateful for the festivals that were held. Where else could I hear and enjoy actor Anthony Quinn, humorist Erma Bombeck, the Baroness Maria von Trapp and Maya Angelou, all in one short evening of joy?

Father, the lessons learned at the festival will be remembered for years to come. May those who listened appreciate You more. —OSCAR GREENE

Digging Deeper: DEUT. 32:1–3

Sat 5   *There is no fear in love; but perfect love casteth out fear....* —1 JOHN 4:18

Our son John had only one thing on his wish list that wasn't electronic. When he struggled with his feelings at school, a therapy dog had brought him comfort and companionship, and he wanted one of his own. We had boarded dogs for a week over the last two summers to see how our other kids would take to a canine companion. They took.

I, however, was another thing entirely. A nip when I was two had given me a fear of dogs. And then there was the matter of sociability: Dogs are extroverts and the proper pets for extroverts; not for an introvert like me. But listening to John talk about dogs and seeing the delight of the other children with our boarders softened me up.

Julia and I made a deal with John. If he'd make the effort to do well at his new school, we'd get him a dog. Julia checked local shelters on the Internet and found Amsterdam, a yellow Lab/golden retriever mix, ten months old, housebroken, neutered and friendly.

Now I can be seen most days at our local dog run, watching Amsterdam find his place in our neighborhood canine society and taking my own tentative steps into the society of owners. I'm still not used to being greeted at the door by a nuzzle and a wagging tail, but I'm growing to love it.

And John? His first report card came a week after Amsterdam. He earned his dog!

Lord, thank You for using Amsterdam to remind me
that my heart need never stop growing.
—ANDREW ATTAWAY

Digging Deeper: GEN. 1:23–25

Sun 6

For every beast of the forest is mine,
and the cattle upon a thousand hills.
—PSALM 50:10

Most days, rain or shine, I take my German shepherd Elijah walking in what I call "my place." It's a beautiful, solitary, overgrown trail, winding between the Harpeth River and a weather-beaten cliff where, I'm told, a pair of bald eagles once nested.

One morning, under a cloudless blue sky, I was walking and counting my blessings, thanking God for all the things that are mine, including my place and Elijah, who was chasing small prey and marking territory in the time-honored fashion of his kind. When I'd finished my praying, I walked along in contented silence. A line from a verse dropped into my heart in that still, small voice I knew as God's:

Walk humbly with your God.

"What are You saying to me, Lord?" I asked. But all I heard were birds and the crunching of leaves under my feet. Finally, I came to the river, clear and sparkling, a playground for Elijah. He rushed in, leaping and splashing, lost in his play. Above me yellow and gold leaves danced in the air. *The moment is so perfect! I wish I could roll it up and keep it for myself!* And that's when the blinders fell off, and I saw it written everywhere: in the sky, the trees, the river, in every blessing I'd been counting.

"Walk humbly with your God" means trusting Him enough that if tomorrow I lose it all, I know that in God I still have everything.

Father, as Your child, I hold tightly to Your hand, but lightly to what You give. —SHARI SMYTH

Digging Deeper: EXOD. 19:4–6

Mon 7

Through him then let us continually offer up a sacrifice of praise to God, that is, the fruit of lips that acknowledge his name.
—HEBREWS 13:15 (ESV)

Staring back at me from the bathroom floor is a pile of dirty clothes. Specifically, size-large gym shorts, one sweaty workout shirt, an undershirt, well-worn briefs and haphazardly balled-up socks. As usual, the mass of neglected garments sits not inside but *beside* the hamper, clear evidence that my husband has been on the scene.

Today, as I stare back at the messy mound, I fold my arms across my chest and smile. Laugh, even. I catch myself elbowing past annoyance and choosing gratitude instead.

I once heard a radio talk-show host doling out advice to a sourpuss bride who had called to tattle on her clutter-hound husband. "It sounds to me like you've got two options," the host said. "You can live in happiness with a sometimes-frustrating husband or you can live in sparkling cleanliness alone." The comment went deep, both for the caller and for me.

Besides the relationship between humankind and God, marriage is the only covenantal bond noted in Scripture. Which I assume means it's a connection prized by God. I want my attitudes and my actions to show that I prize it as well, and I'm realizing more and more that part of how that gets worked out in my life is by knowing what things to focus on and what things can stand to be overlooked.

And so despite occasional golf clubs in the kitchen, spare sunflower seeds dotting the floorboard of the car, unwashed dishes left stacked in the home office and derelict duds strewn about the bathroom floor, I thank my heavenly Father for giving me a man to know and be known by, to love and be loved by, to serve and to be served by each day. My darling husband may be prone to untidiness, but untidy companionship carries a certain appeal when it involves such a magnificent human being.

> *Thank You, Lord, for eyes to see an abundance of*
> *blessings all around.* —ASHLEY WIERSMA

Digging Deeper: ESTHER 1:19–21

Tue 8

As the Scriptures say, "If you want to boast, boast only about the Lord." When people commend themselves, it doesn't count for much. The important thing is for the Lord to commend them.
—2 CORINTHIANS 10:17–18 (NLT)

I was staying over at a friend's house and helped put her two pajama-clad boys to sleep. But first, I was touched as I listened to them say their prayers, in which they blessed everyone from Uncle Bob ("He's a soldier, you know, God.") to Twinkie, their pet yellow canary. I went to sleep with a smile, after I'd said my own prayers. *Her life seems so picture-perfect, Lord. I wish I had a beautiful house.*

The next morning, I was impressed when we sat at the kitchen table, for as soon as the boys were handed their bowls of cereal, without prompting, they bowed their heads and were silent. "Wow," I said to my friend, "they're saying grace!"

My friend burst out laughing. "They're not saying grace. They're counting Cheerios!"

"What do you mean?" I began but was interrupted by the younger boy's cry.

"*Moooom!* He got forty-four Cheerios, and I only got thirty-nine!"

That problem was quickly remedied when my friend put her hand in the box and sprinkled a few more in the bowl . . . and my problem of envy was quickly remedied too by a short prayer: "God, I do like her house and her boys—even her dog. But I like my own life too. Help me to remember to say thank you more often and not 'count Cheerios.'"

Lord, remind me to count my blessings often and that to compare is to despair. —LINDA NEUKRUG

Digging Deeper: Ps. 128

Wed 9

> "*Now that I, your Lord and Teacher, have washed your feet, you also should wash one another's feet.*"
> —JOHN 13:14 (TNIV)

Recently my mother-in-law started "storying"— as she calls lying—about how I used to cut her fingernails. I had never cut her nails.

God knew she needed it. Alzheimer's and arthritis made the task impossible for her, and her nails were frighteningly long and ragged.

Nevertheless, it took weeks and many more tellings before her fantasy was realized.

It wasn't so horrible. Just as she described, I took her skinny fingers in mine and *clip, clip, clip,* it was done. And they did look pretty and nice. We both savored the improvement.

Immediately afterward, though, she started talking about her feet. She removed her fuzzy socks to reveal bulbous yellow toenails so long they curled under and twisted in every direction. That was too much for me.

No way was I touching my mother-in-law's fungal-looking feet, despite my growing certainty that doing so was precisely what God wanted. I wrestled with myself for weeks. In vain. Finally, following a nurse friend's advice, I took her to a shop to have the deed done professionally.

There, throne-like pedicure chairs loomed above little foot tubs. I was sure this wouldn't work. But somehow, between us, the staff and I managed to hoist her up there, and soon a no-nonsense pedicurist was grinding and massaging away, chatting comfortingly as she worked.

My mother-in-law was in heaven, during and afterward, and the women who took care of her there humbled me to my fastidious core.

Thank You, my foot-washing brother and Lord, for stooping to help me and for loving me, despite my weaknesses and failings. Thank You, too, for providing others who daily take Your easy yoke upon their shoulders and squat to do what needs to be done. —PATTY KIRK

Digging Deeper: JOHN 13:11–13

DIVINE ABUNDANCE

Thu 10   *... The everlasting God, the Lord, the Creator of the ends of the earth....* —ISAIAH 40:28

G od's country." I first heard this expression when I moved to Wyoming in the mile-high foothills of the Wind River Mountains. Bottle-blue sky spread over red rock buttes. Silvery-green sage-brush vistas stretched for fifty miles. Snow-capped nine-thousand-foot peaks drew my eyes upward every day.

Some thirty years later, I visited Reykjavik, Iceland, where I took a shuttle bus to my hostel. On my right, low volcanic rock encrusted with lichen swept inland for miles under lowering cloud. To my left, the metallic-blue North Atlantic rolled to the horizon. When I lowered my window and drank in the minty fresh air, the driver caught my gaze in his rearview mirror and smiled. "First trip to Iceland?" I nodded. "It's God's country!" Of course, I agreed and told him about the American Rockies.

Just two weeks later in the soft-pink wash of French twilight, I arrived at the train station of Collioure, a small port where the Pyrenees tumble into the Mediterranean. The guidebook assured me that my hotel was perched on a cliff at the far end of the bay. The taxi driver hopped out, stashed my bags and opened the front door. Sitting side by side, chatting companionably in French, we wove through the narrow streets, a jumble of three-story, terra-cotta-tiled houses adorned with wrought iron balconies and geraniums. At last, we emerged by the undulating teal-green Mediterranean, gilded in sunset pinks. I gasped. My driver smiled, nodded and whispered: "Yes, yes. It is God's country, no?"

Wyoming, Iceland and France are just the beginning. Surely, God's country is revered through the ends of the earth.

Lord of all Creation, we praise You for Your handiwork throughout the world.
—GAIL THORELL SCHILLING

Digging Deeper: Ps. 50:1–6

Fri 11

"In that day I will respond," declares the Lord—"I will respond to the skies, and they will respond to the earth; and the earth will respond to the grain. . . ." —HOSEA 2:21–22 (NIV)

My e-mail box remained stubbornly empty. Still no answer from the friend I'd written to. I checked my voice mail. I'd left messages for several people, but none had responded yet.

I was struggling with a tough decision and desperately wanted a friend's perspective. I'd reached out—through a variety of technologies. Everyone I sought out was busy or not home or didn't have time to answer. For days, I felt that my request for help, insights and just plain friendship had disappeared into a black hole. I didn't like the feeling of sharing, asking and opening myself up and getting no response.

But the hard truth is sometimes that the response I long for doesn't come. Friends forget to return a call or put off answering an e-mail. Children don't remember to reach out, and the longed-for Mother's Day card may not come. A spouse may be distracted by a phone call from work in the middle of a moment of heartfelt sharing.

What a profound gift God offers us when He promises to always be attentive to us and to respond. The Almighty God of the universe cares deeply and intimately for us, and when we call out to Him, He's never too busy. Not only that, but His response isn't a generic word of comfort or encouragement. He responds to us in unique ways, tailored for our specific situation.

Lord, I'm so grateful that You long to hear from me and respond with such tenderness to each problem I bring You. Remind me to turn to You when I feel alone. —SHARON HINCK

Digging Deeper: ISA. 54:4–6

October

Sat 12

"I will go before you and make the rough places smooth...."
—ISAIAH 45:2 (NAS)

O ne crisp October morning, my husband Rick suggested we ride his motorcycle through the north Georgia mountains. I'd played passenger near our home, on mostly straight roads. This was different.

He unloaded his bike from the pickup truck and hopped on. With shaky legs, I teetered on the foot peg and climbed behind him. Peering over the steep cliff, I clamped onto his waist like an octopus. "I'm not sure about this."

"You'll be fine."

"Go really slow."

Every time Rick steered into a curve, I leaned the opposite way. Before long, he pulled over and stopped. "What are you doing?"

"Helping you balance. If I don't, we'll fall."

"Relax. Lean *with* me, Julie."

Stuck on some backwoods road miles from the truck, I didn't have too many options. *He's been riding for years. Maybe, just maybe, he knows what he's doing.*

Then I did the unthinkable: I gave in. I stopped keeping vigil for oncoming cars and relaxed my shoulders. For the first time that day, I noticed the perfectly blue sky, apple-red leaves twirling in the trees and the faint aroma of chimney smoke. I began leaning into the curves when he did, far to the left and back to the right—the black pavement racing closer beneath us. I couldn't understand how it worked, but we didn't fall.

That's the moment the thrill came. When I chose to let go and stopped trying to control the motorcycle—the same way I'd often handled life. I kissed the back of Rick's neck. "Thank you. You were right. I had fun."

Lord, I don't want to miss any adventures You've planned for me. Surely, You see the twists and turns in the bumpy road ahead. —JULIE GARMON

Digging Deeper: Ps. 20:6–8

Sun 13

And since we know he hears us when we make our requests, we also know that he will give us what we ask for.
—1 JOHN 5:15 (NLT)

I'd always been curious to visit the Western "Wailing" Wall in the Old City of Jerusalem. I didn't expect how deeply moved I would be.

Built as a retaining structure on the western flank of the Temple Mount by King Herod two decades before Christ's birth, the wall has taken on tremendous significance in the centuries since. Jews came here initially to lament the destruction of the temple by the Romans. Now, the wall is a place of prayer. Pieces of paper with prayer requests are slipped between the cracks of the ancient stones.

At the last minute, I decided to write out some prayer requests of my own, filling up a scrap of paper at lunch with the Guideposts Holy Lands Tour group. I carried the paper with me all afternoon, to the Church of the Holy Sepulchre, believed by many to be the site of Golgotha, and down the Via Dolorosa, the path along which Christ carried His Cross.

It was dusk when we arrived at the Temple Mount. Across a great courtyard the wall stood, illuminated, a fifteen-story relic of an ancient time. Yet it felt so alive and contemporary.

I was uncertain of the protocol. Orthodox Jews were bowing and praying rhythmically. Finally, I walked up and tucked my prayer requests deep in a crevice. Then with my fingertips I touched the stones.

A tremendous peace swept over me. I bowed my head and let the feeling take me, a sense of reassurance and love utterly unexpected in its power, both a whisper and a roar. Finally, I stepped back. I looked up and saw the prayer requests in every nook and cranny, hundreds, maybe thousands. And

I thought about how long this wall had stood, like God's hand, taking our cares from us.

Lord, I pray at a wall that has survived for two thousand years and heard the prayers of millions. Let my humble prayers join that chorus praising Your goodness. —EDWARD GRINNAN

Digging Deeper: 2 CHRON. 6:39–41

Mon 14

"Do not let your hearts be troubled. You believe in God; believe also in me. My Father's house has many rooms; if that were not so, would I have told you that I am going there to prepare a place for you? And if I go and prepare a place for you, I will come back and take you to be with me that you also may be where I am. You know the way to the place where I am going."
—JOHN 14:1–4 (NIV)

I sat quietly at his bedside, keeping watch. Mr. Li, an elderly man, was a nonresponsive patient in end-of-life hospice care. There seemed nothing I could do for him but to be present.

Maybe he knows I'm here, I thought, as I talked to him about the sunshine outside the window and his uneaten lunch. No one knows how much the dying can hear, but we are told that hearing is the last of the senses to leave the physical body.

A couple of hours passed, both of us quiet. Then, quite suddenly, without moving, Mr. Li said three words: "I die Shanghai."

He was dying, and Shanghai was more than seven thousand miles away from New York City. Hospice workers are taught to do whatever the patient asks whenever possible. The watchword is comfort but in this case I was helpless. His wish, I knew, could not be granted. But maybe it already had been.

"God moves in a mysterious way," we often sing, "His wonders to perform." I wondered if He had taken the spirit of this quiet patient as he moved nearer to his death and given him a vision of his home city.

I shouldn't have been anxious. Mr. Li was still quiet, but I was sure I saw a half-smile on his gaunt face. I had no difficulty in imagining him in Shanghai, in a quiet courtyard or on a busy street.

May we have faith that the sick and the dying rest in Your comfort, Lord. —BRIGITTE WEEKS

Digging Deeper: JOB 29:12–14

THE GIFT OF TREES

Tue 15

"Now these were the visions in my mind as I lay on my bed: I was looking, and behold, there was a tree in the midst of the earth and its height was great."
—DANIEL 4:10 (NAS)

Do you ever have moments of feeling arrogant or entitled? One time I recall is a summer afternoon, riding in a neighbor's sporty blue convertible, hair blowing in the breeze. As we sped down the highway, I seemed to absorb the car's elite persona. *Yeah, you, move over!* I noticed but pretended to ignore the admiring attention we got. I turned into a real road queen.

Nebuchadnezzar was proud king of a vast Babylonian Empire several hundred years before the birth of Jesus. He was "flourishing in his palace" when he dreamed of a great tree reaching to the sky, visible to the whole earth. It had beautiful foliage and fruit, and "all living creatures fed themselves from it." But in his dream the tree, except its stump and roots, was cut down.

The king called for the prophet Daniel to interpret his vision. Nebuchadnezzar learned he was the tree and was going to be cast into the wilderness.

His kingdom would be restored when he recognized that it is "heaven that rules." Seven years later he honored God, saying, "All His works are true and His ways just, and He is able to humble those who walk in pride" (Daniel 4:37).

I never did ride in that flashy convertible again. And then about a year ago, the old car I drive acquired a really smashed rear end. I get lots of attention . . . the humbling kind.

Lord, pride invades, demands and alienates. I'd much rather have a humble heart with You there.
—CAROL KNAPP

Digging Deeper: Ps. 29:3–5

Wed 16   *If I speak in the tongues of men or of angels, but do not have love, I am only a resounding gong or a clanging cymbal.*
—1 CORINTHIANS 13:1 (NIV)

Isaac was the passionate and irrepressible Israeli guide on one of our Guideposts Holy Lands Tour coaches. One morning as we headed for Nazareth, he pulled a tarnished coin from his pocket. "This coin, a shekel, is at least two thousand years old," he said, holding it aloft before asking us to pass it among ourselves. "Hold it tightly for a moment and feel yourself connected to its history, and I will tell you a story."

Isaac bought the coin from a reputable dealer for nearly five thousand dollars. "When my wife saw the credit card bill, she threw me out of the house. She was furious!"

Isaac went to live with his mother for a month before he was able to convince his wife to take him back.

It took her a long time to cool down, but Isaac's wife finally understood his passion, his spiritual yearning for this coin. And when it finally reached my hands, I did too. I could barely make out the head of Tiberius or the engraving. I held the coin tightly. Had it circulated through Jerusalem? Could this coin have scattered when Christ overturned the moneychangers' tables at the temple? Had an apostle touched this coin? Mary? Even Jesus?

As we passed through Cana where Christ performed His first miracle and where there is a beautiful little church, Isaac pulled out his cell phone, called his wife and shouted, "I love you!" He explained he always does this when he passes the "most famous wedding spot on earth." He certainly believed that a woman who understood why he had to have that coin, and forgave him his extravagant purchase, was a woman who truly loved him.

Lord, I am connected to You in so many ways and Your love is the true coin of the realm. It makes all things possible. —EDWARD GRINNAN

Digging Deeper: 1 PET. 1:3–12

Thu 17

Thanks be to God for his indescribable gift!
—2 CORINTHIANS 9:15 (NIV)

My family was sitting around my daughter's kitchen table. Danita's a busy doctor, and the rest of us—my wife Rosie, son Ryan and grandson Lil' Reggie—were enjoying having her to ourselves for the day.

I mentioned a few of my health issues, including the fact that I'm going to need a hip replacement soon. I thought they'd be sympathetic and listen, but Danita started right in. "Daddy, are you eating healthier? You know you need to stay away from some of your favorite fried foods. Are you exercising on a regular basis? If you lost ten pounds, your hips would thank you."

I was completely caught off-guard. All of the years of being Danita's father, I've been looking out for her interests. What friends were good influences on her; was she taking care of herself and not working too hard at the hospital; was she connected to God and a loving faith community? Now the tables had turned. I sputtered in response and tried to justify my situation. But that didn't faze Danita. "Are you at least walking every day? You know, Daddy, you need to do all you can to strengthen this hip naturally before you consider surgery."

It was hard to be held accountable. And as I listened to her, I reflected on the goodness of God Who gave me a daughter who not only is a physician, but who cares for me and looks out for my good.

Lord, help me to listen to You as I learn how to listen to others who love me. —DOLPHUS WEARY

Digging Deeper: JOB 42:14–16

Fri 18

"I have told you these things, so that in me you may have peace. In this world you will have trouble. But take heart! I have overcome the world."
—JOHN 16:33 (NIV)

A wave of terror rushed through my body when I heard my mother say that word.

"Cancer?" I repeated into the phone. "Papi has cancer?"

Mom did her best to assure me that the doctors caught it early enough, but that didn't stop my tears. All I wanted to do was get on a plane to Florida and run into my father's arms.

"Karen," my mother said, with an uncharacteristic calm in her voice, "he's going to be fine." The absolute peace and assurance in her voice did more than calm me down; it puzzled me.

Growing up, my mother thought every bump, cough or pain was cancer. "Oh no, no," she'd say, frantic with worry as she'd examine us. "That doesn't look right. You need to get that checked!" She'd completely freak out over a small rash on my arm or a stomach bug, but now my father had cancer and she was calm?

For a moment it angered me. With all the years of her overreacting over nothing, she finally had a real reason to panic. Yet there was no hint of worry in her voice. The anger left just as quickly as I realized how unnatural this was for her. Only God could create such a shift in her response.

Thank You, Lord, for the peace only You can give.
—KAREN VALENTIN

Digging Deeper: Ps. 89:7–9

Sat 19

Weeping may endure for a night, but joy cometh in the morning.
—PSALM 30:5

I've known lonely. I've worked hard all day, trying my best to serve others, only to come home to an empty house, a microwave dinner and silence.

I remember once saying to my sister Keri, "Maybe I'll just move in with you and Ben and sleep on your couch forever."

I'm fortunate now. My wife Corinne has known lonely too.

When we married, we shared many of the same dreams, centered around a longing to have a safe, happy home where love was always waiting. Already, I was approaching forty and Corinne was thirty-eight, and more than any other thing, we prayed that having a sibling for Harrison might be part of God's plan for us.

Five months after we wed, His answer came. "Brock, we're going to have a baby," Corrine said.

"Wow, Dad, I always wanted a little sister!" Harrison added.

Our due date quickly approached, and before we knew it, we were in the hospital, welcoming our new baby girl. I was speechless as the nurse handed Mary Katherine Kidd to her proud momma. Corinne looked up into my eyes. I wanted to say something profound but "You did it" was all I could manage.

Corinne's eyes were filled with joyful tears as she shook her head and softly pointed upward, saying it better than I could have hoped: "No, Brock, it was God Who did this for us."

Thank You, Father. Thank You. —BROCK KIDD

Digging Deeper: ROM. 12:1–3

Sun 20

Let your light so shine before men, that they may see your good works, and glorify your Father which is in heaven. —MATTHEW 5:16

It was a formal affair, and the auditorium was full of people dressed in sequins, lace and tuxedos. That night, my daughter Lanea (pronounced la-NAY-uh—no one ever gets it right at first) was dressed in silver evening shoes and garnet-colored earrings and dress. A proud mama, I sat next to her as she was honored as a finalist for a Lamplighter Award for her community service.

For the past several years, Lanea has carried a walkie-talkie instead of a purse, and traded in her pumps for tennis shoes as she climbs stadium steps at the Durham Bulls Athletic Park, where she oversees Durham's annual Project Homeless Connect. She has made the event a day where guests receive medical and dental care, haircuts, eye exams, housing and job assistance, and a warm delicious meal—all for free.

I hold my breath when her category is called: the John Hope Franklin Humanitarian Award. An image of Lanea and her team flashes on the screen, along with photos of other nominees in her category. They have all done marvelous things.

The presenter fumbles opening the envelope. I see him struggling to pronounce the name written there and I know.

Lanea stands and, in shock, makes her way to the stage. My baby is a winner!

Lord, help us to let our lights shine, and may our lights reflect on You! —SHARON FOSTER

Digging Deeper: 1 TIM. 6:17–19

Mon 21

We are hard-pressed on every side, yet not crushed; we are perplexed, but not in despair.
—2 CORINTHIANS 4:8 (NKJV)

The recession has been hard on me. A recent news report stated that single women my age are the hardest hit. Unemployment is particularly high for anyone over fifty-five, and our singular resource is consequently exhausted. Our medical bills are increasing, our energy diminishing. Our homes are worth half to two-thirds of what we paid for them. And while this past summer I did find work driving motor coaches in Alaska, I'm back to unemployment.

The hardest part is that existence becomes, by necessity, self-serving. Every thought, deed and choice revolves around staying fed, getting your medications, keeping a roof over your head. It's all about you. I find it isolating and untenable.

Two weeks ago I woke to a childhood memory verse: "In all thy ways acknowledge him, and he shall direct thy paths" (Proverbs 3:6). *Great, God will tell me what to do!* But the rub—I have to acknowledge Him, which means . . . Give him a nod, as in, "Hi, I see You"? I pulled out the dictionary. Who knew? *Acknowledge* can mean "admit, give in, concede." Perhaps concede to God that this recession is nothing I can fix, no matter my unrelenting pursuit and weary strategizing to the detriment of all else. Was it time to simply let go?

Within twenty-four hours, I put my house on the market. I'll be unemployed and homeless and taking a 40 percent financial loss, but I can no longer tight-fist what little I have left. It's no way to live and it's making me narcissistic. Better to concede and let God direct my way.

> *Letting go of my only asset is scary, God.*
> *Please honor my fragile trust as I concede to*
> *Your greater understanding.*
> —BRENDA WILBEE

Digging Deeper: Ps. 80

Tue 22

Be very careful, then, how you live—not as unwise but as wise, making the most of every opportunity, because the days are evil. —EPHESIANS 5:15–16 (NIV)

We had one rainy day after another in October. October, that blissful month when the leaves turn russet and gold, the sky should be a slate blue, the temperatures in the midfifties.

My son William was flying in for a brief visit before Halloween. "Let's go hiking," I e-mailed him. "I'll take a day off."

"Great plan, Dad," he e-mailed back.

I blocked out Thursday on my calendar, moved some meetings, Googled for information on nearby hikes and picked my outdoorsy friends' brains. Tuesday, Will arrived on the red-eye, a Tuesday that looked like it would be stunningly, achingly beautiful. I dashed to the office, glanced at the weather in between e-mails. Wednesday: rain. Thursday: rain. Today: gorgeous. Maybe this father-son bonding moment under cerulean skies was not meant to happen.

Unless we did it today. I hardly had a chance to poll the Supreme Being when an afternoon meeting got canceled. Surely, a sign. I called home. "Will, let's go hiking now," I said.

"Sure," he replied, groggy from his catch-up nap.

"I'm out the rest of the day," I e-mailed my colleagues.

"Anything wrong?" one asked from her BlackBerry.

"Everything right," I e-mailed back.

At three o'clock that afternoon, Will and I were on top of a mountain, an eagle floating beneath us, the wind at our backs, the shared water bottle our reward for a rigorous ascent up 1,600 feet of granite. "My muscles are really going to hurt tomorrow," I told Will.

But today. We had today.

Thursday it poured rain.

Help me, Lord, to make the most of every day.
—RICK HAMLIN

Digging Deeper: 2 SAM. 22:29–34

Wed 23

He that shewed mercy on him. . . .
Go, and do thou likewise.
—LUKE 10:37

BOOM! At the sound of the explosion I looked in the rearview mirror and groaned. Smoke and rubber fragments were spewing from one tire on my heavily loaded stock trailer. A blowout—just what I didn't need.

There isn't enough grass on our ranch, so the family I work with and I spend a lot of time on the road hauling cattle to and from the summer range. We travel together with two trailers, but as luck would have it, I was the last one out and had to shut the gates. Now the others were miles ahead, oblivious to my predicament.

"Why now, God?" I grumbled under my breath and got out the wrench and the spare.

A shiny, new Chevy sped past. Minutes later, a tricked-out Ford pickup flew by like I wasn't even there. I was almost finished when an old, beat-up VW bus with mismatched doors wheezed to a stop behind my trailer.

"Need he'p, missy?" the thin, stooped man asked. His shirt was threadbare, and he appeared to have gone a while between meals. He looked like he needed more help than I did.

I thanked him and assured him all was well. As he went on his way, I found myself thinking of the parable of the Good Samaritan. It wasn't the priest or the Levite who helped the Jew; it was the lowly Samaritan. *I see why now, God, and I'll do the same for others.*

Lord, never let me forget to help others and bless those who remember to help me. —ERIKA BENTSEN

Digging Deeper: LEV. 19:32–34

October

Thu 24

"I baptize you with water for repentance, but one who is more powerful than I is coming after me...."
—MATTHEW 3:11 (NRSV)

Because we live in New London, Connecticut, the river flowing by our city is, naturally, called the Thames. No one will ever mistake New London for old London, nor would anyone gazing off our porch think they were watching London's Thames. Nevertheless, our small city has a busy little river. All manner of water vessels pass by our windows: freighters, oil barges, even the occasional cruise boat. Most interesting to me are the submarines. The Naval Submarine Base is upriver, and right across from us is the submarine manufacturer Electric Boat. So if we glance out at the right time, we can see a sub coming home or going out.

Subs are awe-inspiring and a little frightening. When I see them leaving, I pray for the men and women in that small, powerful space and for the families left behind. When they return, I thank God for their safety and pray for their reunions.

Perhaps it's my imagination, but I've noticed that the departing subs appear grim, rushing to the ocean to submerge for months. On the other hand, when they return, some submariners climb out onto the top of the vessel after it surfaces. They wave and shout, anticipating the welcome awaiting them at the base. The returning subs move more easily, as though in recognition of safety, of coming home.

I think it's that way with God and me. When the world's tensions, violence and greed draw me from God and my loved ones, I am harsh, filled with dread. But when I return to God, I rejoice, relieved and grateful for the welcome awaiting me. I rest once again in God, my home.

Almighty God, You are my home. If the world draws me away, bring me back to You so that I may rest and rejoice in Your Presence. —MARCI ALBORGHETTI

Digging Deeper: DEUT. 11:11–13

Fri 25 *Keep at it till the finish. Don't drag your feet....* —HEBREWS 6:9 (MSG)

I couldn't make myself begin the dreaded task of organizing my closet, tossing out clothes, lining up shoes.... Mulling over my lack of enthusiasm early one morning, I avoided the grueling task by going outside to get the newspaper.

On the front porch, I saw that the pesky chipmunks had declared war on my pansies in the small planter... again. The tiny, steadfast creatures attacked whatever I planted. I sometimes imagined them in the bushes, smirking and singing victory in their high-pitched cartoon voices. I wasn't about to harm them; they often peeked in the windows at me curiously. But now it had become a war of them against me.

I'd plant artificial flowers, which I abhor, if I had to. But I'd win. Carefully, I selected plastic pansies, packing dirt firmly around them.

The next morning, checking my planter, I was astonished. The tenacious creatures had pulled up and scattered flowers, spilling dirt all about.

Sitting on the porch step, in my pajamas, defeat settled over me. *The chipmunks keep at it, don't they?* a silent voice seemed to suggest.

Back inside, I walked directly to my cluttered closet, sat on the floor and picked up a pair of shoes, then another. I'd begun! Several hours later, my closet looked amazing.

Jesus, no wonder they call You Teacher!
—MARION BOND WEST

Digging Deeper: ACTS 6

Sat 26

And we are anxious that you keep right on loving others as long as life lasts, so that you will get your full reward. —HEBREWS 6:11 (TLB)

I'm not crazy about change. I like my environment and the people around me to stay the way they are.

But then, suddenly, my friend Norma's husband Herb died in his sleep.

After his death, Norma, in her mid-eighties, decided to sell their home and move to an assisted-living high-rise. We'd been seeing so much of each other at the pool and going out for breakfast or lunch, that I was upset she was leaving my neighborhood. But she's a feisty gal who has always handled adversity and life's changes with grace and courage.

Then, right after Norma decided to move, two other friends, George, age ninety-three, and Evelyn, nearly ninety, decided to sell their villa in the block next to mine and also move to an assisted-living place. Again, I was devastated. My two dear friends and I had had many delightful lunches and dinners together. We'd chatted up a storm as we swam side by side in the community pool for hours at a time. They'd inspired me with stories about the two places where they volunteer each week, Menorah Manor, a nursing home, and the Largo Cultural Center where they were still ushers for all the live productions as well as tour guides. But they, too, needed extra care.

And so I had to let go of the close neighborhood bond with my all-time-favorite seniors. I learned that moving on doesn't mean friendships end. Norma, George and Evelyn are still close friends whose strong faith in God helped them and me see that life is a progression and that change is a blessing.

Lord, help me to be graceful and accepting when the time comes to make drastic changes in my life. And meanwhile, please keep an eye on Norma, George and Evelyn. —PATRICIA LORENZ

Digging Deeper: PROV. 18:24

Sun 27

Love must be sincere. Hate what is evil; cling to what is good. Be devoted to one another in love. Honor one another above yourselves.
—ROMANS 12:9–10 (NIV)

I was shopping for a new watch recently when I recalled the watch I received as a gift when I was a nursing student. I was celebrating my nineteenth birthday at my boyfriend's home. I sat perched on the edge of the ottoman in the living room while David retrieved a small, shimmering gold box.

Hovering over me was David's mother. Harriet knew what the box contained and couldn't wait for me to open it. Ever so slowly, I lifted the lid. Inside was a delicate gold nurse's watch that featured a sweeping red second hand. "So you can check your patients' pulses easier," Harriet explained, her heart bubbling over. "Here," she said, beaming, "check my pulse. I want to be your very first patient."

Back then, I accepted Harriet's enthusiasm as Harriet just being Harriet. She was a woman of quiet grace and gentle beauty who always delighted in others' good fortune. But recently I ran into Harriet's daughter, and she explained that it wasn't second nature at all. Harriet actually made a conscious effort to be happy for others' successes.

That means I can emulate Harriet, not just admire her. When a friend buys a showroom sedan that puts my cobbled-together car to shame, I can truly delight in her happiness. And when a co-worker lands the dream assignment that would have been perfect for me, I can respond just like Harriet, my heart bubbling over with love.

Keeper of my dreams, Lord, give me an applauding heart when others do well. —ROBERTA MESSNER

Digging Deeper: PROV. 17:8, 22, 27

Mon 28 *Jesus Christ is the same yesterday, today, and forever.*
—HEBREWS 13:8 (NKJV)

Recently, I was in Minnesota, working on a project about the role of faith in people's lives, and I spent a couple of days with a man who would probably be classified by most of us as a "have-not." Like so many Americans, he has spent the past couple of years battling long spells of unemployment and foreclosure. He has burned through most of his savings. He has even suffered a falling-out with his family. In his story, there was pain galore.

But there was also more. He was recounting the last couple of years of his journey in great detail as we sat in a cozy booth at a local Italian restaurant. Our food came—monstrously large piles of sausage and peppers and onions and cheese, all sautéed into mountains of steaming goodness, capped with beautiful overeasy eggs and served with browned slices of Italian bread—and he asked if he could say grace. "Thank you, Dad," he prayed, in a voice as soft as the melting butter on our toast. "Thank you..."

I honestly don't remember what exactly he prayed for after that, because I was so struck by the contentment in his voice. The spirit in which he approached God amazed me—from the intimate way he called on Dad to his complete lack of a complaining spirit. Somehow, amid a season of so much uncertainty, he still clung to thankfulness.

To most reporters, there's no news in that prayer—nothing to see or write about. But maybe that's apropos, because the news is fleeting, focusing on things that pass away. This man's relationship with his heavenly Dad? That will endure.

Thank You, Dad, for all the blessings in this life . . . most of all, Your faithfulness. —JEFF CHU

Digging Deeper: GAL. 4:5–7

Tue 29

"Blessed are the pure in heart, for they shall see God."
—MATTHEW 5:8 (NKJV)

W ork has been wonderful—launching a whole new line of inspirational products for Guideposts called Hope Springs has required my constant involvement and attention to every detail. By the time fall arrived, I still had a whole lot of vacation days left. Being far away from Hope Springs when it was at such a nascent stage just didn't work, so a remote or exotic vacation was out of the question.

My husband Matt and I arrived at a happy solution. We'd take one week to go to our favorite spot: on the coast of Maine, looking over Blue Hill Bay. I awoke that Monday, grateful for some quiet, unscheduled time, and glanced out the big glass door. To my great amazement and sheer delight, I saw not one, not two, but three bald eagles soaring by! I was mesmerized.

And then the phone rang with a jolting jangle of noise, interrupting my reverie. It was an important question from the office and the request for a conference call later in the day. Through my annoyance, I said an angry prayer: *Lord, help me please!*

I looked up and saw the eagles, remarkably, still there. One swooped down, caught a fish, came to roost on the big pine tree on the bank directly in front of me and began to eat its meal. It was an inspiring sight to see, even if it was to the eagle just a matter of going about its business. It went about its business . . . and now it was time for me to do the same.

Thank You, Lord, for providing work to do in Your service, wonders of nature to remind me of Your majesty, and the great fortune to live a life rich with both. —ANNE ADRIANCE

Digging Deeper: ECCLES. 3:1–13

Wed 30

"I will search for the lost and bring back the strays. . . ."
—EZEKIEL 34:16 (NIV)

My son, his two young daughters and I hurriedly headed to a University of Colorado football game because the girls wanted to see the live buffalo mascot run across the stadium to start the game. As we drove down a side street, I saw a small, white dog darting back and forth.

"Stop!" I said. Reluctantly, Derek pulled over. I quickly jumped out, scooped up the shaking dog, and checked the tag; her name was Mia. We called the phone number, but there was no answer so we left a voice mail.

"Now what?" all three asked me because this rescue operation was obviously my idea. We ended up backtracking to their house, put the dog in the backyard and went on to the game with two disappointed little girls; we'd missed the buffalo run and kickoff.

I knew why I felt so passionate about saving Mia. Several weeks earlier, my own beloved golden retriever got out of our house and quickly disappeared. Frantically, I searched the neighborhood. Finally, I returned home to find a phone message from our veterinarian's office: "We have your dog. A lady brought him in because our name is on one of his tags." I arrived at the vet's office a few minutes later where I burst into tears when my dog came bounding out of a back room.

After the game, we drove back to their house, and there was Mia still waiting in the backyard. We agreed Derek and the girls would keep Mia and hope for a phone call.

An hour after I got home, my phone rang. "They came to get Mia!" my granddaughters both exclaimed at once. "A mom and dad and two little girls. They were gone, and she got out and wandered two whole miles from their home. They were so happy we found her! They kept saying thank you!"

I did too.

> *Lord, what a blessing to be part of the picture when the lost is found in Your creation. Thank You.*
> —CAROL KUYKENDALL

Digging Deeper: PROV. 3:26–38

Thu 31

You who are young, be happy while you are young, and let your heart give you joy in the days of your youth. . . .
—ECCLESIASTES 11:9 (NIV)

Joey, my five-year-old, announced that he was going to make his own Halloween costume. Then he proceeded to set up shop on the kitchen counter, asking for construction paper and a glue stick.

After a half hour, he asked me to dump out two cereal boxes so he could use them for robot arms. I normally would have said no, imagining weeks of eating smooshed cereal, but I was so intrigued by the process that I carefully poured cereal into storage bags and handed over the boxes.

A while later, he asked for glitter glue and masking tape. Then it was pipe cleaners. Then watercolor paints.

After two hours of intent work, I saw nothing but a huge mess. But my son beamed up at me and told me he was almost finished and that it had turned out *exactly* like he had hoped.

Ten minutes later, he jumped out of his chair to try on the costume. He taped boxes to his arms, a mask to his forehead and construction paper shoes onto his sneakers. Then he strutted into the kitchen and proudly showed off his creation.

Joey looked great. And while his mask may be taped on and his costume probably won't hold up well in a thunderstorm, I'm letting him wear it on Halloween. After all, I can't bear the thought of him wearing a store-bought costume when he's so joyful about his creation.

Lord, thank You for children who see the world so joyfully that we can't help but feel happy too.
—ERIN MACPHERSON

Digging Deeper: GEN. 2:2–4

GIVING THANKS

1 _____

2 _____

3 _____

4 _____

5 _____

6 _____

7 _____

8 _____

9 _____

10 _____

11 _____

12 _____

13 _____

14 _____

15 _____

16 _____

17 _____

18 _____

19 _____

20 _____

21 _____

22 _____

23 _____

24 _____

25 _____

26 _____

27 _____

28 _____

29 _____

30 _____

31 _____

November

I urge, then, first of all, that petitions, prayers, intercession and thanksgiving be made for all people—for kings and all those in authority, that we may live peaceful and quiet lives in all godliness and holiness.

—1 Timothy 2:1–2 (NIV)

OPERATION THANKFULNESS

Fri 1   *On this mountain the Lord Almighty will prepare a feast of rich food for all peoples....* —ISAIAH 25:6 (NIV)

I *sure am glad it's not last November*, I thought as I took plates out of the china cabinet. The previous Thanksgiving I had snapped a photo to post online of the thawed raw turkey still sitting cold and bluish in a cooking bag on Thanksgiving night. Dinner had been canceled because our son John was in the hospital, trying to knock out a nasty intestinal inflammation so he wouldn't need emergency surgery. Gordon and I ended up eating hamburgers at a fast-food counter that was the only place open at the hospital.

The rest of our family, who had been "uninvited" to our dinner, scattered. Our son Jeff and his wife Leah and daughter Kendall hastily found a restaurant that was serving turkey. Our other son Chris called up a young woman he'd recently met who had mentioned she was going to a huge family dinner.

Yes, I was definitely glad it wasn't last November. I set a plate for John, thanking God that he was now the picture of health. Then next to Chris's plate, I set one for his girlfriend Grayson. We all loved her and they were quite serious. Suddenly I realized that it was our canceled plans one year ago that had brought the two together.

As I set down Gordon's plate, I had a fresh perspective on canceled plans. Even when big days are ruined by illness or by being apart from our loved ones, God's chances aren't ruined for bringing some new and unexpected good out of them.

Father, I offer to You my plan today that didn't turn out the way I wanted. Thank You that You can turn it into a day of blessings in Your wise and wonderful bigger-picture-of-life way. Amen.
—KAREN BARBER

Digging Deeper: Ps. 65:10–12

Sat 2 *I will hear....* —EXODUS 22:27

My phone is beyond description. It's a computer, a camera, a flashlight and a Solitaire game. There are applications for everything. There's a dog repeller, a talking gerbil, a recipe finder and a weather channel. I can listen to college lectures, get directions to wherever I want to go and check the price of an item in the grocery store.

But there's one application that stands out far beyond the rest. It lies somewhere between wild fantasy and total wonder and has, in a strange way, connected me to the presence of God.

Ocarina is a flute that you can play on your phone by blowing into the microphone and touching the finger-rings that appear on the screen. But there's more. Tap the globe on the app's menu and suddenly you are in outer space, looking down on our planet. From that vantage point, you hear the plaintive sound of people all around the world playing their flutes. You see their songs spiraling toward heaven in shafts of light. Somewhere in South America, Bart is playing "Amazing Grace"; in Florida, Mattie's playing "Summertime"; and in China, E is playing a haunting melody that I do not recognize.

As Avala plays "Twinkle, Twinkle, Little Star" on some tiny Pacific island, I see her song as a prayer and, high above, God listens, gathering our prayers, never missing a single chord.

Beyond the words, He knows the location, the name, the face, the heart, of every prayer. Every wish, every longing that wafts across the galaxies flies straight to His ear.

Once more I spin the globe on my iPhone screen...in Australia, DX is playing "Love Divine, all loves excelling, joy of heaven to earth come down...."

I stand amazed, Father. But You already know that, don't You? —PAM KIDD

Digging Deeper: Ps. 62:11

Sun 3

Serve the Lord thy God with all thy heart and with all thy soul.
—DEUTERONOMY 10:12

To those who've never delighted in the companionship of a McNab cow dog, a cousin of the Border collie, this breed has the intellect of a Mensa member, the cunning of Sherlock Holmes, the work ethic of Mother Teresa, a "till death do us part" kind of loyalty and, with my Blue Dog, the finely tuned hearing of a bat.

Blue Dog comes with me as I go about my daily chores on the ranch. The thing I've noticed most often about him is he's always listening for commands. It doesn't matter if I'm talking with someone else, talking to myself or talking to him. If Blue Dog hears a command at any time, he's prepared to spring into action, whatever it is. And it doesn't have to be meant as a command.

I was fixing fence the other day, and when I finally finished splicing the broken wires, I said, "That's it." I must have run my words together because Blue Dog heard "sit" in the middle of those other syllables and immediately sat, watching me with his steely brown eyes, ready for my next instruction.

Another time Blue Dog was in the back of the pickup, I'd gotten out to close a gate. Someone came by and told me I could leave it open and I answered, "Okay." Blue Dog immediately sprang from the truck. *Okay* is his word to unload.

Blue Dog can be snoring on his bed in my house, but if he even thinks he hears a command, he'll leap to his feet and be ready for action. I've learned to be careful of what I say because I know, whether he is asleep or awake, Blue Dog has one ear trained on me at all times, ready to obey.

Dear Lord, if only I would serve You like a cow dog, always listening for Your instruction and ready to spring wholeheartedly into immediate action, with all my heart and soul. —ERIKA BENTSEN

Digging Deeper: EPH. 6

Mon 4   "*Can any one of you by worrying add a single hour to your life?*"
—MATTHEW 6:27 (NIV)

I didn't realize what I had done until I was getting dressed at the gym before work and looked down at my feet: one blue sock, one black.

It is a peril of the season now that the sun is rising later. I get dressed in the dark so as not to disturb my late-sleeping spouse Julee.

There's our dog Millie to be walked, and a cycling class at the gym across town I need to get to fast if I have any hopes of snagging an open bike. All this rushing around in the dark and now it had finally happened: I'd had a wardrobe malfunction.

I supposed I could run home and retrieve a matching pair . . . but, no, there was that early meeting I scheduled. Well then, I could stop at some store and buy a pair of socks, a drug store or something because legitimate clothing stores don't open until ten o'clock and by then, I was sure, my day would be destroyed. *What if one of the participants at this meeting noticed?* I would lose all credibility. *Who wants to do business with a man who can't put on the same color socks?*

By now I was walking in the general direction of my office, still uncertain of my course of action. I looked around me. A multitude of pedestrians were making their way to their jobs in almost an equally multitudinous array of clothing. People wear the craziest stuff to work these days, proud to demonstrate their personal style, to show a little bit of who they are by how they dress.

What was I so worried about? Maybe I thought this minor variation in hue revealed some inner

chaos or lack of consistency. Maybe I thought I
had to be perfect.

I went about my day with my different colored
socks and not a soul noticed. After a while, neither
did I.

*Lord, I can get so hung up on the small stuff that I let
it ruin a day that is yet another perfect gift from You.
Help me stay focused on the beauty and purpose
of life and let the little stuff go.*
—EDWARD GRINNAN

Digging Deeper: GAL. 1:10

Tue 5

*We take captive every thought to make
it obedient to Christ.*
—2 CORINTHIANS 10:5 (NIV)

When I was pregnant, my husband and I read
a book that convinced us children under two
years of age should not be exposed to television,
something about hampering the fragile neurologi-
cal systems that were still working hard to develop.
So after Prisca was born, we made sure that whenever she was in a particular room, the television was
turned off.

We were mocked by family and friends alike ("Just
let her be normal, for goodness' sake!"), but we stuck

to our guns, explaining (with a grin) that Prisca's ensuing brilliance in years to come would put all naysayers in their place.

Several months into this technology ban on my daughter's life, we entered a local department store. Prisca was seated in her pillowed shopping-cart cover, enjoying the stimuli surrounding her, when we happened upon the TV aisle. Realizing the unfettered enthusiasm that scores of screens would elicit from my poor, TV-deprived child, I stopped the cart and simply stared at Prisca, who was staring up at those screens. *"Hooo!"* she said, bouncing excitedly in her seat. *"Hooo! Hoooo! Hooooooo!"* Eyes danced and arms flailed as fat fingers reached for the epicenter of her euphoria, twenty-five big-screen, flat-panel TVs.

Between giggles, I tried in vain to pull Prisca's attention back to me, but poking her, prodding her, rattling her favorite toys, singsonging her name out loud could not possibly be more interesting than the newfound font of her fanciful joy. Eventually, I rolled her away toward the less-exciting mouthwash aisle. But something about her reaction stuck with me the rest of the day. The thought of being *that* riveted and transfixed, *that* captivated and consumed—I want God to be able to get my undivided attention just...like... *that*.

Father, captivate me today. —ASHLEY WIERSMA

Digging Deeper: ISA. 45:21–23

Wed 6 *The Lord says, "I will guide you along the best pathway for your life. I will advise you and watch over you."*
—PSALM 32:8 (NLT)

Our son Timothy was doing a semester in Italy, and we got a cheap flight to visit him in Parma in the dark, dank month of November. I found myself a bit distracted during a tour of the ancient city. I was worried about family thousands of miles away and thinking God was just as far. Tim's host mother took us into the old church of San Giovanni Evangelista (St. John, the Evangelist) to see the frescoes.

All the lights were off, and the only person around was an old monk. "Could you turn the lights on, please," our Italian host said, slipping him a ten-euro note.

With a little grumbling, the monk began flipping on lights and pointing. "Here," he said, gesturing to the dome above us, "is a vision of God painted by the great artist Correggio." We looked up at the ceiling to a magnificent fresco of Jesus descending from heaven, a stunning vision of blue sky, clouds and angels in paradise.

Then the monk led us to the altar and the choir benches. He had us look back to the dome. "As you can see from here, we cannot see God or His heaven."

It was true. The glories of the dome weren't visible from this angle. All we could see was John, the evangelist, at the bottom of the dome, writing.

He paused for us to consider the lesson. When you're in the dark, when you're not sure what the right thing to pray for is, when your family feels very far away, you still have something to focus on: the Word of God, the stories recorded by His followers such as John.

"God is at work even when we can't see it," the monk said. He flipped off the lights and escorted us outside to the dim November day.

God, let Your Word be my guide. —RICK HAMLIN

Digging Deeper: REV. 22:4–6

Thu 7

"And whoever gives one of these little ones only a cup of cold water in the name of a disciple, assuredly, I say to you, he shall by no means lose his reward." —MATTHEW 10:42 (NKJV)

A few months ago, someone sent me a video on the Internet about a six-year-old girl named

Taylor who needed a seizure-assistance dog to protect her during her almost daily seizures. The dog, according to the e-mail, would cost about one thousand dollars. I was struck by how cheerful this little girl was, in spite of the adversity she was facing. A corporation for which I was giving a motivational speech the next week agreed to donate the money, and that, I figured, was that.

But then we got word back from Taylor's mother that there had been a miscommunication: The highly trained puppy wouldn't cost one thousand dollars, it would be ten thousand dollars.

This was a staggering sum, and I didn't know anyone who could or would donate that much money. And then I felt like God was telling me: "You're right. You don't *personally* know anyone who would give that much. But that doesn't mean hope is lost."

I frequently make Internet videos and am fortunate enough to have a relatively large viewership. So I made my own video about Taylor and put it online. People across the world fell in love with her just as I had, and four days later, we had raised the entire amount.

Taylor just received her puppy a few weeks ago. She named it Heaven.

It struck me as such an appropriate name, because there can't be anything much closer to heaven on earth than being the recipient of kindness and generosity, especially when it comes from total strangers.

Lord, thank You for giving me the opportunity in this life to be both a giver and a receiver of kindness and generosity. —JOSHUA SUNDQUIST

Digging Deeper: DEUT. 10:12–14

Fri 8

Now your attitudes and thoughts must all be constantly changing for the better.
—EPHESIANS 4:23 (TLB)

I'm on a purging kick," I proudly told my daughter when she stopped by to check our progress on re-painting and recarpeting our bedroom. *Purging* is a verb lifted right out of my Bible study, and it means to "rid oneself of sin." But I was applying it to my task of getting rid of stuff we'd been accumulating for the last thirty years.

My daughter rolled her eyes as she surveyed the stacks of books and files and pictures and clutter strewn out across the bedroom floor. "Good luck!" she said on her way back out the door. Soon, I knew that I needed more than luck to complete my task. I quickly felt overwhelmed at the enormity of my goal.

Take the books, for instance. I'd highlighted some text in many of them, which proved I'd read them. *Then why am I not more brilliant?* I lamented as I flipped through some pages. *Or more like Jesus? Have all those words made any difference in shaping me?*

Discouraged, I moved on to the boxes filled with photographs. I had no idea where or how to start. Surely I didn't have enough time left in my life to sort through them all.

So I turned to tackle the closet, but that was like taking a walk down memory lane: the T-shirt from the first race I ever ran; the dress I wore to our daughter's wedding; those pants that fit perfectly when I felt the thinnest in my life. How could I get rid of any of those?

I realized that my purging could not be accomplished quickly. Purging oneself of a critical spirit or the need to be right is not completed with a single decision in one day. Rather, it's a constant, lifelong process. The important thing is to merely keep making progress.

Lord, some purges are never completed,
but I'm determined to make progress.
—CAROL KUYKENDALL

Digging Deeper: MATT. 6:19–21

DIVINE ABUNDANCE

Sat 9   *He shall deliver the needy....*
      —PSALM 72:12

Food stamps! It was a bitter blow to my pride and independence—and me, a college graduate. Yet, when my meager resources and child support evaporated a couple of years after the divorce, I was forced to seek assistance. I hid behind last year's magazine in the welfare office and waited my turn.

"Now, now," said the caseworker, picking up on my agitation, "a situation like this is exactly what food stamps are for. Besides, most people use them for only about eighteen months before they're back on their feet." Not only did her encouragement fall flat, I drove twelve miles to the next town where few knew me to purchase groceries with those embarrassing stamps.

Despite my cheery façade and avoidance tactics, my tightly knit community knew my situation. A few days before Thanksgiving, the doorbell rang, and I faced folks from church lugging a charity basket containing a turkey, all the fixings and extras. While the kids dug through and squealed in delight at marshmallows for the yams, I fought back tears of shame. As the caseworker predicted, within a year and a half our family's finances improved enough that I no longer needed public assistance. Boxes from church, however, continued to arrive for the next several years. During that time I became, if not comfortable, then accepting of friends helping to feed us. After all, charity is just another word for love.

Gracious Lord, You provided manna in the desert for Your children long ago and You provide for us still. I am humbled by Your faithfulness.
—GAIL THORELL SCHILLING

Digging Deeper: 1 COR. 13

Sun 10

After the earthquake came a fire, but the Lord was not in the fire. And after the fire came a gentle whisper.
—1 KINGS 19:12 (TNIV)

On Sunday, I went into the church social hall to speak to a girl from the youth group. The noise was deafening. About fifty people were talking to one another, and I had to shout to ask my question.

Then I read this passage from 1 Kings. I wasn't able to hear God's gentle whisper in the noisy social hall. So how did I expect to hear Him in the time I carve out of my loud, busy life?

I did an experiment. I had heard about *lectio divina,* a spiritual practice that involves making time and space for God to speak to you. I took my Bible outside, sat in a lawn chair and read a verse over and over. I contemplated various phrases and words. I paid attention to anything that jumped out at me. I asked God how He wanted me to apply what I learned. And then I was silent, still, knowing that God is.

Just as I'd had a hard time hearing the girl in the church social hall, I'd had a hard time hearing God in the midst of my busy life. But in the quiet of the backyard, the Holy Spirit spoke to me through the Word. The time I carved out, the quiet space I retreated to, made all the difference in being able to hear God and know what He wanted from me.

Lord, speak to me through that powerful whisper You revealed to Elijah. Open my heart to what You have to say to me. Amen. —CAMY TANG

Digging Deeper: Ps. 85:7–9

Mon 11

You must teach them to your children and talk about them when you are at home or out for a walk. . . .
—DEUTERONOMY 6:7 (TLB)

"Did you enjoy the parade?" I asked a friend. "No!" she replied. "When the veterans marched by, some teenagers were talking and laughing. When I asked them to be quiet, they ignored me. It was disgraceful!"

At first I shared her outrage. During World War II, my pilot-father spent months in a German prison camp. My brother Mike fought in the Gulf War, and my friend Orlando spent twenty years as a submariner. Don, my husband, served a two-year Army stint during the Cuban missile crisis. My friend's husband is a Vietnam veteran, and children of other friends have been in Iraq and Afghanistan. Veterans deserve respect!

But as I thought further, I wondered, *Do those teenagers know any veterans? Do they know about the sacrifices made for their freedom? Have they heard about the good works soldiers do overseas and at home?* My own grandchildren know, but not all families have a history of military service. The only knowledge some children have is what they see in movies or on the Web—not always accurate or flattering.

I'm going to a Veterans Day program and dinner today, and in the coming year I'll watch a couple of parades and attend memorial services where veterans present the colors. I'm going to seek out young people and introduce them to some of our veterans. I'm confident that a living history lesson will make a big difference in their attitudes.

Thank You, Lord, for soldiers and veterans and for all those who honor them and teach others to do the same.
—PENNEY SCHWAB

Digging Deeper: PSS. 18:46–50, 29:11; 2 THESS. 1:3–4

Tue 12 *Joshua . . . said to them . . . "Each of you is to take up a stone on his shoulder. . . . When your children ask you, 'What do these stones mean?' tell them. . . ."*—JOSHUA 4:4–7 (NIV)

A 180-year old chestnut tree blew over in high winds one day not long ago in Amsterdam. That I learned of this in a Chicago newspaper meant that this wasn't just any ordinary tree. It was the chestnut tree the Jewish girl Anne Frank wrote about several times in the diary she kept while she and her family hid from the Nazis during World War II. Located just outside her window, the tree became for Anne a powerful symbol of the life and freedom she could not experience in her cloistered existence.

As I read the story of the fallen tree, my eyes drifted to a small stone I keep on my bookshelf. The stone is about as ordinary a rock as you'll ever see, a chip of gray masonry without any distinguishing beauty. But because it was given to me as a reminder of faithfulness by a group of Croatian Christians I visited almost two decades ago, as they sought safety in their church while war raged all around them, this little chip of brick has become a symbol of faithfulness to me. Every time I look at it—and I've put it in a place where I see it every day—it reminds me: God is faithful, no matter what.

For centuries, God's people have used ordinary objects as powerful reminders of the deep and abiding presence of God. The story of how Joshua asked the children of Israel to collect stones to remember God's deliverance across the Jordan River is but one of many examples.

Stones, trees... the object isn't as important as the principle. What do you use to remind yourself every day that God is faithful, no matter what?

Help me to see Your faithfulness today, God, in whatever You place before me. Amen.
—JEFFREY JAPINGA

Digging Deeper: GEN. 7:8–9

Wed 13

Now godliness with contentment is great gain.
—1 TIMOTHY 6:6 (NKJV)

My son Henry shines a flashlight on the living room rug. He flicks the beam of light back and forth until he rouses our cat Frank, who jumps up out of a sound sleep and pounces on the radiant circle. Henry laughs, picking up the pace. With a quick twist of the wrist, he casts the light the distance of the room. "Go, Frank! Go!" Henry squeals.

I scan the circulars that have come with the morning's newspaper. There are lots of toys the boys want for Christmas. An expensive food processor that's out of my price range would be great for me, since the one I have only works on one setting. There's a set of plates that catches my eye. *How wonderful it would be to have a perfect, full set for when we have company!*

Henry slows the pace of flashing and shines the light back and forth. Frank's paws meet the beam, and he puts his face right in the center. Exhausted, Frank lies down and Henry, tired of playing, puts down the flashlight.

I look up from the newspaper just as a scrap of sun shines through the window. Frank runs to that too. He settles down right in the light, closes his eyes and stretches to show his belly. He looks so peaceful; I put down the paper and join him.

In the warmth of the sun, I listen to Frank purr and my mind turns to the sales circular. I sometimes make the mistake of thinking something I buy will make me content; energy spent chasing the wrong light.

Dear Lord, You are the Source of contentment.
Help me to bask in Your true light.
—SABRA CIANCANELLI

Digging Deeper: 1 TIM. 6:5–7

Thu 14 *For no one can lay any foundation other than the one already laid, which is Jesus Christ.*
—1 CORINTHIANS 3:11 (NIV)

Like many kids, I often misheard song lyrics and stories. (Apparently, Elton John was admiring "the sweetest eyes I've ever seen," not the "sweetest pies I've ever seen." Huh. Sweetest pies made sense to me.) Anyway, one Christmas I listened to a priest talk about how Jesus was born in a stable . . . and I didn't know that was the end of the sentence. I thought it was an adjective: "Jesus was born in a *stable family*" or "Jesus was born in a *stable environment.*" It took me a while to realize that *stable* meant "barn."

Which is ironic, because Jesus wasn't born in a stable anything. Oh, I'm certain Mary and Joseph were swell parents, but I can't imagine life in the first century was known for constancy and peace. Like most everywhere in that era, Palestine was probably full of short, hard-scrabble lives ekeing out subsistence on the edge of the desert. Add to that some Roman oppression and rampant disease, and the only stable thing in Jesus' life must have been the relentless Mediterranean sun.

And yet… And yet and yet and yet. And yet a first-century itinerant preacher spoke about taking care of one's brothers and sisters, of doing what the Samaritan would do. He said that the lowest of the low—mustard seeds and the meek—would one day blossom. It must've sounded crazy. It still sounds crazy. And maybe twenty centuries later our seemingly sturdy lives could use a little crazy to remind us that what seems stable could be gone tomorrow and what seems ethereal might be the solidest thing we own.

> *Lord, You were born in a stable, but preached compassion and redemption. Give me the strength to overcome my seed-sized faith and become a messenger of love.*
> —Mark Collins

Digging Deeper: Isa. 26:1–4

THE GIFT OF TREES

Fri 15
Then they came to Elim where there were twelve springs of water and seventy date palms, and they camped there beside the waters.
—EXODUS 15:27 (NAS)

I remember learning in school that Plains Indians wasted nothing of the buffalo they hunted. In the Bible there is a staple tree . . . the date palm. These trees supply building materials, shelter, shade, food and fuel for desert people. Their leaves are woven into mats and baskets. Their highly nourishing fruit (a female palm produces two hundred pounds of dates a season) can be dried and stored several years.

Palms, having a long tap root, are able to reach deep for their water source. The Israelites fleeing Egypt must have been overjoyed to come upon the springs and lush date palms of Elim. In their journey through unfamiliar wilderness, forty years worth, they would develop a deep tap root.

I'm not a person who readily embraces the unknown. Moving from a suburban home in eastern Washington to a trailer house in the woods of Alaska . . . flying to an Arctic island in January for the birth of a grandchild . . . traipsing off to Los

Angeles as caregiver for my one-hundred-year-old aunt, I had to do some intense reaching for God in these times just to have the courage.

When I learned a Judean date palm seed, found preserved in a jar for two thousand years, was thriving after being planted in Israel's Arabah desert, I thought its tap root must be very strong. Trusting God for the unknowns that seem to never go away, believing He is with me for His good purpose, are making my faith root strong like that.

> *Every strength I muster is sourced in You, Lord.*
> *Inspire me to reach deep.*
> —CAROL KNAPP

Digging Deeper: Ps. 92:12–15

Sat 16

"Other seed fell into good soil and brought forth grain, growing up and increasing...." —MARK 4:8 (NRSV)

Serving as the birth partner for my friend Connie was quite an experience. I'm not a big kid person, but after going through two pregnancies and births with her, I enjoy my friend Connie's sons R.J. and Jett. They are serious little boys, and I get a kick out of their perceptions and reactions, especially to each other as they are less than fourteen months apart. I've been surprised by how much I learn from them.

A veteran of day care, R.J. had just turned three when it came time for his brother to enroll. That first Monday, Connie dressed them and put both into car seats, explaining to R.J. that Jett was going to school with him. R.J. was beside himself. As soon as they were out of the car, he grabbed Jett's hand, telling everyone, "This is my brother!"

On Tuesday, R.J. watched curiously as Connie once again dressed his little brother and put him in the car. Once at day care, R.J. dutifully took Jett's hand and led him in, reminding a few people, "This is my brother." On Wednesday, R.J. started to walk into the day-care center without Jett. Connie took Jett by one hand and R.J. by the other and began to walk with them. R.J. stopped in his tracks, gave Jett an annoyed glance, looked up at Connie and asked, "What, no babysitter at home anymore?"

When I finally stopped laughing, it occurred to me that I can be like R.J. with my faith. I get all jazzed up about a Gospel passage, a great sermon, an interesting service opportunity. Then it's full speed ahead for me; I want to tell everyone and do everything! But time passes. The words fade. The work gets hard. And there's no babysitter to take up the slack. That's when I have to rely on God to keep me going.

Lord, help me to remember that Christianity is not a game of show-and-tell. Give me the spirit and faith to get in and stay for the long haul.
—MARCI ALBORGHETTI

Digging Deeper: ROM. 4:19–22

Sun 17

Join with me in suffering, like a good soldier of Christ Jesus. No one serving as a soldier gets entangled in civilian affairs, but rather tries to please his commanding officer.
—2 TIMOTHY 2:3–4 (NIV)

One of the great things about my ministry at Guideposts is working with military chaplains. During my recent visit to the US Marine Corps Recruit Depot in Parris Island, South Carolina, I saw firsthand their mission in action. They make Marines who are committed to their core values in service to the country.

The first thing the drill instructor does is take full control of the recruits. In the first few days, they learn a new vocabulary, the rules of engagement, and how to eat, shower and wear their uniforms the Marine way. If recruits arrive at boot camp over-weight, the drill instructor will put them on a diet.

My visit got me thinking that I, too, like a recruit, must surrender, follow and be willing to give up control to God. The control factor often gets in the way of God turning me into one of His finest disciples. I don't always want to pray or read my Bible or respond kindly or forgive people who say hurtful things to me. Jesus said, "Whoever loses his life for my sake will find it" (Matthew 10:39). Some days this seems like a tall order.

On my last day, I attended the graduation at the Peatross Parade Deck. What a sight as hundreds of recruits lined up to officially become US Marines. I felt proud to be American and humbled by their courage and commitment. I headed home, ready to discover the changes that take place when I submit to God's love.

Dear God, help me to daily submit to Your loving leadership, so You can transform my heart for Your glory. —PABLO DIAZ

Digging Deeper: MATT. 8:5–10

Mon 18   *"Am I not allowed to do what I choose with what belongs to me? Or are you envious because I am generous? So the last will be first, and the first will be last."*
—MATTHEW 20:15–16 (NRSV)

Just before bedtime, my nephews, five and three years old, broke out the Candy Land board, determined to squeeze in one game before being marched upstairs to their rooms. Things were not going well for Caleb, the three-year-old. He didn't get the playing piece he wanted. Then he started to fall behind. "It's not fair. I want to win!" he said in a voice apparently meant to make sure that even the neighbors knew.

I say that kind of thing all the time in my head. In school, I saw fellow students who didn't do the work but charmed their way into their teachers' favor. In the office, I've seen folks improve their standing with the boss not by the quality of their work but through the skill of their self-promotion. But one of the hardest lessons to learn is that life is not fair.

As Caleb eventually made his way to bed, I thought about the parable where Jesus addresses our concept of fairness and meritocracy—by which I mean He destroys them. He tells the story of the vineyard workers, who each agree to a day's wage but then grumble when those who work fewer hours receive the same wage.

This parable is a warning against envy, a reminder to shift our perspective and a signal that God does not view fairness as we do. When I grumble about fairness, the focus is on myself; it's totally me-centric. But the truth is, I have already received far more than I deserve in the gift of knowing Christ. What would be truly fair? Punishment for sin? Life may not be fair, but God is just. I may want to win, but in a venture far more significant than a game of Candy Land, it's only through God that I ultimately can and will.

> *Lord, cultivate in me a humble servant's heart.*
> —JEFF CHU

Digging Deeper: PHIL. 2

Tue 19

> *Then he said to them all: "Whoever wants to be my disciple must deny themselves and take up their cross daily and follow me. For whoever wants to save their life will lose it, but whoever loses their life for me will save it."* —LUKE 9:23–24 (NIV)

Of all the places I had been on this Guideposts tour of the Holy Lands, from Ephesus to Jerusalem, the ruins of Masada, 1,300 feet above the Judean desert, challenged my notion of faith.

Masada. The very name conjures synonymity: sacrifice, courage, defiance, martyrdom. Originally built by King Herod, he died before he could avail himself of his impregnable fortress.

From atop the terraced ruins I could look to the Dead Sea, just as the Zealots must have done when the imperial legions laid siege to their mountaintop redoubt after the failed uprising in Jerusalem. They held out for three years. In the end they watched Jewish slaves, whipped and beaten, build a siege ramp against the western ramparts, the most vulnerable to an assault. There were thousands of Roman troops and only 980 of them...men, women, children.

The rest of the story is history. Rather than be captured, enslaved and made to renounce their God, these Jews took their own lives. And now, to stand upon the ground where that sacrifice was made unnerved me.

It occurred to me that seige of Masada prefigured the thousands of Christians who would willingly go to their deaths at the hands of the Romans in the coming centuries. Virtually all of the original disciples died martyrs' deaths, and most of the early saints were martyred. These followers of Christ took their faith to their graves. Staring out across to the Dead Sea, I couldn't help but ask myself, what would I have done for my faith?

Lord, You willingly gave Your earthly life for our eternal salvation. May the life I lead today show me worthy of these great sacrifices.
—EDWARD GRINNAN

Digging Deeper: PHIL. 1:20–22

Wed 20 "*So do not fear, for I am with you;
do not be dismayed, for I am your
God. I will strengthen you and help
you....*" —ISAIAH 41:10 (NIV)

It was time to do math. "It's too hard!" wailed
Stephen.

"It's hard but not *too* hard," I replied.

"I can't do it! It's too hard!" came the wail again.

"It's not too hard *with help*," I said. I've been here
before, having guided each of my children past fear.
By now I have a whole arsenal of sayings: "You'll
only get better if you practice." "There's a reason every pencil has an eraser." "Scary isn't the same as impossible." Lately I've added, "As long as there's not
a tiger behind that door, you can walk through it."

I know how to do this, but frankly it's tiring. I
think of my friends, none of whose kids seem to
get derailed by fear, and wonder, *Is parenting really
supposed to be this difficult?* My frustration billows.
I indulge it until another thought blows in: Even
for moms, *hard* isn't the same as *too hard*. The fact
that parenting is more challenging than I'd like it
to be doesn't mean it's impossible. And I do have
help—if I remember to ask for it.

So I give Stephen's shoulders a rub and say, "Tell
you what: Before we begin math, let's pray." We
turn our attention away from multiplication and
toward heaven, away from fear and toward hope.

November

We open the door and find that what we thought was a tiger was, in fact, a tiger-shaped worry. And then we go on to do the task set before us.

Lord, make my confidence in You bigger than my fears.
—Julia Attaway

Digging Deeper: Ps. 146:4–6

Thu 21

The voice of the Lord is powerful.... —Psalm 29:4 (esv)

My home state of Mississippi is—and has been—divided by race. What's sadder than that is the church is also divided. We have churches for white people and we have churches for black people. And we don't often reach across these racial boundaries to encourage one another as brothers and sisters in Christ.

I'd been feeling down recently about the progress that the organization where I was working had been making. I've dedicated my life to Mission Mississippi's calling—to encourage black and white Christians to love across the barriers of race. However, I don't always see tangible progress or evidence that we're making any headway.

While sitting in my doctor's waiting area the other day, my wife and I noticed a woman looking in our direction. Suddenly, she got up and walked right up to us. "Are you Dolphus Weary?" she asked. Once I confirmed this fact, she continued, "I thought I recognized you. You preached at the church I attend in Natchez. What you are doing is so vital, significant and wonderful. All of us need to love each other, no matter what race we are."

I was totally blown away and encouraged. This woman had heard me preach of love, peace and reconciliation. One by one, we can change even a state like Mississippi.

Lord, Your voice and Your Word are powerful. May I learn how to rejoice with thanksgiving in all You are doing. —DOLPHUS WEARY

Digging Deeper: GAL. 3

Fri 22

Do all things without complaining and disputing.
—PHILIPPIANS 2:14 (NKJV)

I arrived at church for a planning meeting with two toddlers in tow. In the narthex, one broke free and ran off, while the other clung to my legs, whining.

Pastor Miller came out to greet us with a warm smile. "How are you today?"

I huffed a strand of bangs out of my eyes and winced against a growing headache. "The kids are running me ragged."

His eyes twinkled. "But isn't it wonderful that they can? How difficult to be a parent with a child too ill to run and play." I absorbed that new perspective.

So many of the challenges I complained about were only in my life because of much greater blessings. Could I shift my focus to them and spend a little less time on the complaining?

In the coming days, it became a bit of a contest for me. Each time I heard myself protest about something, I looked for the blessing I was missing. The car stalled out on a cold morning, but that problem only existed because we had a car and didn't need to take a bus to work. My calendar stressed me out with a packed schedule, but it was a gift that we all had the health to participate in so many events. My husband had to work late, but the fact that he had a job was a blessing. Piles of laundry, dishes to wash and bathrooms to clean were no longer a reason to complain but a chance to thank God for the bounty in my life.

Heavenly Father, thank You for all the gifts You've poured into my life. When my day feels difficult, help me notice the blessing behind the challenge and turn my complaints into praise.
—SHARON HINCK

Digging Deeper: Ps. 5

<u>*Sat 23*</u> *Therefore, to him who knows to do good and does not do it, to him it is sin.* —JAMES 4:17 (NKJV)

When my nephew Alex was on break from college, he accompanied me to a store to purchase an apartment-size refrigerator for the tiny kitchen in my log cabin. As the two of us hoisted it down from the checkout counter, the clerk, a new employee, became flustered and neglected to scan my purchase. Instead, she focused on two large cans of coffee I was buying. I started to point out the error to her, but her supervisor was nearby and I feared she'd get in trouble. *I'll call the store later and report it anonymously,* I told myself.

By the time Alex and I were loading the refrigerator into my car, I was already rationalizing not telling anyone about the oversight. After all, that same establishment had cheated me out of a hundred dollars recently when they didn't reimburse my money on a faulty appliance I returned. *This just evens the score,* I whispered, trying to soothe my conscience.

After we hooked up the refrigerator, I felt like I owed Alex an explanation. "About that refrigerator they didn't charge me for," I began as I scrubbed a counter that didn't need scrubbing at all. "It's one of those tricky situations in life. I'm praying that God will show me what to do."

Alex's mouth tilted into a question. "Do you really need to pray about it, Aunt Roberta? Don't you already know what to do?"

All at once, I remembered something Dr. Martin Luther King Jr. once said: "The time is always right to do what is right."

For me that time had arrived. "Let's have some coffee, Alex. After that, I believe we have an errand to run."

Help me never to confuse what is easy, Lord, with what is right. —ROBERTA MESSNER

Digging Deeper: PROV. 11:3–5

Sun 24

Remember me, O my God, for good!
—NEHEMIAH 13:31 (NKJV)

I was in the church basement, cleaning up after a coffee hour hosted by another parishioner, when Mr. Fetridge happened by. The church's door-keeper and unofficial handyman, Mr. Fetridge kept an eye on things. After glancing around the kitchen, he summarized his view: "You're a good worker. Not everybody is."

I accepted his compliment for myself but also on behalf of my father, who expected his children to pitch in and taught us how to get a job done right.

He faithfully pastored a church, which we cleaned every Saturday; I made sure the hymnbooks stood face-out and straight in the racks. I had to burn the trash but only when the wind died down. He kept a big garden; I had to pull weeds without disturbing the carrots. We owned a Chevy; he showed me how to apply polish with an even, circular motion and then rub it all invisible.

I didn't always appreciate my father's directives. He could be harsh and overbearing. It would be easy for me to harbor negative memories, but I've chosen to dwell on the positive aspects of his fathering and the valuable lessons that wended their way into my character. He instilled his love for Christ, and he modeled how to be a good and disciplined worker. As he neared death, he talked of his need for grace.

This morning, walking from my Chevrolet to church, I imagined my dad looking down from above. His eyes asked a question. I answered with a smile. His request mirrored Nehemiah's last recorded words: *Remember me, O my daughter, for good.*

Lord, continue to draw me to a deeper appreciation of the best of my family heritage. —EVELYN BENCE

Digging Deeper: JOHN 13:33-35

Mon 25

Now faith is being sure of what we hope for and certain of what we do not see. —HEBREWS 11:1 (TNIV)

For years, my sister and I have been discussing the Christian faith in which we were raised. She wants to believe but can't. She offers all the arguments against faith that once stymied me: the unlikelihood of Jesus' Resurrection and miracles; God's apparent meanness in such Old Testament stories as the flood and the demand that Abraham sacrifice his only son; the countless people in the world who've never heard about Jesus, who are, she worries, damned.

"I believe Jesus was a good man but nothing more," she tells me, echoing my own past doubts.

She's certain only about what she doesn't believe. "I don't believe in heaven. And I sure don't believe in hell."

Her biggest faith impediment is the source of most God-knowledge others offer her: the Bible itself. Her main exposure to it is what we heard read in church as children. Whenever she tried reading it since those days, she says, she found it obscure and boring and soon gave up.

"The Bible was just made up by some guy," she complains, "like all the other holy books out there."

"Worse than that," I commiserate. "It was written by a *bunch* of guys we know next to nothing about." That used to be one of my big problems.

The only encouragement I can offer her in her quest to know for certain that God exists is the vague and implausible story of my own return in adulthood to the faith of my childhood. How I ended up in a Bible study class peopled by older misfits who took me on as their evangelism project. How I read the Bible, really read it, for the first time. How we discussed, argued, laughed. And how God took over from there, as I saw it, reassuring me that my hope was all the certainty I needed.

Thank You, Father, for honoring my quest to know
You by transforming my meager hope into faith.
Help me know how and when to intervene in others'
quests to know You. —PATTY KIRK

Digging Deeper: DEUT. 4:29, 39–40; JER. 29:12–14

Tue 26

"Your hands shaped me and made me. Will you now turn and destroy me? Remember that you molded me like clay. Will you now turn me to dust again?" —JOB 10:8–9 (TNIV)

I'm currently going through a difficult time at my part-time job. My supervisor tends to remember extra things she needs at the last minute and piles it onto the work I already have. And if I don't complete it all before I leave, she gets annoyed. It makes for a very stressful environment.

At Bible study one night, the discussion came around to suffering. I realized I should have a better attitude, because I have hope in Christ that things will eventually get better.

The next day I received an e-mail from my supervisor, who seemed unreasonably irritated. But instead of my initial impulse to send a defensive response, I sent one asking her to clarify what she wanted, when she wanted it and how she wanted it done.

She answered in more cheerful language, as if she was in a better mood. The result was I was less stressed and able to get her what she needed.

I know our relationship isn't completely fixed, but I have hope. I, along with Jesus, am working to make things better—in my situation and in my heart.

Lord, thank You for watching out for me and being at work in my life. Help me to trust in You. Amen.
—Camy Tang

Digging Deeper: Isa. 64:8

DIVINE ABUNDANCE

Wed 27   *They shall still bring forth fruit in old age....*
—PSALM 92:14

My daughter Tess no longer phones me for turkey roasting advice. She knows to remove the bag inside and can also replicate Mom's stuffing and whip up golden gravy tastier than my own. Not only that, she's taught her sister Trina to do the same. I definitely feel less needed by my children. I joke that I'm no longer CEO for our family, just a trusted consultant. But my levity hides my feelings of no longer being essential as I age.

To ease my melancholy, I strolled the grounds of the Canterbury, New Hampshire, Shaker Village, a once-thriving community deemed "heaven on earth" by the believers who lived there. During my training as a tour guide for the village, I learned that the orchard established in 1917 had been a mainstay of this community by providing apples to sell, preserve and serve, especially as pies enjoyed at breakfasts.

Now, nearly one hundred years after being planted, most of the trees continue to bear fruit. Windfalls of Duchess of Oldenburg, McIntosh and

November

Newton Pippins litter the grass. One stunted tree—gnarled, leafless and blackened by fire—draws me closer. Unbelievably, two red apples dangle from its uppermost bough. It's alive!

The startling image stays with me and reminds me that even though I've aged, I too, am very much alive.

Eternal God, may I use well whatever years You grant me. —GAIL THORELL SCHILLING

Digging Deeper: Ps. 90:12–17

Thu 28   *When he had given thanks, he broke it [the bread]. . . .*
—1 CORINTHIANS 11:24 (RSV)

Thanksgiving. Say the word and thoughts fly to turkey, Pilgrims, Native Americans.

When I think of Thanksgiving, I envision lists, carloads of groceries, days of cooking. The thought alone makes me deliriously happy!

My holiday goes like this:

"Hey, Keri. It's Momma. Have you decided what you want for Thanksgiving?"

"Ben, name your dish."

"Herb, are you sticking to speckled butter beans?"

After the initial polling come recipe gathering and grocery buying. It's then that I settle in for my weeklong cooking marathon. With one oven, the planning is complicated, but I glory in the challenge. And when T-Day rolls around, I am ready. The spread is profuse, the leftovers last through the entire weekend and, yes, the work is overwhelming.

So, you ask, why?

My answer is simple: I'm giving thanks!

When we gather around the long makeshift table, fancy with fall leaves Abby has gathered to nest Harrison's pinecone turkeys, I look around and see the faces of those I love most. Beyond the biggest turkey I can buy is Bebe's cornbread dressing with giblet gravy, Brock's mashed potatoes with skins, David's candied sweet potatoes and my sweet potato casserole. Keri gets both macaroni and cheese and fresh turnip greens.

Every dish, you see, is my personal gift, my prayer of thanks, my gesture of caring.

After all, what better way to say "I love you" than "Here, Ben, are rutabagas made just for you."

*Come sit with us, Father, and
know our thanksgiving.*
—Pam Kidd

Digging Deeper: 1 Chron. 16:33–35

Fri 29

These commandments that I give you today are to be on your hearts. Impress them on your children. Talk about them when you sit at home and when you walk along the road, when you lie down and when you get up.
—DEUTERONOMY 6:6–7 (NIV)

For Thanksgiving this year, my family did something we hadn't done before. We celebrated with my dad's extended family out in Long Island, where he had spent most of the summers of his childhood, and nearby the summer home my family had until I was six.

We rarely see Dad's family, so I knew very few people out of the thirty or so who were there, including my great uncle who had christened me and presided over my parents' wedding, a cousin my age whom I could barely remember from play-dates, and many more whose faces were completely unfamiliar. We had a nice Thanksgiving, but I was used to having a closer family experience.

Then, the next morning, Dad took my mother, brother and me around town, showing us the places he'd gone with his brother all those years ago. He brought us by the old grocery store that was still serving customers, the stretch of beach that used to be deserted, and the barnhouse they'd played in during the summer it was unoccupied.

Finally, he took us by our old house where I'd had some of the best times of my childhood, where my brother and I created plays with stuffed animals, and our dad told us long stories.

This house meant something to us that no one else in the world could share. The relatives I'd seen this week, for all their generosity and kindness, hadn't felt like family. Now I understood why. Family comes not just from blood but also from shared histories, the cherished memories that remind us we are forever partners in life.

Thank You, God, for the blessings of memory and family. —SAM ADRIANCE

Digging Deeper: GEN. 1:28–31

Sat 30

Then I will give them a heart to know Me, that I am the Lord; and they shall be My people, and I will be their God, for they shall return to Me with their whole heart.
—JEREMIAH 24:7 (NKJV)

I had succeeded in getting a Wednesday evening last-row-in-the-balcony ticket to *Fiddler on the*

Roof on Broadway, so I was happy about the trip home from Penn State to suburban Philadelphia. For a while though, I thought I would have to cancel and eat the ticket because I had been ill with a stubborn case of the flu. But I got well enough right before I was scheduled to go home.

The day after I arrived, I took the train to New York City, had a quick dinner, and showed up early at the Majestic Theatre to stand around in the lobby and enjoy being there.

Almost as soon as the show started, when Tevye began singing "If I Were a Rich Man" to God, I realized I had chills. I was afraid that I was getting sick again, but I ignored it because there was no way I was going to walk out on this show now that I was here.

When intermission came, the chills went away, but they came back during the second act. I realized it wasn't illness. I'd enjoyed musicals before. This time, however, I was watching my own family's history, our Sabbath joy, our foibles and superstitions, the *shtetl* life of my forebears. It wasn't just a Broadway show, it was my heritage.

When I hear Tevye talk to You, Lord, I know my
people have always done it and that I can too.
—RHODA BLECKER

Digging Deeper: Ps. 89:14–16

GIVING THANKS

1 _____

2 _____

3 _____

4 _____

5 _____

6 _____

7 _____

8 _____

9 _____

10 _____

11 _____

12 _____

13 _____

14 _____

15 _____

16 _____

17 _____

18 _____

19 _____

20 _____

21 _____

22 _____

23 _____

24 _____

25 _____

26 _____

27 _____

28 _____

29 _____

30 _____

December

So then, just as you received Christ Jesus
as Lord, continue to live your lives in him,
rooted and built up in him, strengthened in
the faith as you were taught,
and overflowing with thankfulness.

—COLOSSIANS 2:6–7 (NIV)

GOOD NEWS OF GREAT JOY

Sun 1

[Joseph] went there to register with Mary, who was pledged to be married to him and was expecting a child.
—LUKE 2:5 (NIV)

FIRST SUNDAY IN ADVENT: PREPARING OUR HEARTS

Come, Thou long-expected Jesus" says the Christmas hymn, and usually when I hear it, I think of how long the people had waited for their Messiah. But no one could have waited for Jesus' birth with more anticipation than Mary. It's been a while, but I remember what it was like to be pregnant. Nine months to ponder questions that can't be answered until the baby arrives; the same kinds of questions Mary might have asked. *Am I truly prepared? How will this baby change my life?*

It all came back to me when a young co-worker was pregnant, with some new concern or question every day. One day she was telling Jeanne, the most experienced mother in our office, that she wished the waiting didn't have to take so long. "Think of it as a gift," Jeanne said. "God gives you nine months to get comfortable with the idea that your life is never going to be the same!" That's a decidedly uncomfortable—but accurate—thought.

Advent provides a similar opportunity: four weeks to ponder what Jesus' coming into the world means to me. Christmas is one day of excitement and joy, as is the day of a baby's birth—a rush of emotions that passes in a blur. But Advent brings time to consider how the birth of this baby will change my life. *Can my faith grow stronger? Can I truly become more like Him?* Each year, the season of Advent gives me a fresh opportunity to welcome Jesus and think about how I can be changed because of Him.

Loving Jesus, although I think of You now as a baby, You have the full-grown power to change me. Use this time of Advent to prepare my heart for Your arrival.
—GINA BRIDGEMAN

Digging Deeper: 2 THESS. 1:2–4

OPERATION THANKFULNESS

Mon 2   *"And all the trees of the field will clap their hands."*—ISAIAH 55:12 (NIV)

Every Christmas I get stressed out with so much to do that I've made a point of writing down one unexpected gift of Christmas that has nothing to do with gift-giving or gift-getting.

Finding such a happy moment the Christmas our son Chris spent in Iraq seemed nearly impossible. Then one cold December afternoon, I was standing behind the ropes at the top of the escalators at the Atlanta airport in a crowd of people awaiting arriving passengers. Because I was there to give a business associate a ride to an interview, I hadn't given much thought to how utterly sad and alone I would feel as, one by one, my comrades in the crowd rushed forward to the embraces of loved ones arriving home for Christmas.

I bit down hard on my lip as several GIs in desert fatigues came up the escalator. Then suddenly I heard clap, clap, clap! A man in front of the crowd was applauding. I looked around to see if perhaps a movie star or other VIP was arriving. No. Instead, the clapping man in a red vest that said "USO" stepped forward to shake the GIs' hands. A woman with graying hair skipped toward them and gave each of those tough-looking soldiers a firm grandmotherly hug. They grinned from ear to ear.

I stood transfixed as this clapping duo greeted all the soldiers coming off the escalator as though they were long-lost relatives. My heartwarming Christmas moment had found me.

Maybe I couldn't see Chris this Christmas, but I could participate in the joy and pride I felt for each of the soldiers who came up the escalator. I took off my gloves and began clapping as hard as I could.

Dear Father, thank You that when we rejoice and clap our hands in welcome, our own hearts are filled with the gift of good cheer and gratitude. Amen.
—KAREN BARBER

Digging Deeper: Ps. 47

Tue 3 *For the Lord God will help me....* —ISAIAH 50:7

By the first of December, all my Christmas cards had been mailed... except one. Sadly, I entered the card shop with no real hope of finding the appropriate card for a son in prison. A son who didn't want to see family, didn't write us. A son who was once beautiful, godly, funny, but whose heart had grown cold, hard.

What was there to say at Christmas?

The bell on the door of the shop tinkled merrily as I entered the busy, happy place. I hoped no clerk would ask, "Are you looking for something in particular?" Christmas carols played sweetly. Most everyone smiled, even weary shoppers.

I began my search with my emotions in check, as though shopping for a head of lettuce. *Lord, help me find a card.* God and I both knew it was a half-hearted prayer. A card with a snowy scene caught my eye. A warmly lit house glowed in the far distance. I opened it slowly, daring to hope . . . just a little.

A son moves out of a mother's home, but never her heart.

Merry Christmas, Son. You have always been loved.

Holding the card to my happy heart, I hurried to the checkout counter.

Oh, my Father, You know all about distance between family members. —MARION BOND WEST

Digging Deeper: PROV. 31:1–2, 28, 30–31

Wed 4   *A time to keep silence, and a time to speak.* —ECCLESIASTES 3:7

Every Christmas, I dread losing my voice. I start marking Advent with a record of how many days I've managed to avoid a cold, a cough, a sore throat, some bronchial congestion and the all-dreaded laryngitis. I can't remember a Christmas Eve service when there hasn't been some member of the choir sniffling, sucking cough drops or using an inhaler.

Last year at Christmas I thought I was doing okay, pacing myself like an Olympic athlete, leaving parties early, going to bed at a decent hour. I felt a worrisome tickle in my throat the Sunday before Christmas, but I figured the wise thing to do was soldier on. That evening a group of us gathered at church to go caroling in the neighborhood, a once-a-year event I didn't want to miss. The stapled copies of music were handed out, and we warmed up to "The First Noel." I hoped no one would hear a fraying in my sound. Maybe it would go away. Halfway through our five-block pilgrimage, I was croaking. Soon all I could do was mouth the words.

Why does it always happen? I thought. *And at Christmas, the best time of year to sing?*

But silence has its own rewards. I could watch people watching us: the dad carrying his child on his shoulder like Bob Cratchit holding Tiny Tim, the people who rose from a dining room table and gazed from a window silhouetted by the light, the guys at the hardware store who stepped out from behind their cash register and paused to listen to "O Little Town of Bethlehem."

"You sound terrible," Carol said as we headed home.

"I'll be okay," I whispered. Next year maybe I'd get through the holiday unscathed. For now, I was marveling at "Above thy deep and dreamless sleep the silent stars go by." Wow! What a great line. I must have been too busy singing to notice it before.

Christmas comes in silence, too, Lord. Thank You for showing me that. —RICK HAMLIN

Digging Deeper: LUKE 2

Thu 5   *"Therefore whoever humbles himself as this little child is the greatest in the kingdom of heaven."*
—MATTHEW 18:4 (NKJV)

Public speaking, it is said, is more feared than any other experience, including death. I know from experience it doesn't get any easier with practice. Consequently, when I had to make a small presentation at my husband's retirement party, I was so nervous that I wrote out my few words a couple of weeks in advance and committed them to memory. Nothing to be afraid of, right?

I walked into the circle of guests—and took a deep breath. Instantaneously, my mind went completely blank. The microphone was put into my hand, and I managed to say, "As you know, Edward is retiring." There was no next sentence.

Suddenly, my two-year-old granddaughter Madeline, with a very determined look on her face, stood before me. She pointed firmly. "Mine, mine!" she said. I had no idea what she wanted. She pointed again and reached up at the microphone. It looked like a great toy. Why should Grandma get to play with it all by herself?

The guests began to laugh, and I found myself smiling too. Why was I afraid of speaking in a world that contained such a cute bundle of confidence and determination? I bent down to show Madeline the microphone, straightened up and told the crowd what a great husband, father, grandfather and teacher Edward had been for many years, and how proud his family was of him. The two-year-old public-speaking coach had effortlessly turned panic into poise, laughter into words.

Bless the children at home and abroad, Lord.
Bring them peace and love as they grow.
—BRIGITTE WEEKS

Digging Deeper: ISA. 11:5–7

December

Fri 6

All things were made through him, and without him was not anything made that was made. —JOHN 1:3 (RSV)

For the last few weeks, my husband has spent his evenings forming a miniature mountain. He made wire armature that he covered with plaster and once it set, he gathered twigs from our yard and glued different shades of wool roving to create foliage. Small pieces of wire were fashioned into miniature men that he carefully painted while looking through a magnifying glass.

I've been teasing him, looking in now and then and asking how his molehill is coming. Today he finished, and we delivered it to our brother-in-law Don.

Every Christmas Don creates a perfect miniature village in their spare room. Trains run the route through a perfect world of lighted houses and shops, telephone poles strung with wire. There's even a reproduction of their very own house.

This afternoon when we gave Don the mountain, his eyes lit up and he clapped his hands. He placed it in the spot he'd been saving for it and took us on a tour of the village, pointing out the river his wife painted on the back wall, the frozen lake his son made of glue and glitter, the country store crafted by his dad, and the hand-painted storefronts done by his mom.

Looking down at the miniature village, I noticed the details so lovingly made: the footsteps in the snow, the pen filled with cows eating from a trough, the carolers on the corner. Each element added to the magnificent beauty of the landscape, just like it does in real life.

Dear Lord, today I will notice Your hand in the details that magnify Your love here on earth.
—SABRA CIANCANELLI

Digging Deeper: Ps. 87:1–3

Sat 7

"Lord, what do You want me to do?... "—ACTS 9:6 (NKJV)

Last weekend I started mentally gearing up to host a meal. I've learned that a good dinner party includes people who share common interests but can also bring fresh ideas to enliven the table-talk. I scribbled names of professional women with admirable faith, all lively conversationalists, the ideal grouping.

Even the thought of entertaining can prompt me to tidy up. Skimming through and discarding old magazines, I stared at a headline that made me think twice about the guest list: "Guess Who Ought to Be Coming to Dinner?" I stopped and read the smaller print of the text, about Jesus and His "unacceptable dinner guests." Author Bonnie Thurston asked, "What if I invited folks to dinner and did not worry whether they belonged at the table?"

The question reminded me of a Christmas party I had organized years ago. I invited a number of social misfits. Most of them came. Some of them talked too much. Some hardly at all. They ate well and left full of cheer. Afterward I confided in a friend: "This gathering—I'm questioning my motives."

"What do you mean?"

"I invited them because I thought it might be their only holiday party."

Seeing kindness deeper than patronizing pity, he blessed the event. "That's not a bad reason," he assured.

I admit that I'm not quite ready to let go of my vision for the "ideal grouping." But at least I'm thinking along different lines: "Who ought to be coming to dinner?" It's not a bad question to ask.

Lord, whatever event I'm planning, help me to ask good questions, starting with "What do You want me to do?" —EVELYN BENCE

Digging Deeper: GEN. 18:1–8

GOOD NEWS OF GREAT JOY

Sun 8

*So Joseph also went up from the town of
Nazareth in Galilee to Judea, to
Bethlehem the town of David....*
—LUKE 2:4 (NIV)

SECOND SUNDAY IN ADVENT:
JOURNEYING WITH GOD

When our children were little, we had an
Advent tradition of reading a different
Christmas storybook every night. On Sundays, one
of those included a board game where you moved
your piece along a route that took Mary and Joseph
from their home in Nazareth to Bethlehem. We
always had fun with it, but Ross would get so frustrated when he'd land on a space that said, "Donkey
stumbles—miss a turn" or "Broken bridge—go back
three spaces."

"That's not fair!" he'd cry. I'd tell him that's just
the way the game worked. We all landed on those
spaces occasionally. As he grew, he learned to accept that truth—in the game and in life—especially
living with his sister's chronic illness. While Maria's
Crohn's disease is manageable, when it flares up,
it feels very much like the go-ahead-four-spaces-
then-go-back-three of our favorite board game.

As we approach Christmas, we wonder, *Will it flare up again like a few years ago when she made it home from a hospital stay a few days before Christmas?*

That night Ross came home and sang his "O Holy Night" solo just for Maria in our living room. And when she spent those days before Christmas hospitalized, family and friends came through with meals and all kinds of help.

That's part of the lesson I feel God is trying to teach us along this journey. We may feel that we're missing a turn or taking a few steps back, but we never doubt that God is walking right alongside us as we go.

Lord, I can't pretend this journey is one I would have chosen, but as long as You travel beside me, I know I will make it to the finish. —GINA BRIDGEMAN

Digging Deeper: GEN. 28:13–22

Mon 9   *Give ear to my prayer, O God; do not hide yourself from my supplication.* —PSALM 55:1 (NRSV)

It took me a while to stop being annoyed with the author Richard Paul Evans. One Christmas my mother gave me his book, *The Christmas Box Miracle*. It is a family tradition for me to receive a new Christmas book each year. Mom said this book reminded her of what I was going through as a writer: the frustrations with the publishing industry, financial worries and the disappointment when an editor just didn't seem to be on the same wavelength as I was.

It was a good book. But turning the pages, I started to feel dismayed as Evans described how his first book had come into being, going from a lovely story to the beginning of a multimillion-dollar career. He believed God had guided his every step in this process, directing him to certain decisions, including the counterintuitive choice of an agent who did not share Evans' deep faith. The agent turned out to be the one who launched him into the stratosphere of a successful career. Basically, God told him to bet on the winning horse.

By the time I finished the book, I had a familiar feeling in the pit of my stomach: inadequacy. Why didn't God ever talk directly to me? Why was it that when I had a hard decision to make, all I could hear was the silence of a loving, patient Presence but nary a spoken hint?

I grabbed a branch on my slide down into the dumps. Hadn't God healed me repeatedly of cancer? Hadn't God sent me the kindest, strongest man in the world? Hadn't God given me a diverse group of friends so I never stop learning? Wasn't my life filled with veritable miracles, large and small? Maybe I needed to stop listening so hard for God to speak and start paying attention to how He acts every day in my life.

Loving God, remind me that I don't always need to hear Your voice when my life is filled with Your actions. —MARCI ALBORGHETTI

Digging Deeper: PROV. 10:22–25

Tue 10

Only the living can praise you as I do today.... —ISAIAH 38:19 (TLB)

Postage stamps have always fascinated me, so when I was teaching my college literature class, I pointed out that "nearly all the great American writers have a postage stamp in their honor." I showed several on the projection screen, from Henry Wadsworth Longfellow and Edna Ferber, to James Baldwin and Emily Dickinson.

"If you do something that inspires a postage stamp, you can count yourself a success," I suggested. "But you have to be dead a few years to get one. Maybe that's because we don't always know who is great until they are gone." I quoted British statesman Joseph Chamberlain loosely: "Some people are like mountains. You have to get back a ways to see how big they are."

At the end of the semester, students were filing out of my classroom, and a shy young woman dropped an envelope on my desk as she passed by. When they were all out of the room, I opened the envelope and smiled. My student had designed a large postage stamp with my picture on it and a mountain in the background. At the bottom of the stamp was the quote from Chamberlain and attached was a note: "Mr. Schantz, thanks for a wonderful class. Krissy."

I was deeply touched by her gesture but especially pleased that she gave it to me while I am still alive!

We don't know how long the people we admire and love will be around. And at my age, I don't know how long I myself will be around to tell them how much I appreciate them. Sometimes I don't say anything because I'm afraid I will sound mushy. Often it's easier to find a card that says it for me. But today is the time for me to say something, before the door is forever closed.

Dear God, You are the best. Thanks
for a wonderful life.
—DANIEL SCHANTZ

Digging Deeper: 2 COR. 4:6–18

Wed 11

But the stranger that dwelleth with you shall be unto you as one born among you, and thou shalt love him as thyself.... —LEVITICUS 19:34

My son Chase pulled his red wagon, and I helped navigate the bumps and curbs as we marched on our street in Newport, Rhode Island. Snow and ice threatened to overturn the wagon and spill its contents on the ground.

Chase was a boy of six, bundled in sweaters, a hooded coat and gloves as protection against the icy cold. Hours earlier, he and his sister Lanea had been my companions in our small kitchen while I baked sweet potato pies. The recipe was passed from my grandmother to my mother to me. Not only were they a family favorite, but sailors stationed at the nearby US Navy base loved them.

Chase and I delivered the warm pies to an officer hosting dinner for sailors far from home. Though we never met the service members, we made our deliveries several times each year. The joy of offering the gifts to others and the sweet recollection of my son, the baker's helper, leading our holiday procession still keeps me full.

Chase is grown now, but the memory still reminds me to reach out to those around me, especially those in uniform, who may need a touch of home.

> *Lord, as we celebrate the holidays, we thank You*
> *for teaching us the joy of blessing others.*
> —SHARON FOSTER

Digging Deeper: Ps. 41:1; 1 COR. 10:16–17, 24–26, 31–33; PHIL. 2:1–11

Thu 12

For you are great and do marvelous deeds; you alone are God. —PSALM 86:10 (NIV)

Stephen's friend Eli was over this afternoon, and the two boys spent many top-secret hours constructing something. Materials disappeared into Stephen's room: duct tape, string, stomp rockets and pulleys. Occasionally, I was called on to supply paper clips or pipe cleaners. When at last the budding Rube Goldbergs called me to see their masterpiece, I had to stand in the doorway; there was no space left in Stephen's room to walk.

There, from minitrampoline to bunk bed and across the blue carpet was a contraption that could only be described as stunning. "It's a transportation system for small stuffed animals," the boys explained. There were an airlift and a zip line, an elevator and a bus. And the whole thing worked. I know: I was commanded to watch it. Numerous times.

It's kind of amazing what seven-year-olds can come up with. I gazed at the sprawling creation, then smiled at my son, the youngest of the children God created within me. *How did you think of this?* I almost asked Stephen. But I stopped the words as they reached my lips, for the question was actually intended for Someone else.

Father, open my eyes to Your marvelous deeds,
especially the familiar ones I no longer notice.
—JULIA ATTAWAY

Digging Deeper: Ps. 72:17–19

Fri 13

Commit everything you do to the Lord. Trust him, and he will help you. —PSALM 37:5 (NLT)

People line up outside the night before," my co-worker said, "and things have gotten tense, even hostile." That night I could barely sleep. The upcoming Christmas toy sale—to serve needy families in the community—was already stressing me out. I had to coordinate the whole event. With only three months on the job, I wasn't confident I could pull it off.

"Bagels," I mumbled, my eyes wide open in the dark. "Can't forget to preorder them for the volunteers." That and hundreds of other details pecked at my brain like busy chickens. And when I finally did fall asleep, I dreamed of chaos, shouting matches and full-out brawls!

The next day I met with the pastor to go over logistics. My anxiety mounted as I realized how much more I needed to figure out in a few short days. As always, we both said a prayer at the end of our meeting. When it was my turn, I didn't know what to say. What I really wanted to do was cry. "Dear Lord," I said, after a long pause, "help me get through this toy sale." After another long pause, I added, "And help me to have fun."

I arrived the morning of the toy sale at 5:30, and as promised there was already a line outside. Instead of nerves, I was bubbling with excitement. We made hot chocolate for the people in line and pancakes for the volunteers. Once the tasks were delegated, the doors opened and it ran like clockwork. There were Christmas carols in the waiting area, prayer and counseling on the upper floors, and happy shoppers leaving with large bags filled with toys for their children. By the end of the day, I was grateful for getting through the challenge and joyful that God allowed me to have fun, too, just as I'd asked.

*In everything I do, Lord, teach me to enjoy each
moment in my life instead of just getting through it.*
—KAREN VALENTIN

Digging Deeper: ISA. 58:11–14

Sat 14

*"This day is holy to our Lord. Do not
grieve, for the joy of the Lord is your
strength."* —NEHEMIAH 8:10 (NIV)

Today, in the bookstore, I stood in a very long
line, waiting with a few gifts to buy. Passing
time, trying not to get annoyed, I looked around
the store and realized my mom was standing in line
just one man behind me.

I waved at her, and she waved back. I noticed
right away she looked sad. Then, as she lifted up
her glasses and wiped a tear from her face, she said,
"It's the song. This beautiful song."

I couldn't hear any music over the registers
and the distant whistle of a barista frothing milk
in the adjacent coffee shop. "What music?" I asked.

"It's Maria," she said. "Ave Maria."

I looked down at the ground and then at the
man behind me who rolled his eyes, unaware the
woman behind him was my mother and Maria was
my sister who died in her sleep almost four years
ago.

The line moved up, and I felt the wave of sorrow rise. I made my purchase and waited by the doors. By the time Mom checked out, "Joy to the World" was playing. We walked to our cars, and Mom reached in her shopping bag to show me the perfect gift she had found for my niece. A woman holding a little boy passed us, and the boy shouted, "Merry Christmas!"

Mom and I smiled and returned his greeting. "Merry Christmas!"

Dear Lord, the holidays can be a mixed bag of emotions. When grief comes, open Your loving arms and carry me through to joy.
—SABRA CIANCANELLI

Digging Deeper: Ps. 31

GOOD NEWS OF GREAT JOY

Sun 15   *And there were shepherds living out in the fields nearby, keeping watch over their flocks at night.*
—LUKE 2:8 (NIV)

THIRD SUNDAY IN ADVENT: JESUS, THE BRIGHT MORNING STAR

On the night Jesus was born, I can picture the shepherds watching their flocks with single-minded devotion. This was their most important job. Once night fell, perhaps it was their only job. The wise men watched the skies with the same intensity. Nothing was more important than determining the location of this new king's birth.

Watching the sheep, watching a star, watching and waiting with a singular focus. Quite different from life in the twenty-first century when I think of all I find myself watching in a typical Christmas season. I watch my husband Paul's men's choir concert and watch for sales on decorations and the gifts on my list. We watch our neighbor dance in the annual production of *The Nutcracker* and watch our favorite TV specials like *A Charlie Brown Christmas*. Then there's the church concert and a movie or two—after all, would it be Christmas without *Miracle on 34th Street*?

Watching all this makes for a busy season but doesn't necessarily keep my focus on Jesus. Even church concerts and Christmas shows, while carrying the message of Christ's birth, can distract me from focusing on Christ Himself. So I've begun a new habit this Advent. Each evening I walk out my back door, and taking a cue from the wise men, scan the December sky for the brightest object—Sirius, the Dog Star. I watch it for a few moments, and not only do I feel connected to that first Christmas, but it's time each night to focus my heart on the One at the center of it all.

Jesus, You are the bright morning star. Lead me to make You the center of every Christmas season.
—GINA BRIDGEMAN

Digging Deeper: REV. 2:27–29

THE GIFT OF TREES

Mon 16

Then Solomon sent word to Huram the king of Tyre, saying, "As you dealt with David my father and sent him cedars to build him a house to dwell in, so do for me." —2 CHRONICLES 2:3 (NAS)

I spent my high school years in a small logging town in north Idaho. Returning recently to visit, I saw an exhibit with fascinating footage of the last log drive in that area.

Surprisingly, log drives were going on even in the Bible! The cedars of Lebanon grew in the subalpine forests of what was then Phoenicia. They attained heights of one hundred feet and girths of forty feet. Add to this a wood that resists insects and decay, has a fragrant scent, and possesses a grain easy to work with, and it's clear why this slow-growing giant was a major export.

King Solomon contracted with a Phoenician king for a supply of timber to build a "house for the name of the Lord my God" (1 Chronicles 22:7). King Huram agreed they would "cut whatever timber you need from Lebanon and bring it to you on rafts by sea to Joppa, so that you may carry it up to Jerusalem" (2 Chronicles 2:16). Eventually Lebanon's cedars were depleted, leaving the ones yet standing fiercely protected.

I've come to see history as layered rather than linear—the past not stretched along a time line but under, and even beside, the present. So a log drive in Phoenicia's Lebanon occupies space with a log drive in Idaho's panhandle.

The Bible is alive with stories that speak to my life . . . if I quit the idea that they all happened way back when and begin to connect them meaningfully with now.

You, Lord, are very present—and so is Your Book. You meet with me and teach me and share life with me in every story.
—CAROL KNAPP

Digging Deeper: AMOS 9:5–7

Tue 17

For the Lord Himself will descend from heaven with a shout, with the voice of an archangel, and with the trumpet of God. And the dead in Christ will rise first. Then we who are alive and remain shall be caught up together with them in the clouds to meet the Lord in the air. And thus we shall always be with the Lord.
—1 THESSALONIANS 4:16–17 (NKJV)

It was dusk when my friend Sue, my sister Rebekkah and I arrived at the charming blue-clapboard bed-and-breakfast. Our innkeeper Bev met us at the door. A whistling tea kettle, candles glowing in the windows, stereo playing "Joy to the World" and a bubbling pot of gingerbread potpourri welcomed us.

It was Christmastime in Zoar, Ohio, and the past and present were wondrously alive in the tiny village. Zoar was founded in 1817 by a group of two hundred German Separatists seeking escape from religious persecution in their homeland.

The three of us immediately felt as much a part of things as the luminarias lighting the way along the streets housing a bakery, a blacksmith shop, authentic log cabins, the lovely church.

"If earth can be this great," Sue said, "just think how heaven must be." Before long we were speculating on what that day would be like when we are at long last reunited with our loved ones. Would Jesus gather our parents, no longer feeble, and say, "Let's go meet the girls. We don't want them to cross over the Jordan alone"? And what song would the angelic choir be singing as Sue made her grand entrance into that celestial city?

As much as I love my fixer-upper log cabin and adore visiting country inns, I'm just a pilgrim in this weary world. My real home is where Jesus is. The homecoming there will be like no other. How I long to hear Him say, "Welcome home, Roberta. Well done, thou good and faithful servant."

Thank You for the eternal promise of my home in heaven, dear Lord. —ROBERTA MESSNER

Digging Deeper: REV. 21

Wed 18

If many years remain, they must pay for their redemption a larger share of the price paid for them. —LEVITICUS 25:51 (NIV)

Last week, I had to put down my lawnmower. Baling wire and duct tape no longer worked;

the motor gasped its last. I took it up to the trash, dropped it off and saluted.

Ironically, the trash is where I first found the mower, dumped unceremoniously amid garbage cans and recycling bins. I could see the starting switch was missing, so I liberated it from the sidewalk and drove it home. Sometimes people throw things away that really need only a simple fix.

My ever-patient wife Sandee watched as I unloaded my find in the driveway. She sighed and went back inside. She's seen me rescue junk before, usually with spectacularly stupid results. But this time it really *was* a simple fix, and the mower worked . . . and worked and worked and worked, nearly eighteen years in all. Toward the end of its days, it's possible I could've cut the grass quicker with scissors, but I would not give up.

Good thing, too, because I've given up so many things. I've had to say good-bye to more than just mowers. I've sent two out of three kids off to college; I've watched parents and friends move to their Great Reward . . . all that, plus the recently arrived AARP membership. Age has nibbled away at my knees, my hairline, my limitless future.

Luckily I, too, have been rescued—not once, but many times, pulled from some emotional trash heap somewhere by a good family and attentive friends. Compassion is such a simple fix, really. It's surprising we don't try it more often.

Lord, I don't know what years have been allotted for me; I do know that I have received more compassion and love than I ever deserved. Help me see the simple fixes in life, so I can return the favor.
—MARK COLLINS

Digging Deeper: REV. 22:12–14

Thu 19

He who did not spare His own Son, but delivered Him up for us all, how shall He not with Him also freely give us all things?
—ROMANS 8:32 (NKJV)

I adore Christmas. No matter how lean the year, I will have a Christmas savings account. For months I try to figure out the positively best present I can give each family member. The fun doesn't stop there because ratcheting up the anticipation comes next.

"Oh dear, Harrison, you're growing so fast, I'm afraid your present won't fit!" (How can an iPod not fit? Hee-hee-hee.)

And then, there's the trick packaging. I learned from the best. My father once gave my mother a winter cape wrapped in a vacuum cleaner box!

"Corinne, do you have a wish list?" She doesn't know that I'm only searching for clues. My goal is to look beyond the list and find something she hasn't yet imagined.

Christmas, according to some, has become too commercial. There are those who refuse to give presents, and if that's the way to happiness for them, then that's the way they should go. There are those who give to good causes in lieu of presents. That works too. We once gave a family in Zimbabwe a cow as Herb's present, and he liked that a lot.

My bliss requires shiny paper, ribbon and possibly a rock thrown in for mystery. All the while I'm well aware that it's impossible to trump the gift God gave when He sent His Son to teach us how to live. And as for encouraging requests from those I love, I like the precedent my heavenly Father sets. He always manages to give me something better than I ask for.

Father, Christmas is coming. I can hardly wait
to see what You have up Your big sleeve!
—Pam Kidd

Digging Deeper: Rom. 6:23

Fri 20

*Even the sparrow has found a home,
and the swallow a nest for herself,
where she may have her young—a
place near your altar, Lord Almighty,
my King and my God.*
—PSALM 84:3 (NIV)

"Just two more days till I go home for the holidays," my friend said, bubbling over with excitement. She described her family's home, nestled between mountains, her great-grandmother's rocking chair on the sturdy front porch her father built. Tons of family were anxious for her arrival, and I could just picture the bustle and love she'd soon experience.

Where's home for me? I wondered as I said goodbye to my friend and took the train back uptown. *Where could I go to rest and be taken care of?* Home was no longer in Brooklyn where I grew up. None of my family lived there anymore. It wasn't the new condo in Florida, where my parents moved to after their retirement. I'd started my own home in Manhattan with my husband and children, but his emotional distance made me feel like a stranger in that home and eventually he left.

What house could I return to that bore the roots of tradition and family history? The closest thing I could think of was my cousin's big house in the country where we'd gather for most holidays. But now separated from his wife, he lives alone in a small rented apartment and has his kids every other weekend. *When could my scattered family be together?*

I opened the door to my apartment, and my two boys dropped their toys and ran toward me. "Mommy's home!" Brandon screamed. The three of us collapsed on the couch and snuggled. "I guess I am home," I said with a smile.

Help me remember, Lord, that You have placed me where I belong for a purpose. Home will always be in Your loving care. —KAREN VALENTIN

Digging Deeper: 1 PET. 2:3–10

Sat 21

Two are better than one, because they have good reward for their toil. For if they fall, one will lift up the other; but woe to one who is alone and falls and does not have another to help.
—ECCLESIASTES 4:9–10 (NRSV)

The pastor asked us to stand and "pass the peace." Though this ceremony wasn't part of my childhood church experience, I had done it before. You turn to a couple of people next to you, say "Peace be with you," and then it's over and everyone sits down again.

Not at this church. The other parishioners, after greeting their immediate neighbors with smiles and hugs as often as handshakes, left their pews and looked for more friends to share the peace. When they asked my name, I could tell they weren't just being polite. A sweet woman named Brian was especially eager to get me a name tag and help me with anything else I needed. I met Pastor Joseph, smiling broadly, and he told me he was so happy to see me there. Their sincerity was palpable.

I had recently moved to Austin, Texas, and had gone in search of a place of worship. Austin Central was the first one I tried, and it was perfect. Growing up in the Northeast, I was often anonymous in the churches I attended; services were dry and cold. This was a whole new experience for me. I fell in love with what this enthusiastic passing of the peace represented: a community's obvious warmth and its focus on bringing the love of God to the world outside of it.

At the end of every service, the pastor says, "Our worship is over, but the service has only just begun." I knew from my first few moments in this church that these words were true. I had found my new church.

Thank You, Lord, for exposing me
to Your people's love.
—SAM ADRIANCE

Digging Deeper: EPH. 4:1–7

GOOD NEWS OF GREAT JOY

Sun 22 *"Come, follow me," Jesus said. . . .*
—MATTHEW 4:19 (NIV)

FOURTH SUNDAY IN ADVENT:
FOLLOW ME

The word *follow* doesn't actually appear in the Christmas story, but it's a familiar part of it. The wise men followed the star to the manger in Bethlehem. We don't know exactly who they were, but clearly they had studied the stars and had confidence that the one they followed would lead them to the birthplace of a king. Then, in a dream, they were warned not to return to King Herod to tell him what they had found and they followed that advice. They understood that what and whom they followed was very important.

I learned that lesson in a vivid way a few weeks ago. I was part of a caravan traveling to Sedona, Arizona, for a women's retreat. I began following the line of cars from the church parking lot, and as we spread out on I-17, I picked a white SUV to follow and settled in for the two-hour drive. About an hour later, the SUV put on its turn signal and exited the freeway. I followed, although I knew we weren't close to our exit. Then I realized I'd been following the wrong car! Fortunately, I knew the way to Sedona and got back on the right road.

From faith to politics to diets, we're constantly bombarded with messages about what and whom to follow. But over and over in the Gospels, Jesus has one message: "Follow me."

As Advent nears an end and I approach the celebration of Christ's birth, the obvious question is "Where do I go from here?" Jesus provides the answer in two simple words: "Follow me."

Dear Jesus, help me keep my Christmas promise to follow You in my thoughts, words and actions, not just at this special time of year but all the time.
—Gina Bridgeman

Digging Deeper: Ps. 63:7–8

Mon 23

A thousand years in your sight are like a day that has just gone by, or like a watch in the night.
—Psalm 90:4 (NIV)

One Christmas Eve, my siblings and I had just polished off a second serving of

Mom's twice-baked potatoes (basically a dessert themselves) when we heard a rustling at the door. Our eyes widened. As we dashed to the front door, we finally caught her, our own little Santa Claus in the making!

For decades, our family babysitter Renee had been sneaking by our house to leave four Christmas gifts at the front door, one for each of us siblings. In all our years, we'd managed to miss her, but not this time.

We threw open the door to catch a very startled Renee in the process of hanging a bag of four perfectly wrapped presents on the doorknob, her signature gift, a personalized ornament, tucked inside. "We caught you!" the four of us fully grown adults yelled as we danced and hugged her.

Renee laughed as she heard how greatly her gifts—small in monetary terms but huge in their representation on our tree—had impacted our holidays throughout the years. Her presence, sneaky as it was, had signified the true start of the season.

Like God often does, Renee blesses us and shows us her love without seeking anything in return.

How blessed we are, Lord, to have Your team of living angels surround us constantly! Remind us to show love and kindness in return and to do all things for Your glory. —ASHLEY KAPPEL

Digging Deeper: Ps. 118:23–26

GOOD NEWS OF GREAT JOY

Tue 24 — *But the angel said to them, "Do not be afraid. I bring you good news that will cause great joy for all the people."* —LUKE 2:10 (NIV)

CHRISTMAS EVE: GOD'S MESSAGE OF LOVE

I grew up a Christmas Eve person. The most joyful parts of my family's celebration happened on that night. My brothers and I took turns studying each beautifully wrapped package under the tree, trying to guess its contents. The house was filled with the delicious aroma of Mom's special Christmas dinner: turkey, stuffing, cranberries and mashed potatoes. We set out cookies for Santa Claus, fancy Italian ones that my dad's friends sent from his old neighborhood bakery. Then, because I was the youngest,

I was given the special job of placing the Baby Jesus in the manger scene by the Christmas tree.

Later, as we opened our presents, we shared the pure joy of being together as a family—laughing and oohing and ahing over the best gifts. I always seemed to get exactly what I hoped for; at least that's how I remember it. We'd stay up later than usual, but not too late, because we had to be in church in the morning. With warm memories of the night swirling in my head, I'd fall asleep knowing that Christmas Eve was the happiest night of the year.

The message of Christmas Eve with my family was simple: You are loved. Everything they did told me that. The message of Christmas for all of us is the same, God expressing how very much He loves us in one simple but miraculous act: giving us Jesus. That is good news of great joy.

Heavenly Father, once again this Christmas I've received exactly what I hoped for: my Savior come to earth. Thank You, and Merry Christmas!
—GINA BRIDGEMAN

Digging Deeper: MATT. 1:18–25; JOHN 3:15–17; EPH. 5:1–2

GOOD NEWS OF GREAT JOY

Wed 25

> *And the shepherds returned, glorifying and praising God for all the things that they had heard and seen. . . .* —LUKE 2:20

CHRISTMAS: SAVORING GOD'S GREAT GIFT

You know those quaint images of Christmas morning, of children rising before dawn to peek at what's under the tree and then waking their parents to get the festivities started? Well, it was never like that at our house.

Our children Ross and Maria liked to sleep, so even when they were at the most excitable age, Paul and I had to wake them up because *we* couldn't wait any longer. And then instead of indulging in the typical unwrapping frenzy that takes only a few minutes, Ross and Maria liked to play with each gift. He'd want to try out the computer game, and she had to read the picture book. We didn't hurry them because we always enjoyed seeing how much they appreciated each gift.

Those days provide a gentle reminder to consider my own appreciation, especially concerning God's gifts. God loved the world and everyone in it so

much that He gave us His Son, a gift we are reminded of every Christmas.

My children aren't little anymore, but the lesson
they taught me lives on. Today, I plan to take my
time savoring God's great gift of Jesus and showing
my appreciation for Him—as I worship in church
this morning and later take a few extra moments
for my daily prayer. I can't think of a better way to
spend Christmas.

*Not just this one special day, Lord, but every day, I
will take the time to appreciate all You have done
for me, giving You glory and praise.*
—GINA BRIDGEMAN

Digging Deeper: Ps. 100

Thu 26

*For He shall give His angels charge
over you, To keep you in all your
ways.* —PSALM 91:11 (NKJV)

While shopping at the estate sale of a woman
who was moving to a retirement community,
I happened upon the prettiest gold pin nestled inside yellowed tissue paper in an old, red and gold
gift box. The pin was in the shape of a Christmas
tree, and on its branches were small pearl orna-
ments. A stately rhinestone star crowned the tree.

As I waited for my sister who was still shopping, I noticed a tiny golden angel on one of the branches. "Why, there's an angel on this pin," I said to the white-haired lady who was hosting the sale. "Wait a minute, there are two angels. No, there are three of them!"

"Let me see," the woman answered. She shook her head in amazement. "Why, I've worn that pin going on twenty years now and I've never noticed any angels on it."

As I drove away, above the hushed crunch of gravel, the woman's comment gave me pause. You see, I never noticed the presence of angels in my own life until a passel of them showed up when I failed to engage the emergency brake on my car some years back. My automobile rolled down a hill and was headed for thirty or so shoppers at a neighborhood yard sale... until those angels intervened.

Back then, I thought angels were something that graced other people's lives, certainly not mine. Now, every time I get into my car, I ask God for His angels to protect me as I drive.

This holiday season, I'll be wearing my new angel pin on the collar of my coat. When someone admires it, I'll point out the three hidden angels I've grown to adore. I'll also share with them the promise that God will give His angels charge over them.

*Thank You, thank You, thank You, dear God,
for the promise of Your watchful angels.*
—ROBERTA MESSNER

Digging Deeper: PS. 68:17; MATT. 4:6

Fri 27

*For all flesh is as grass, and all the
glory of man as the flower of grass.
The grass withereth, and the flower
thereof falleth away: But the word of
the Lord endureth for ever....*
—I PETER 1:24–25

My wife Julia loves clean surfaces. Clutter distracts her, unsettles her and makes her grumpy. Alas, for her, she married a man who loves books.

The long wall of our living room is covered with bookcases from floor to ceiling. Three bookcases sit in our bedroom, each with stacks before it. Coffee table, end tables, cabinets and chests—almost everything that can hold a book does. I long ago ran out of strategies to keep them hidden from wifely eyes. Double shelving? Of course. Closets? Just about full. Apartment living has its limitations. But if I wanted to stay married, some of those books would have to go.

So I sadly piled them up in front of the living-room bookcases to await removal—evidence of classes attended, jobs held and passing enthusiasms. (What can I say? I really did mean to learn Chinese.)

One part of my library that I didn't cull is my Bible collection—KJV, NIV, NAS, ESV and a half-dozen more translations remain on the shelves. My mind tells me that the Word is what matters; whether I find it in the Good Book or the Good Download, the message is the same. But the feel, the weight, the smell of a Bible—whether its cover is leather or cloth, its edges gilded or plain—are physical markers for me of the spiritual treasures within, reminders of the time when a particular verse spoke to me with special power.

Lord, no matter how I receive it, Your Word has the power to change my life. —ANDREW ATTAWAY

Digging Deeper: DEUT. 31:11–13

Sat 28

"Peace I leave with you, My peace I give to you; not as the world gives do I give to you. Let not your heart be troubled, neither let it be afraid."
—JOHN 14:27 (NKJV)

My daughter Kate is nothing if not steadfast. "*Mooommmy!* I want to wear the pink dress to school. With the orange boots and the lime green sweater," she whined. I said no. Not only because the outfit was a complete atrocity but also because the pink dress was too small, long sleeved and made out of wool. It was 102 degrees outside.

Kate would not give it up. There was no distracting her. No dissuading her. No changing her mind. At breakfast: "Mommy, I spilled yogurt on my tank top, so can I go change into the pink dress?" In her room: "Mommy, why is my pink dress shoved up there at the top of my closet where I can't reach it?" While we did crafts: "Mommy, look! I drew a picture of myself wearing my beautiful pink dress."

It drove me crazy, but the fact that she's so young yet steadfast in her resolve is kind of admirable. I want to be like that with God. I want my every thought, my every word and my every action to overflow with Him. I want nothing to distract me. No one to dissuade me. And nothing to stand in the way of Christ's perfect peace.

Lord, help me be steadfast in my thoughts today, so everything I do is overflowing with You.
—ERIN MACPHERSON

Digging Deeper: COL. 3

Sun 29

"See that you do not despise one of these little ones. For I tell you that their angels in heaven always see the face of my Father in heaven."
—MATTHEW 18:10 (NIV)

My son Phil and his wife Katie, after having three children of their own, adopted a little girl abandoned on the streets of China. Before getting her, they learned that her osteogenesis imperfecta (brittle bone disease) was far more serious than had been revealed.

"What are you going to do?" I asked Phil as he faced the agonizing choice to give her up.

His voice was full of despair. "I can't abandon her now."

So two-year-old Alice arrived and stole our hearts. Tests revealed fissured bones, and she's since broken four more.

I went down to help out the day of her surgery. Evidence of Phil and Katie's sacrifice for Alice was everywhere. Having given up their spacious two-story home, six people were now jammed into a small fixer-upper. No privacy, no individual space, no place to put coats and toys. They didn't seem to notice.

Seven-year-old Jamie led me to where Alice lay on her mattress, leg splinted, and waiting to go to the hospital. Alice flashed me a happy, pain-laced smile even as Jamie knelt to touch his nose to hers. Then, quite suddenly, his voice quivering and eyes awash with tears, he told me, "It's so sad that she's so breakable."

His voice still quivering, Jamie added, "But what's not sad, Granny, is that she has such a cute face. Don't you think she has a cute face?"

I do, and I kissed her pretty face, my heart bursting with love for this joyous, happy child—and overflowing with gratitude for her parents, unwilling to abandon her.

The blessings, it seems, God, are ours, when we live out our religion, pure and undefiled.
—BRENDA WILBEE

Digging Deeper: DEUT. 7:9; ROM. 8:38–39; PHIL. 2:1–8

Mon 30

To some who were confident of their own righteousness and looked down on everyone else, Jesus told this parable... "The Pharisee stood by himself and prayed: 'God, I thank you that I am not like other people....'"
—LUKE 18:9, 11 (NIV)

My friend was making some poor choices and hurting others in the process. My frustration built because she seemed unwilling to change. I've learned that when I'm angry at someone, it's a good signal to pray. So I began telling God to change my friend's heart, to give her insight, to send circumstances to stop her course. I felt rather virtuous about my prayerful approach.

Until I read Luke 18. In bright "neon" colors, I saw my attitudes enacted by the Pharisee. From my place of superiority, I was happy to direct God to fix someone else.

I'd once attended a Bible study where the speaker addressed an issue I needed to hear, and a friend poked me and said, "I'm glad you're hearing this." Argh! Every defensive cell in my body bristled. Yet now I was doing the same thing to my friend—just not as overtly.

I asked God to show me the right way to pray for my struggling friend, and the word that came to me was *us*. As I thought about the traits causing her poor choices, I realized I had some of the same traits; they just showed up in different ways. Instead of asking God to fix her, I prayed for God to help us and to draw us closer to Him.

Heavenly Father, there is someone in my life I'm having difficulty with. I pray for us both. Help us to draw closer to You, to grow and change, to receive Your grace. Amen. —SHARON HINCK

Digging Deeper: LUKE 6:41–43

Tue 31

Give to the Lord the glory he deserves! Bring your offering and come into his presence. Worship the Lord in all his holy splendor. —1 CHRONICLES 16:29 (NLT)

I got back to our apartment, the afternoon of New Year's Eve, only to encounter a bold note stuck to the refrigerator: GET NEW TOILET SEAT TODAY.

New Year's Eve is funny. When you're young, New Year's is a mandatory excuse to go out. When you get a little older it's an excuse to stay home.

Except now I had big plans. I walked over to our local home supply outlet. "Bathroom fixtures?" I inquired of a floor person, keeping my voice low.

I headed for the appropriate aisle, grabbed the first reasonably priced toilet seat and scurried for the checkout. "Want that toilet seat in a bag?" asked a cashier with a megaphonic voice. "No thanks." It was a decision I would regret. No sooner had I left the store than I ran into a couple I hadn't seen since grad school.

Jeff and Annie had come to New York City from a small town in the Midwest to experience the midnight madness in Times Square. "What glamorous stuff are you up to tonight?"

"Just a quiet evening at home," I said.

We parted ways, vowing to stay in touch. Annie, always the jokester, shouted over her shoulder, "Enjoy your toilet seat!"

Julee was cooking something really delicious-smelling when I came home. "Needs a couple hours still, just enough time to install the toilet seat." Neither of us is handy, but Julee and I got to work. It took us much longer than it would have the super, but there was something incredibly peaceful and, yes, even celebratory about it.

God, another year with You, with Julee and our dog Millie, with our friends and families, neighbors and co-workers, with this whole wonderful, sometimes troubled but always blessed world. What more celebrating can I do but to praise You?
—EDWARD GRINNAN

Digging Deeper: 1 CHRON. 16:24–26; PHIL. 3:13–14

GIVING THANKS

1 _____

2 _____

3 _____

4 _____

5 _____

6 _____

December

7 _____
8 _____
9 _____
10 _____
11 _____
12 _____
13 _____
14 _____
15 _____
16 _____
17 _____
18 _____
19 _____
20 _____
21 _____
22 _____
23 _____
24 _____
25 _____
26 _____
27 _____
28 _____
29 _____
30 _____
31 _____

FELLOWSHIP CORNER

In the midst of a year of transitions, ANNE ADRIANCE of Oldwick, New Jersey, has learned more profoundly that the most important things never ever change. For that, she says, "I am deeply grateful. My husband Matt and I have had one son graduate from college and start a life on his own, and another son live in faraway cities all year long. It's meant we've had to learn new ways of relating as parents, expressing our feelings and sharing our connections as a family. Through it all, my love for my precious family, and my joy in living the life I have before me, has only grown!

The past year has been a time of major transitions for SAM ADRIANCE, who says, "I graduated from college, moved twice, started a new job and got engaged to my longtime girlfriend Emily. I've settled for now in Providence, Rhode Island, where I teach math at a charter school. All the challenges, however, only made me more grateful for those I could always count on for comfort, support and encouragement: Emily, my parents and God. Life has become harder this year—but my reasons to be thankful have only grown."

One of MARCI ALBORGHETTI's favorite lines from a prayer by theologian Paul Tillich is "Let a grateful mind protect us against national and personal disintegration." The prayer really resonates with Marci, who observes, "It's easy to find reasons in life to feel disappointed, but it is much more difficult—and much more positive and faithful—to find reasons for gratitude. Like many Americans these days, Marci and her husband Charlie, of New London, Connecticut, have worked to find reasons for giving thanks.

"It's been a year of new beginnings," writes ANDREW ATTAWAY of New York City. "A new dog for the family, new schools for John (a devoted computer gamer), Mary (growing in strength and technique as a dancer), Maggie (who's blossoming as a writer) and Stephen (now a proud Cub Scout), the beginning of her senior year at MIT for Elizabeth, and new opportunities for Julia and me. It doesn't seem possible that I'm turning sixty-five this year; the Lord says, "Behold, I make all things new" (Revelation 21:5), and I'm sure He has many new and wonderful things in store for me." You can keep up with what's new in Andrew's life at aattaway.com.

This has been a manna year for JULIA ATTAWAY of New York City, who has practiced looking to God for sustenance one day at a time. "When life is tough, I find it helps to take time to consciously look for the bright spots in each day. There is always something to be thankful for," she writes. Her son John has returned home from a year in a residential placement, and Elizabeth continues to thrive at MIT. Mary's dancing grows stronger and more beautiful, while Maggie and Stephen are as wonderfully quirky as ever. Julia is in the process of returning to full-time work, so changes lie ahead for her three homeschooled children.

"We're grateful that after serving in the Army, our son Chris returned to Georgia where he received an MBA from Emory," says KAREN BARBER of Alpharetta, Georgia. "Now he's entering another new phase of his life after proposing to a wonderful young woman named Grayson. Looking back, I realize that Chris's deployment led me in an unexpected direction when I started the militaryprayer.org website. Through it I discovered the power of the Internet to help us pray during new life challenges. This led me to start another prayer ministry: www.prayerideas.org. On our site, people from all over the country share practical ideas on ways of praying that have worked for them."

EVELYN BENCE of Arlington, Virginia, thanks God for a good, solid year—no mountaintop vistas or rough-terrain trips. "But then there was the May weekend in Duck, North Carolina, when two friends and I sipped hot coffee as we watched the sun rise over the Atlantic. And an August sibling gathering on a scenic New York lake. My day-to-day concerns focus on my editing business, my church community and a young neighbor girl with special needs with whom I play every day. When I entertain, she greets guests on the stoop with a shy smile."

When ERIKA BENTSEN of Sprague River, Oregon, is asked why she got into cattle ranching, her usual reply is: "Because I want all of my wrinkles to come from smiling!" She explains, "I really get attached to the animals in my care. Although ranching is a far cry from a simple life, I'm surrounded by God's creation and there's no other place on earth I want to be. I am so blessed and thankful that God has guided me into joining the Guideposts family so maybe, just maybe, I can share with others the enthusiasm He instills in me every day."

RHODA BLECKER and her husband Keith live in Bellingham, Washington, where they are very active in synagogue life. Rhoda's five published books (as Roby James) are still finding audiences, and she considers Keith her perfect first reader. She divides her time among her treadmill, reading, writing and herding cats. Keith does all the cooking, because Rhoda is a danger in the kitchen.

GINA BRIDGEMAN of Scottsdale, Arizona, is happy and grateful to return to the pages of *Daily Guideposts* after a one-year hiatus. In that time, son Ross graduated from Belmont University; Maria is a high school junior who would tell you the best thing that happened this year was learning to drive. "This past year, in my absence from *Daily Guideposts*, I realized how thankful I am for its readers, who wrote and called to check on me and my family," Gina says. "They truly are like an extended family across the country, and I give thanks to God for putting them in my life."

The past year has been one of adventure and exploration for JEFF CHU of Brooklyn, New York, who says, "I've had the chance to take a remarkable journey around America for a journalistic project on faith. I've visited twenty-eight states, taking in vistas from a thunderstorm sweeping across the Kansas plains to the golden high desert of northern Arizona. I've talked to people of every denomination and none, and I've worshiped in churches far different from my own. Through it all, I've gained an appreciation for the resilience of faith, especially amidst great struggle, and I've come to understand my own belief better."

"This has been an incredible year of beginnings," writes SABRA CIANCANELLI of Tivoli, New York, a writer and editor whose articles have appeared in *Brain, Child: The Magazine for Thinking Mothers, The Mom Egg, Daily Guideposts: Your First Year of Motherhood, How to Fit a Car Seat on a Camel* and other publications. "My youngest has started kindergarten and my fourth grader has started playing an instrument! For the first time since the boys were born, I'm rediscovering and grateful for the gift of free time."

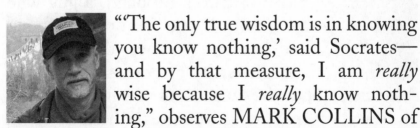

"'The only true wisdom is in knowing you know nothing,' said Socrates—and by that measure, I am *really* wise because I *really* know nothing," observes MARK COLLINS of Pittsburgh, Pennsylvania. "My daughters have to program my iPhone, I can't remember where I put my glasses, and I've forgotten *The Maine*, the Alamo, and most state capitals." Fortunately Mark remembers the most important items—his seminary-faculty wife Sandee; college senior Faith, 21; college sophomore Hope, 20; and high-schooler Grace, 16.

PABLO DIAZ of Carmel, New York, says, "Every day I give thanks to the Lord for protecting my son Paul from a deadly car accident and for his amazing recovery. His life is a constant reminder of God's grace to our family. Elba and I will be celebrating our thirty-second wedding anniversary this year. Christine continues to enjoy her city apartment. When I am not doing ministry at Guideposts or playing tennis, you will find me preaching at churches or speaking to groups. You can learn more about my ministry at pablodiazspeaks.com."

BRIAN DOYLE is, in order, a dad, a dad, a dad, a husband, a guy who attempts to be a decent friend and son and brother, the editor of the University of Portland's *Portland Magazine*, and the author of twelve books of all sorts of inky misadventures. Brian lives in Oregon with his family and a dog the size of Utah who somehow managed to lose one fang. How in heaven's name do you lose a fang, I ask you that? I mean, really.

"For more than ten years it has been my pleasure to be part of the *Daily Guideposts* family," says SHARON FOSTER of Durham, North Carolina. "What a treat to meet so many of you as I travel. In that time, both of my children have grown into adulthood." For the past few years, Sharon has been hard at work on a historical novel, *The Resurrection of Nat Turner*. The research, which took four years longer than she anticipated, required quite a bit of detective work. For more information, visit www.theresurrectionofnatturner.com.

Giving thanks for everything began as an awkward form of discipline for JULIE GARMON of Monroe, Georgia. "After reading Ann Voskamp's *One Thousand Gifts*, I began carrying around a small green gratitude journal. At first I doubted the power of something so simple. I jot down anything and everything to praise God for: a pink stripe across the morning sky, daffodils blooming at Mom's house, Dairy Queen ice cream tonight, two doe in the backyard. When I'm praising Him, it's impossible to fret. My husband Rick and I celebrated thirty-three years of marriage in December."

OSCAR GREENE of West Medford, Massachusetts, is grateful for his interesting and varied life. Twenty-eight months after his marriage, he entered the US Army, later serving in the final campaign on Luzon Island in the Philippines during World War II. Following discharge from the army, Oscar joined General Electric Company. Going on to become a senior technical writer, he retired in 1981. A published writer, his work has appeared in newspapers, magazines and anthologies. He is the author of *House of Strangers*, *Hampton and the War Years*, and *From Homecoming to Twilight*.

"I never feel I really get to know and experience a city until I get a little lost in it," says EDWARD GRINNAN, editor-in-chief and vice president of *Guideposts*. He's had plenty of opportunities to get lost in the past year. Besides traveling the US, promoting his Guideposts book *The Promise of Hope: How True Stories of Hope and Inspiration Changed My Life and How They Can Transfom Yours*, Edward led a group of 150 *Guideposts* readers to visit holy sites in Turkey,

Greece and Israel. "To actually walk in the footsteps of Jesus and Paul, Peter and John the Baptist deepened my faith in ways I am just beginning to truly fathom."

Manhattan resident RICK HAMLIN writes, "Our older son Will has moved on from his first job out of college to his second, while our younger son Tim graduates from college this spring (God willing) to come back home to New York. I happily celebrated my fourth anniversary of open-heart surgery by running to work, about eight miles. I find that if I pray for others as I run, I forget how tired I am and I can focus on people who really need help. In April, my book *Ten Prayers You Can't Live Without: How to Talk to God about Anything* will be published by Guideposts. I'm excited to share some lessons on prayer that I've learned with the *Daily Guideposts* family."

It's been one year since JIM HINCH and wife Kate packed their New York City apartment and moved to California, where Kate started a new job as rector of an Episcopal church in San Jose. They traded tall buildings for tall mountains and an ocean of people for the ocean itself. Jim writes, "We miss our New York friends and city life, but the kids especially love our new quiet neighborhood. Frances, who turned five this year, learned to ride her bike and swim this summer. Benjamin, who is two, was thrilled to discover the cable cars in San Francisco. I'm still writing and editing for Guideposts. And I finished a novel for children. It's been a year of stepping out in faith for everyone. God's presence has been the one constant. As always, He remained steadfast and steady."

SHARON HINCK is an award-winning novelist but is new to writing for *Daily Guideposts* and happy to share some of the ways God delights and surprises her each day. She and her husband are adjusting to empty nesting and make their home in Bloomington, Minnesota. Sharon has two novels in her Christian fantasy series that released in 2012 and welcomes visitors to www.sharonhinck.com.

When you work closely with students, as JEFFREY JAPINGA does as associate dean at McCormick Seminary, graduations mark not only years of service—2012 was Jeff's fourth on McCormick's faculty—but a kind of academic thanksgiving. What made 2012 a little more special was appreciating the first group of graduates Jeff had guided through the full program. But if you know Jeff and his family, you'll know that his moments of deepest thanksgiving, for life and faith, family and accomplishment, come right about sunset on the beautiful Lake Michigan beach near their home.

Thankfulness has been measured in heaping spoonfuls this year for ASHLEY KAPPEL. She and her husband Brian moved from Florida to Alabama, where they both found dream jobs and purchased their first home. Ashley is thankful that, after moving six times in three years, she can finally put away the packing tape for a while! Being in Alabama allows her to spend more time with her family, which makes her most thankful of all. She's looking forward to another year of adventures, when she plans to increase their household by adopting a puppy with whom she intends to share her morning walks.

"Just when we thought life couldn't get any better," writes BROCK KIDD of Nashville, Tennessee, "Mary Katherine Kidd was born into our lives. Her proud big brother Harrison, now 12, is a huge help as he reads to her and keeps her laughing. Corinne and I are blessed to have both sets of parents living nearby." Brock continues to enjoy his eighteenth year in the investment business, and when he's not in the office, he tries to be in God's great outdoors as much as possible.

This year, PAM KIDD and her family discovered that turkey and dressing are not criteria for giving thanks since they have had more thanksgivings than they can count! Brock, Corinne and Harrison welcomed little Mary Katherine into their family, Pam's mother recovered rather miraculously from brain surgery bolstered by near-father Herb's loving care, and both David and Pam set out on personal adventures that defined the tone for this amazing time of transitioning from minister and wife in Nashville, Tennessee. Although real estate for Pam and daughter Keri has been slow, they manage to feed lunch to almost a thousand children every day in faraway Zimbabwe. You can see their work firsthand at childrenofzimbabwe.com.

For PATTY KIRK of Westville, Oklahoma, this year has been one of transitions. The younger of her two daughters, Lulu, has joined her sister Charlotte in faraway Boston, where both are now college students: Lulu, a first-year student in comparative literature at

Harvard, and Charlotte, a sophomore in chemical engineering at MIT. Patty has not been able to properly enjoy empty nest syndrome, a stress-free condition she has been fantasizing about ever since her daughters were in their tweens, because her mother-in-law, who lives on the Kirk farm, has now reached the stage of her Alzheimer's disease where she needs daily help and company from both paid caregivers and Patty and her husband. Reflecting on gratitude over the past year has helped refocus her attention on God's astonishing love.

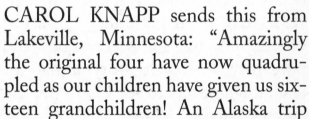

CAROL KNAPP sends this from Lakeville, Minnesota: "Amazingly the original four have now quadrupled as our children have given us sixteen grandchildren! An Alaska trip yielded my kind of rich: eight-year-old granddaughter Sarah and I stayed up till all hours writing stories. In Texas I met cute Chloe—our first African American granddaughter. Also in the mix: Terry's and my fortieth wedding anniversary, back where we began in north Idaho. My sweet mama will soon be ninety; what a gift to have her so long. What a gift to have my husband forty years. What a gift to have four children and sixteen grandchildren. What a gift to know and love the Gift Giver."

CAROL KUYKENDALL of Boulder, Colorado, says, "Gratitude comes easily when I consider that both my husband Lynn and I have survived late-stage cancers and are currently getting good test results. I've realized this year that gratitude is an attitude that takes practice to become a habit. I'm more able to practice the gratitude-attitude when I remember something I heard years ago: I'm not thankful *for* all circumstances (such as a flooded basement) but I can be thankful *within* all circumstances (such as the quick response of a plumber). This year we've been grateful for the birth of another grandchild, for some traveling, and for my opportunity to teach storytelling workshops that encourage others to see God's presence in their life circumstances."

PATRICIA LORENZ, who has lived in Largo, Florida, for nine years, says, "I am so thankful that Jack, my hunka-hunka-burnin'-love, talked me into moving to Florida in 2004. In November 2011, when Jack, almost 75, proposed to me on bended knee, I knew just how many amazing things I had to be thankful for. That he can still get down on one knee is one! One of my pleasures in life is traveling and giving speeches to all sorts of groups. Writing and speaking keep me thankful. Jack, my family and my friends keep me joyful."

"This past year has been a time of healing for my husband and me," reports DEBBIE MACOMBER of Port Orchard, Washington, and Vero Beach, Florida. "Healing from a tragedy no parent should ever have to endure: the loss of a child. Looking back on the aftermath of Dale's passing, I can see God's hand and am grateful for His guiding each member of our family in what was most certainly our darkest hour. Thanks to God's grace, once again we are finding joy in our lives. Last spring Wayne and I took our first vacation as a couple in twenty years, and as I write this all the Macombers are planning to participate in an annual run in Port Orchard as a tribute to Dale, who was passionate about running." Debbie and Wayne continue to serve on the Guideposts National Advisory Cabinet. Debbie's novels consistently earn berths on national best-seller lists, and her inspirational books touch people on many levels.

"Sometimes between football practice and kickboxing class, between teaching my kindergartener to read and my newborn to self-soothe, I forget to pause and reflect on the abundance I have," says ERIN MACPHERSON of Austin,

Texas. "But God truly has blessed me this year—in big ways, such as the birth of my precious son Will and the publication of my first book, *The Christian Mama's Guide to Having a Baby*—and in small everyday ways, such as the handwritten cards my kids draw for me, some encouraging talks with my precious friends in my church community group or even a few unexpected date nights with my husband. I am truly grateful."

"This has been a year of tremendous gratitude for me," says ROBERTA MESSNER of Huntington, West Virginia. "I have finally managed to be successful at losing weight." Roberta's sister-in-law Ellen has served as Roberta's coach. "When I grumbled to her that I couldn't lose more than a pound a week, she told me, 'Just think, Roberta. If you lose a single pound forty-five weeks out of the year, that's forty-five pounds at the end of the year.'" So Roberta took the challenge. Her weight loss thus far? Seventy-nine pounds. And the best thing is, she doesn't feel like she's on a diet. That's a lot to be grateful for.

LINDA NEUKRUG lives in Walnut Creek, California, with her two cats Prince and Junior. Every morning, Linda tries to walk a mile along Iron Horse Trail, which backs up on her house. During that time, Linda tries to focus on all that she is grateful for, giving thanks for such God-given basics like the ability to walk along the path, to see the trees blooming, to greet some of her "trail friends" (people she sees only while walking), to hear the birds singing in the morning before the car horns start honking. And, most of all, Linda is thankful that God gave us all that very important sixth sense. No, not clairvoyance! Something far more important: a sense of humor.

Although it has not been a perfect year, PATRICIA PUSEY of Halifax, Vermont, says she has been grateful for her love of family, faith and friends. "Busyness consumes my days and at times it feels like the clock rules my life. But then I am reminded that my faith runs my life, and for that I am thankful. Our beautiful family, which includes ten wonderful grandchildren ranging in age from twenty-one to newest grandson Ronan born in June, consumes our love and all the hours of the day that are not spent here on the farm running Shearer Hill Farm Bed & Breakfast and caring for our special-needs daughter Brittany. God is good, and for that we give thanks daily!"

DANIEL SCHANTZ was given the permanent title of professor emeritus when he retired in the spring of 2011 after forty-three years in the classroom at Central Christian College in Moberly, Missouri. Dan says, "It is deeply gratifying to hear about former students of mine who are serving in churches, benevolence and mission fields all over the world. It's the best 'pension' I could want." Now that both Dan and Sharon are retired from teaching, they have been taking some day trips and doing more relaxing things. For Dan that means biking, gardening, writing and auto mechanics. For Sharon that includes quilting, cross stitching and corresponding with friends and family.

"Give thanks for downsizing from five rooms to one? Absolutely!" says GAIL THORELL SCHILLING of Northwood, New Hampshire. "My simplified lifestyle allows me more freedom for writing and travel. This summer I enjoyed a month-long writing retreat at the Jentel Artist Residency Program in Wyoming, followed by a visit with my son Greg in Los Angeles. How thankful I am that my newfound flexibility lets me enjoy frequent overnight visits with my mother, children and friends. Since daughter Trina and her husband Steve cooked for Thanksgiving, I spent the morning literally counting blessings. By entry 150, I knew the list was infinite."

"I'm trying to cultivate an attitude of gratitude," writes PENNEY SCHWAB of Copeland, Kansas, "and it's helping me appreciate how truly blessed I am. I thank God for the successful knee-replacement surgery that allowed Don to walk Oklahoma State University campus pain-free when we attended the fiftieth anniversary of his graduation. It's a privilege to be mother of three and grandmother of six. This year I lost my dear friend Bob Dennis, my mentor during much of my working life. I'm immensely grateful for the wisdom he shared, the guidance he gave and his witness that he was ready to go home and is now with our Lord."

This past year ELIZABETH SHERRILL and her husband John, of Hingham, Massachusetts, celebrated their sixty-fifth wedding anniversary. "Looking back over the decades with the confidence of hindsight, we found we could give thanks for the hard times as well as the joyful ones." Another wedding celebration took place in March, when their daughter Liz married Dana Kintigh. "Widow and widower have found each other, and John and I have a bigger family than ever. Holidays now are a matter of how many extensions will fit on the dining-room table."

SHARI SMYTH of Nashville, Tennessee, says she has learned a lot about gratitude from her daughter Sanna, who is a recovering alcoholic and quick to tell her mother, "Being thankful is one of the lifelines to sobriety." Shari says, "It's also a lifeline for me and my all-around health and from Sanna I'm learning to practice it. I'm grateful that my husband Whitney is still my best friend and that our children Wendy, Laura, Jon and son-in-law Glen continue to do well and be so involved with us. Not to mention our grandson Frank, who shines more joy into our lives than I can say. And most especially I'm thankful to God from Whose hand all these gifts have come."

"There was much for which to be thankful this past year," says JOSHUA SUNDQUIST of Washington, DC. "I had my first anniversary with my first girlfriend, which is surely something to celebrate! I continue to be blessed with opportunities to share my story in front of national and international audiences through my speeches and my memoir *Just Don't*

Fall. I also have become increasingly active with the American Amputee Soccer Team." He recently helped with a soccer clinic to join new amputees from Haiti and the US armed forces. Visit him at joshsundquist.com.

"It is indeed a year to give thanks!" MELODY BONNETTE SWANG of Mandeville, Louisiana, writes. She recently graduated with a PhD in educational leadership from the University of Southern Mississippi. "I was filled with such thankfulness as I walked across the stage," states Melody, "and, somehow, in the huge coliseum, I heard my family cheering!" That cheering section included Melody's children Misty, Kristen, Christopher and Kevin; their spouses; her 81-year-old mom; sister Sandi and brother-in-law Bob; and seven of her grandchildren. Melody is especially thankful for her husband's support while she earned her degree. "I never could have finished my doctorate in two-and-a-half years without his hard work," says Melody. "He has his doctorate, too, so we now jokingly call ourselves a 'paradox.'"

JON SWEENEY is an author, editor and popular speaker with a wide range of interests. His newest book is a work of popular history telling the story of Pope Celestine V: *The Pope*

Who Quit: A True Medieval Tale of Mystery, Death, and Salvation. Since 2004 he has been the associate publisher at Paraclete Press in Massachusetts. He is the author of many books, including *Verily, Verily: The King James Bible—400 Years of Beauty and Influence.* He writes often for the magazine *America* and blogs regularly on the Religion page of *The Huffington Post.* Today he is married; lives in Woodstock, Vermont; and has three children: a daughter in college, a son in high school and a baby daughter.

 CAMY TANG grew up in Hawaii and now lives in San Jose, California, with her engineer husband and rambunctious mutt Snickers. She used to be a biologist, but now she writes full time, is a staff worker for her church youth group and leads a worship team for Sunday service. This past year she's been learning to be thankful despite the washing machine breaking down at exactly the wrong time and her father having back surgery. Thanks to friends expressing God's grace, she's found grace in trying circumstances and strength in frustration. When she's not reading a book on her e-book reader, she's knitting socks, training for her second marathon or scolding her dog for chewing her shoes.

KAREN VALENTIN says, "My father is cancer free! It's just one of the many things I'm giving thanks to God for. God has opened a door to work with inner-city children at Graffiti Ministries, a position that is fulfilling, exciting and a means of financial and emotional support for my family. And although it was difficult, I give thanks for the storm that God used to strengthen and grow me into the woman He's called me to be." Karen lives with her two young sons in New York City and is the author of *The Flavor of our Hispanic Faith*, *Hallway Diaries* and her children's books series Allie's World.

This year has been a whirlwind of activity for SCOTT WALKER of Macon, Georgia. One of his programs at Mercer University, Service First, is quickly accelerating. Service First sends Mercer graduates internationally for one year to do specific service projects. Says Scott, "I am thankful to be energized by their young passion for dreaming dreams and seeing visions." His children are now grown and living in Columbia, South Carolina, and Washington, DC. Scott's wife Beth remains ever youthful and loves connecting Mercer students with Study Abroad opportunities and exchange programs. "We are grateful to blend our life and work, preparing another generation to go about doing good."

DOLPHUS WEARY of Richland, Mississippi, writes, "In March 2011, we took our second trip to Liberia, and after returning I was diagnosed with malaria. After going through six months of blood-thinning medicine, I was scheduled for a right hip replacement. With so many people praying for me I was able to give God thanks throughout the process. Our daughter Danita got married in May 2012. Ryan continues to work as a computer data manager for a construction project, and yes, Lil' Reggie is seven years old and in the second grade. We are blessed by him every day. I am now engaged full-time with Rosie in developing REAL Christian Foundation as a connector of resources for rural Christian ministries in Mississippi. My second book—*Crossing the Tracks: Hope for the Hopeless and Help for the Poor in Rural Mississippi and Your Community*—came out in June 2012."

BRIGITTE WEEKS of New York City says, "I have settled into retirement, which for me means I am now very busy—and thankful for that blessing. I am teaching English as a second language to students from all over the world;

working in an inpatient hospice unit in a big city hospital, where I see families giving thanks both for the lives of loved ones and for the peace and comfort of hospice care; and learning to be a lay minister in my church. My husband Edward also retired and we are hard at work figuring out how to live together full time! While I am teaching English, he is learning Spanish. And always growing and changing are five grandchildren, one of whom, young Benjamin, is now reading Wimpy Kids books all on his own. I hardly have time to count my blessings!"

In the early seventies MARION BOND WEST of Watkinsville, Georgia, heard about thanking God for everything. She says this year she rediscovered the powerful principle. Here are some of the things she thanked God for: His hand remaining on son Jon in prison and that God's peace is beyond logic; the continuing of son Jeremy's amazing five-year restoration from addictions and bipolar disorder; the restoration of a portion of her energy, zapped by autoimmune diseases; a husband who doesn't care if she's mostly given up on cooking; the fresh ideas God gives her before sunrise; a change of heart, after nearly deciding for the first time she didn't want to bother with a Christmas tree this year—"and the beauty it radiated in our home and my heart."

For freelance-writer ASHLEY WIERSMA, this is her debut effort with *Daily Guideposts*, and in a year filled to overflowing with kindly rivals, the invitation to participate has itself given her yet one more in a long list of reasons to give thanks: relocating with her husband back home to Monument, Colorado; watching their baby girl become a generous and gregarious toddler; sensing God's lavish provision as she sorted out how to maintain a rigorous writing schedule even as a wee one giggled underfoot; finding unexpected blessings in the midst of bidding a loved one a forever farewell. The twelve months that have just passed are months marked by the shake-your-head-in-grateful-disbelief sensation that comes from sharing intimacy with a great God.

BRENDA WILBEE of Birch Bay, Washington, will be saying good-bye to Guideposts this year. She would like to thank all who've been corresponding with her and adds, "I hope we can continue! This past year my family has seen happiness amidst heartache. My granddaughter Alice, now three, has brittle-bone disease. After breaking her legs twice while trying to walk, she's had steel rods inserted into her bones to straighten and strengthen them. She's now walking without mishaps! I'm grateful that despite the gravity of her situation and having been abandoned on the streets of China, Alice now has a family who loves her, the best medical care available, and hope for her future. Truly my family can say, 'In all things give thanks.' I hope and pray your families are experiencing similar happiness amidst heartache. If you'd like to keep in touch, my e-mail is Brenda@BrendaWilbee.com."

 During all the years TIM WILLIAMS worked as a victims' advocate for Mothers Against Drunk Driving and as an EMT-firefighter in Durango, Colorado, he was immersed in tragedy. Now that he is retired, Tim says God has allowed him to slowly embrace the concept that tragedy can be the exception and not the rule. "I give thanks every day for absence of death and injury in my life. I am so grateful for the routine of having a wife who is healthy, sons who are safe, and seven brothers and sisters who thrive along with their spouses and dozens of children and grandchildren. The health and safety of those I love may be routine, but it will never be dull to me!"